Pathways to Prosperity for Adolescent Girls in Africa

Reproducible Research Repository

A reproducibility package is available for this book in the
Reproducible Research Repository at
https://reproducibility.worldbank.org.

Pathways to Prosperity for Adolescent Girls in Africa

Kehinde Ajayi and
Estelle Koussoubé, Editors

WORLD BANK GROUP

ISBN (paper): 978-1-4648-2061-8
ISBN (electronic): 978-1-4648-2062-5
DOI: 10.1596/978-1-4648-2061-8

Cover, illustration of people: Generated by Adobe Firefly, July 16, 2024, from the prompt "Vector image of an African adolescent female, smiling, looking into the horizon." Subsequent modifications made using traditional design tools. Images also used on chapter opening pages.

Cover, background art: © World Bank; created using traditional design tools.

Library of Congress Control Number: 2024917593

Contents

Chapter 3. What Do We Know about Improving Human Capital Fundamentals among Adolescent Girls in Africa?   121

Ioana Botea and Kehinde Ajayi, with contributions from Karen Austrian, Chiara Pasquini and Sara Troiano

Spotlight 3. Quality Implementation of Safe Spaces Programs   147

Karen Austrian and Sara Troiano

Chapter 4. What Do We Know about Enhancing Economic Success among Adolescent Girls in Africa?   159

Wei Chang, Estelle Koussoubé, and Clémence Pougue Biyong, with contributions from Kehinde Ajayi and Chiara Pasquini

Spotlight 4. Focusing on Change: Analyzing the Political Economy of Adolescent Girls' Empowerment Initiatives in Africa   193

Michael Kevane and Estelle Koussoubé

Chapter 5. Conclusions   207

Kehinde Ajayi, Estelle Koussoubé and Fatima Zahra

Boxes

Figures

Maps

Tables

Foreword

In today's dynamic global landscape, investing in adolescent girls is not just a moral imperative, but a sensible economic decision. Evidence-based interventions tailored to adolescent girls' unique needs have the power to catalyze transformative change that reverberates across generations and communities. Because adolescence is a time when key decisions are made that have long-lasting impacts, relatively small investments can change the whole trajectory of a life and thus can have high returns.

At this pivotal moment, with 23 percent of the world's 1.2 billion adolescents residing in Sub-Saharan Africa, the need to act is urgent: millions of adolescent girls across the continent are at crucial turning points in their lives. Despite Africa's vast potential for prosperity, a stark reality remains: 26 percent of adolescent girls ages 15 to 19 in Africa are neither working nor in school, and 27 percent are married or have a child. In comparison, 9 percent of African boys in the same age range are neither working nor in school, and fewer than 3 percent are married or have a child.

Recognizing the multifaceted nature of the challenges presented by this reality, the Center for Global Development, the Population Council, and the World Bank Group have come together to help countries forge a path forward. The rigorous analysis in this report provides clear routes to evidence-based policy that will not only bolster girls' human capital but also empower them economically, laying the groundwork for sustainable progress.

Pathways to Prosperity for Adolescent Girls in Africa offers hope by distilling actionable recommendations based on rigorous evidence of impact. By delineating various pathways to success and examining the implications for policy and practice, this report charts a course toward tangible, lasting change.

At its core, this endeavor is about unleashing the untapped potential of adolescent girls as catalysts for Africa's economic development. The report recommends a set of strong, yet affordable actions to ensure girls' success, such as:

- Promoting girls' economic success through proven and promising multisectoral interventions.
- Focusing on the most vulnerable girls.
- Adopting a holistic approach in the design of interventions.
- Addressing data and evidence gaps to enable stakeholders to better understand what works.

Illuminating the crucial journey toward achieving empowerment for adolescent girls, this report calls upon policy makers, practitioners, researchers, community leaders, and global partners to turn vision into reality. We invite you to join us in helping countries usher in a future in which every African girl can thrive. Together, let us harness the power of data-driven investment to shape a brighter tomorrow for generations to come.

Rachel Glennerster
President
Center for Global Development

Thoai D. Ngo
Vice President, Social and
Behavioral Science Research
Population Council

Victoria Kwakwa
Vice President,
Eastern and Southern Africa
World Bank

Ousmane Diagana
Vice President,
Western and Central Africa
World Bank

CGD CENTER FOR GLOBAL DEVELOPMENT   POPULATION COUNCIL Ideas. Evidence. Impact.   WORLD BANK GROUP

Acknowledgments

This report is the result of a collaboration between the World Bank's Africa Region Gender Innovation Lab, the World Bank's Human Development Practice Group, the Center for Global Development, and the Population Council. It was prepared by a team led by Estelle Koussoubé and Kehinde Ajayi and composed of Henrietta Asiamah, Karen Austrian, Ioana Botea, Wei Chang, Riddhi Kalsi, Michael Kevane, Chiara Pasquini, Clémence Pougué Biyong, Laura Rossouw, Léa Rouanet, Vrinda Sharma, Sara Troiano, and Fatima Zahra. The team is grateful for the overall guidance and support provided by Andrew Dabalen, Aparajita Goyal, and Michael O'Sullivan, with contributions from Amit Dar, Daniel Dulitzky, Rachel Glennerster, Markus Goldstein, Trina Haque, Thoai D. Ngo, Dena Ringold, and Albert Zeufack.

Peer reviewers were Kathleen Beegle, Eleonora Cavagnero, Coralie Gevers, Nicola Jones, Berk Özler, and Idah Pswarayi-Riddihough. Administrative support was provided by Parwana Mowahid, Kenneth Omondi, and Rose-Claire Pakabomba. Nelsy Affoum coordinated the communication and dissemination planning, with contributions from Amy Copley Geist. Beatrice Berman provided production guidance and support throughout the report-writing process.

The team is grateful for feedback and insights from Sarah Baird, Juan Baron, Judith Bruce, Shubha Chakravarty, Thomas de Hoop, Flore Martinant de Preneuf, Rani Deshpande, Diva Dhar, Aletheia Donald, Isabella Micali Drossos, Safaa El Tayeb El-Kogali, David Evans, Ian Forde, Tihtina Zenebe Gebre, Silvia Guglielmi, Kelly Hallman, Margareta Norris Harrit, Caroline Kabiru, Daniel Kirkwood, Scherezad Joya Monami Latif, Diana Lopez, Vandras Luywa, Rachel Marcus, Iain Menzies, Miriam Muller, Benedetta Musillo, Arindam Nandi, Lucia Nhampossa, Brenda Oulo, Ana Maria Oviedo, Amber Peterman, Rachel Pierotti, Luc Razafimandimby, Christophe Rockmore, Justin Sandefur, Hugues Setho, Natacha Stevanovic, Jozefien Van Damme, Waly Wane, David Seth Warren, the World Bank's Gender Group, and participants at the concept note review, authors' workshop, and decision review meetings. The team also benefited from seminar comments from an extensive group of colleagues at our institutions.

The team is additionally grateful to the many organizations that shared their perspectives with us during the writing process, including BRAC, Kasha Global, Plan International, and the United Nations Children's Fund.

The team thanks Nzilani Simu for excellent graphic design support and Luz Carazo, Ariana Ocampo Cruz, and Federico Sanz for valuable research assistance. The team is also grateful to the World Bank's Publishing Program, including Amy Lynn Grossman, Michael Harrup, and Jewel McFadden; and to Nora FitzGerald for initial copyediting.

The team would like to acknowledge the generous support of the Umbrella Facility for Gender Equality (UFGE), a multidonor trust fund administered by the World Bank to advance gender equality and women's empowerment through experimentation and knowledge creation to help governments and the private sector focus policy and programs on scalable solutions with sustainable outcomes. The UFGE is supported with generous contributions from Australia, Canada, Denmark, Finland, Germany, Iceland, Latvia, the Netherlands, Norway, Spain, Sweden, Switzerland, the United Kingdom, the United States, and the Bill and Melinda Gates Foundation. The team also expresses its gratitude for the generous support of the Global Financing Facility for Women, Children and Adolescents, a country-led global partnership committed to ensuring all women, children, and adolescents can survive and thrive. The Population Council team gratefully acknowledges funding from the Danish Ministry of Foreign Affairs.

This report is part of the African Regional Studies Program, an initiative of the Office of the Chief Economist for the Africa Region at the World Bank.

Finally, the team would like to thank the adolescent girls, their families, and the communities who participated in this study. This report would not have been possible without their willingness to share their experiences and insights.

About the Editors and Contributors

Kehinde Ajayi is a senior fellow at the Center for Global Development (CGD) and director of CGD's gender equality and inclusion program. Previously, Kehinde coordinated research initiatives on women's economic empowerment, youth employment, social protection, and childcare in the World Bank's Africa Gender Innovation Lab. Before joining the World Bank, she was an assistant professor of economics at Boston University, a visiting assistant professor at Duke University, a faculty research fellow of the National Bureau of Economic Research, and a Fulbright fellow in Nigeria. She holds a PhD in economics from the University of California, Berkeley, and a BA in economics and international relations from Stanford University.

Henrietta Asiamah is a research economist at Statistics Canada and was also a World Bank Africa fellow. Asiamah has experience in economic research, teaching, and policy garnered from working with the African Women's Development Fund in Ghana and various Canadian policy organizations. Her research focuses broadly on development economics in areas such as the impact of foreign aid on women's empowerment in Sub-Saharan Africa, the measurement of childhood chronic poverty, and the long-term consequences of childhood poverty for future life prospects. Her research has been published in peer-reviewed journals, including the *World Bank Economic Review* and *Child Indicators Research*. She holds a PhD in economics from the University of Guelph in Canada and a BA in economics and statistics from the University of Ghana.

Karen Austrian leads Population Council's Girl Innovation, Research, and Learning Center, a global research hub that generates, synthesizes, and translates evidence on adolescents to support investments that transform their lives, especially those of girls. Prior to stepping into this role, Austrian led a portfolio of projects designed to empower girls in east and southern Africa.

She develops, implements, and evaluates programs that build girls' protective assets, such as financial literacy, social safety nets, and access to education. Austrian is the principal investigator for two large, longitudinal, randomized controlled trials evaluating the impact of multisectoral programs for adolescent girls—the Adolescent Girls Initiative–Kenya and the Adolescent Girls Empowerment Program in Zambia—and led the Council's work assessing the social, health, education, and economic effects of COVID-19 on adolescents and their households in Kenya. She is also actively involved in ensuring that evidence on adolescence is used by global, national, and local stakeholders, having provided guidance on using data for girls' programs and policies to the Policy and Strategy Unit of Kenya's Executive Office of the President and line ministries; the World Bank and bilateral, multilateral organizations; private foundation partners; and international, national, and community organizations. Before joining Population Council in 2007, Austrian cofounded and directed the Binti Pamoja Center, a program to empower adolescent girls in the Kibera slum of Nairobi, Kenya. She has a master's in public health and a PhD in public health and epidemiology and lives in Nairobi, Kenya.

Ioana Botea is a senior economist in the World Bank's Social Protection and Jobs Global Practice. She has more than 10 years of experience in designing, implementing, and evaluating social protection programs, with a focus on safety nets, economic inclusion, and women's empowerment. Botea has managed operations in Cameroon and Gabon and coauthored global and regional publications on social protection and gender. Previously, she worked in the World Bank's Africa Gender Innovation Lab, where she conducted impact evaluations on what works in reducing gender gaps. Prior to joining the World Bank, she worked for Innovations for Poverty Action in Morocco. She holds an MPhil from the University of Cambridge.

Wei Chang is an economist in the World Bank's Africa Region Gender Innovation Lab. Her work focuses on evaluating development and health interventions in low-resource settings for women's and girls' empowerment, often through cross-disciplinary research in collaboration with governments. Before joining the World Bank, she worked in the area of research on public health in Sub-Saharan Africa and the United States, both at the Harvard University School of Public Health and the University of California, San Francisco. She holds a PhD in health policy and management from the University of North Carolina at Chapel Hill and master's degrees in social work and public health from Washington University in St. Louis.

Riddhi Kalsi is a consultant at the World Bank and a PhD student in economics at Sciences Po, Paris. Her dissertation focuses on labor economics, with a particular emphasis on inclusive empirical analysis. Her current research in France delves into the intersection of privatization with the gender pay gap. She has held multiple teaching appointments in graduate-level econometrics at Sciences Po. Prior to completing that degree, she worked at *Harvard Business Review* in an editorial capacity and at Harvard Business Publishing Corporate Learning as a management specialist. Kalsi holds a master's degree in economics from Sciences Po and a BA with honors in economics from Miranda House, Delhi University.

Michael Kevane is a professor in the Department of Economics at Santa Clara University. He has published articles in *Proceedings of the National Academy of Sciences, World Development, Economic Development and Cultural Change,* the *Review of Development Economics,* and the *American Journal of Agricultural Economics.* One of his areas of interest focuses on how libraries promote reading, with articles published in *LIBRI: International Journal of Libraries and Information Studies, World Libraries,* and *Bulletin des bibliothèques de France.* Kevane is a coeditor of *Kordofan Invaded: Peripheral Incorporation and Social Transformation in Islamic Africa,* the author of *Women and Development in Africa: How Gender Works,* and a coauthor of *Rural Community Libraries in Africa: Challenges and Impacts.* He is past president of the Sudan Studies Association and codirector of Friends of African Village Libraries.

Estelle Koussoubé is a senior economist in the World Bank's Africa Region Gender Innovation Lab, where she leads the research agenda on youth employment and adolescent girls' empowerment. She currently works on impact evaluations of adolescent girls' and women's empowerment programs and on youth employment programs, as well as on agriculture and genderbased violence prevention programs in Sub-Saharan Africa, to inform the design and implementation of effective programs and policies to reduce gender inequality. Before joining the World Bank, Koussoubé was a junior research fellow at the French National Research Institute for Sustainable Development and Paris-Dauphine University, where she worked on the Nopoor Project. She holds a PhD in economics from Paris-Dauphine University.

Chiara Pasquini is an evaluation specialist who has applied her quantitative background to different research methodologies and topics ranging from economic inclusion in Uganda to child labor in Ethiopia and women's empowerment in Afghanistan. Previously, she worked on randomized controlled trials in developing countries for Innovations for Poverty Action and other research centers, gaining substantial field and measurement experience. Pasquini has been a consultant for the World Bank since 2018, supporting a wide range of data-based tasks, such as managing randomized controlled trials and analyzing national-level data sets for project design and policy. Her thematic expertise covers social protection and jobs and female empowerment in Sub-Saharan Africa and South Asia. She holds a bachelor's degree and an MSc in economics from Bocconi University in Italy.

Clémence Pougué Biyong is a research analyst in the World Bank's Africa Region Gender Innovation Lab. Her studies focus on health behavior, women's mental health, the economics of care, and gender-based violence. Before joining the World Bank, she worked on the *Africa Development Dynamics* report at the Organisation for Economic Co-operation and Development. Pougué Biyong holds a PhD in economics from the University of Paris 1 Panthéon-Sorbonne and master's degrees in economics and law from University PSL Paris Dauphine and École Normale Supérieure.

Laura Rossouw is a development and health economist who has worked for several South African academic institutions over the past 10 years and often consults for international organizations, including the World Health Organization and the World Bank. She is currently employed as a senior researcher in the Health Economics and Epidemiology Research Office at the University of the Witwatersrand. Rossouw's research has focused on demand-side and behavioral factors related to health outcomes and health-seeking behavior, specifically those related to maternal, sexual, and reproductive health; gender economics; and adolescent health and well-being. She has also worked extensively on the use of fiscal policies to improve health outcomes, specifically policies targeting alcohol and tobacco use, and more recently the use of fiscal policies to improve access to menstrual hygiene management.

Léa Rouanet is a senior economist at the World Bank, where she is the deputy head of the Africa Gender Innovation Lab. She currently leads several impact evaluations aiming to identify and address gender-based constraints to economic activity in Sub-Saharan Africa, with a focus on adolescent girls' empowerment and skills development programs. She also leads the conceptualization and execution of the lab's research uptake strategy and supervises all analysts within her team. Rouanet's research has been published in a number of peer-reviewed journals, including *World Development, Economic Development and Cultural Change, Economics Letters, Journal of*

Economic Behavior and Organization, PLOS One, and *Economic History of Developing Regions.* Before joining the World Bank, she was a PhD candidate and research fellow at the Paris School of Economics, where her research focused on nutrition, child mortality, fertility, and gender preferences in Africa. She holds a PhD from the Paris School of Economics.

Vrinda Sharma is a consultant for the World Bank and a PhD student at the Paris School of Economics. Her work focuses on the economics of water and climate change, especially understanding agricultural adaptation to changing water quality in developing countries. Previously, as a predoctoral researcher at École Polytechnique, she studied demographic transitions in Sub-Saharan Africa. Sharma holds a master's degree from the Paris School of Economics and a BA in economics from Kirori Mal College, Delhi University.

Sara Troiano is a senior economist in the World Bank's Social Protection and Jobs Global Practice. She leads the East Africa Girls' Empowerment and Resilience Program and the program's Evidence Hub, coordinating analytical products, capacity building, and knowledge exchange on girls' and women's empowerment across the region. Troiano has been working on jobs and education investment projects, with a specific focus on inclusion of women and youth, in Africa, Europe, and Latin America. She has published research on education, social policies, and demography. She holds an MSc in development economics from Barcelona Graduate School of Economics, an MSc in sociology and demography from Pompeu Fabra University, and a degree in economics from Bocconi University.

Fatima Zahra is a social demographer with expertise in transitions to adulthood among adolescents in low- and middle-income countries. She is currently an associate at Population Council's Girl Innovation, Research, and Learning Center. Her research lies at the intersection of gender, education, health, and empowerment. At present, she serves as the technical lead on a range of projects, including impact evaluations of child marriage interventions in the Dominican Republic, India, and Niger; a systematic review examining causal links between education and health; and this report. Prior to joining Population Council, she was a postdoctoral fellow in the Population Studies Center at the University of Pennsylvania. Zahra holds a PhD in sociology with a specialization in demography from the University of Maryland and a master's in communication with a focus on health and social change communication from the University of Southern California.

Key Messages

- Africa holds the key to its own prosperity: investing in the untapped economic potential of adolescent girls.

- To succeed, adolescent girls must obtain the skills, resources, and agency they need for autonomy and prosperity in adulthood.

- The reality, however, is different for adolescent girls in Africa. Currently, 40 percent of 15- to 19-year-old girls in Africa are out of school and not working or are married or have children, compared with 12 percent of boys in the same age range, highlighting the urgent need for action.

- This report recommends six strong but affordable sets of actions to ensure adolescent girls succeed:

  1. **Improve adolescent girls' health and education** by reducing out-of-pocket costs, expanding access, and providing youth-friendly services.

  2. **Promote their economic success** through proven and promising multisectoral interventions that integrate technical and life skills training with employment support, tailored to labor market demands and contextual factors.

  3. **Make the most vulnerable girls the priority,** ensuring that no one is left behind.

  4. **Adopt a holistic approach** to the design of interventions for adolescent girls, recognizing the multidimensional nature of empowerment.

  5. **Address data and evidence gaps** to inform effective policies and programs.

  6. **Foster collaboration and mobilize support** from diverse stakeholders to achieve sustainable impact.

- By implementing these recommendations between now and 2040, African countries could unlock an additional $2.4 trillion in income. With the right investments and support, adolescent girls could be the drivers of Africa's economic transformation.

Executive Summary

Why Prioritize Pathways to Prosperity for Adolescent Girls in Africa?

Africa is the world's youngest region.[1] It holds the key to its own prosperity: investing in the untapped economic potential of its adolescents, particularly its adolescent girls. More than one-fifth of the world's adolescent girls (ages 10 to 19)—145 million—reside in Africa, and this share is expected to increase to more than one-third by 2050 (United Nations Department of Economic and Social Affairs, Population Division 2024). For Africa to win the battle against poverty and achieve sustained economic growth, strategic investments are imperative. These investments must flow to adolescent girls, equipping them with the human capital fundamentals, enabling resources, and agency essential to live economically prosperous adult lives.

Despite their potential, adolescent girls in Africa face distinct gender-specific challenges that significantly affect their economic prospects. The region has the highest incidence of child marriage for girls globally, with one in three African girls marrying before the age of 18. Notably, West and Central Africa are home to 7 of the 10 countries with the highest prevalence of child marriage worldwide (UNICEF 2022). Furthermore, although some progress has been made in the past 25 years, these improvements have primarily benefited the wealthiest households; child marriage rates continue to rise among the poorest in Africa (UNICEF 2023). Child marriage is often associated with early childbearing and a higher fertility rate over a girl's lifetime, with significant negative consequences for both girls and their children across various domains, including health and their future labor market outcomes (Petroni et al. 2017; Wodon et al. 2017).

A reproducibility package is available for this book in the Reproducible Research Repository (https://reproducibility.worldbank.org).

Gender gaps in Africa emerge before adolescence and widen during the transition to adolescence and then adulthood. Although there are relatively small gender gaps in schooling among 10- to 14-year-olds in most African countries, girls are typically more likely to participate in household work and boys are more likely to participate in paid work. In the older-adolescent group (ages 15 to 19), a significant number of girls in Africa (26 percent) are neither working nor in school, compared with about 9 percent of boys. Additionally, about 22 percent of these girls are married, compared with only 1 percent of boys. As these older adolescents transition into young adulthood (ages 20 to 24), the gender disparity becomes even more pronounced. Among young women in this age group, 56 percent are married with children, whereas fewer than 16 percent remain in school. In contrast, young men are more likely to continue their education or enter the labor force, and 71 percent remain unmarried without children (figure ES.1).

Adolescent girls' empowerment is not just a matter of human rights; it is also a valuable investment. This report reveals that every dollar invested in adolescent girls' empowerment can generate more than a tenfold return in economic impact. The net benefit of such investments amounts to approximately $2.4 trillion. This stands in contrast to the total cost of investing in the next two generations of girls across all countries, which amounts to less than $200 billion (Rossouw et al. 2024).

How can countries—in particular, African countries—build a pathway to prosperity for adolescent girls? This report seeks to answer this key question. Drawing on recent initiatives and rigorous research geared toward identifying and addressing the distinct challenges faced by adolescent girls in Africa, the report presents new analyses and a comprehensive conceptual framework for understanding, measuring, and improving adolescent girls' empowerment. This approach considers the diverse range of experiences and needs among adolescent girls, taking into account factors such as their educational status, marital status, and whether they have children. The report concludes by charting a course of policy action to build pathways to prosperity for adolescent girls.

FIGURE ES.1 The Transition from Adolescence to Adulthood Is Starker for Girls Than for Boys

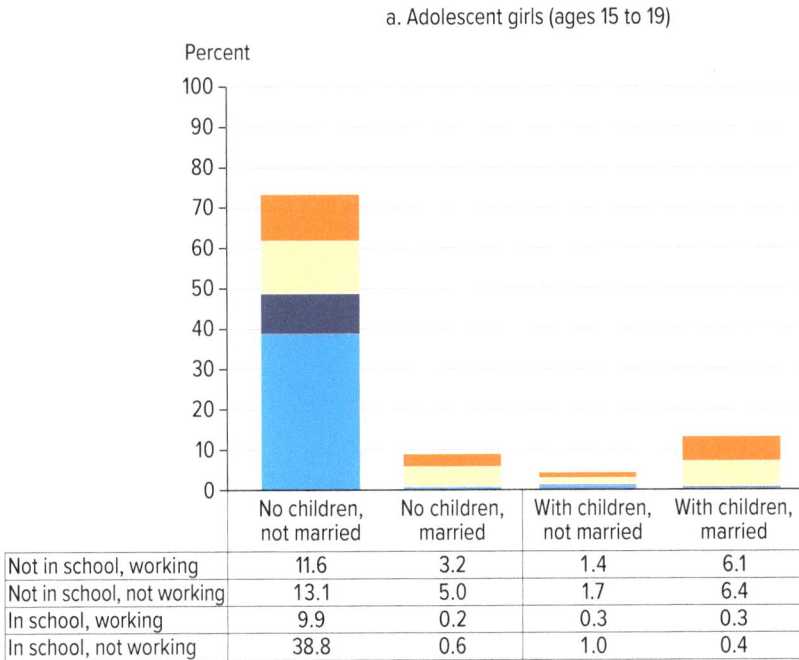

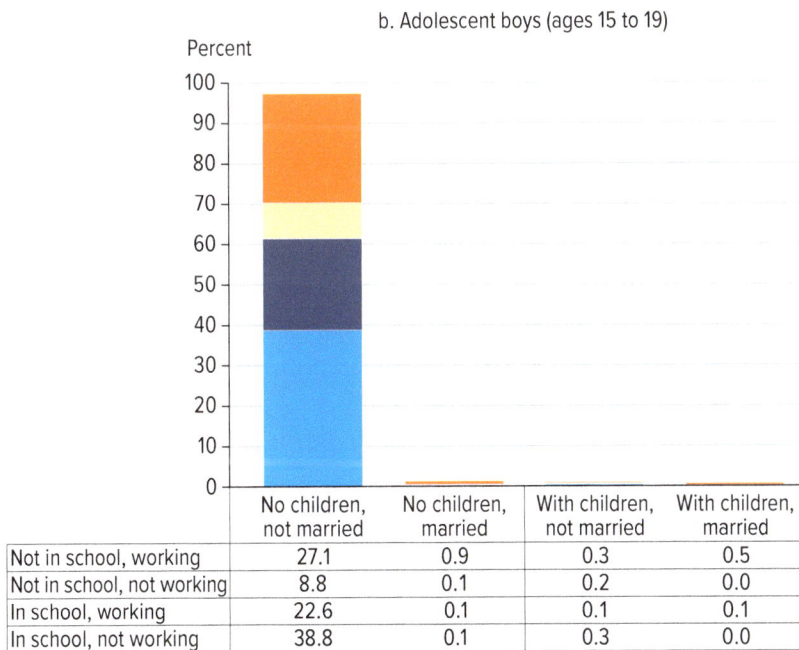

a. Adolescent girls (ages 15 to 19)

Percent

	No children, not married	No children, married	With children, not married	With children, married
Not in school, working	11.6	3.2	1.4	6.1
Not in school, not working	13.1	5.0	1.7	6.4
In school, working	9.9	0.2	0.3	0.3
In school, not working	38.8	0.6	1.0	0.4

b. Adolescent boys (ages 15 to 19)

Percent

	No children, not married	No children, married	With children, not married	With children, married
Not in school, working	27.1	0.9	0.3	0.5
Not in school, not working	8.8	0.1	0.2	0.0
In school, working	22.6	0.1	0.1	0.1
In school, not working	38.8	0.1	0.3	0.0

■ In school, not working   ■ In school, working
■ Not in school, not working   ■ Not in school, working

(continued)

FIGURE ES.1 The Transition from Adolescence to Adulthood Is Starker for Girls Than for Boys *(continued)*

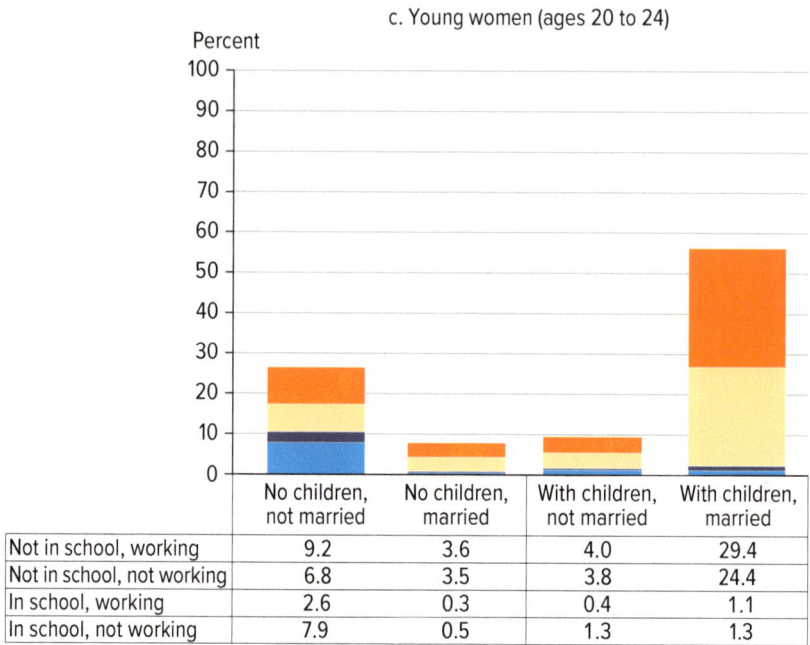

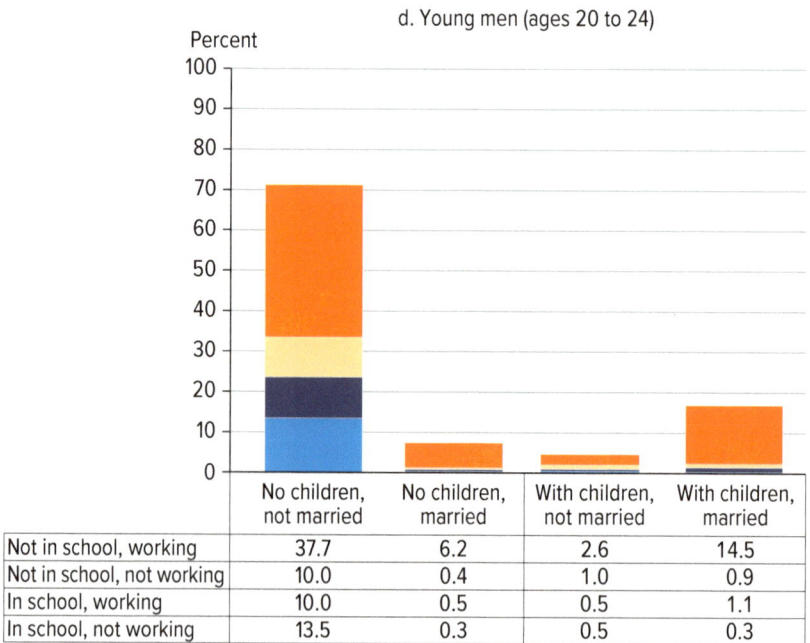

c. Young women (ages 20 to 24)

Percent

	No children, not married	No children, married	With children, not married	With children, married
Not in school, working	9.2	3.6	4.0	29.4
Not in school, not working	6.8	3.5	3.8	24.4
In school, working	2.6	0.3	0.4	1.1
In school, not working	7.9	0.5	1.3	1.3

d. Young men (ages 20 to 24)

Percent

	No children, not married	No children, married	With children, not married	With children, married
Not in school, working	37.7	6.2	2.6	14.5
Not in school, not working	10.0	0.4	1.0	0.9
In school, working	10.0	0.5	0.5	1.1
In school, not working	13.5	0.3	0.5	0.3

- ■ In school, not working
- ■ In school, working
- ■ Not in school, not working
- ■ Not in school, working

Source: Original figure for this report, based on data from USAID's Demographic and Health Surveys (DHS), accessed March 17, 2024, https://www.dhsprogram.com.

What Does Adolescent Girls' Empowerment Mean?

Empowering adolescent girls holds critical importance for poverty reduction and economic growth in Africa. However, achieving this goal demands a departure from the conventional business-as-usual approach. Women's empowerment frameworks have laid the foundation for conceptualizing the dimensions of empowerment for both women and girls. However, what it *means* to be empowered is different for girls and women. Adolescent girls differ from women in significant ways within and across the main dimensions of empowerment: resources, agency, and achievements. Relative to women, girls' access to resources, such as financial institutions or sexual and reproductive health services, is constrained, as is their capacity for making decisions and setting goals.

Even among adolescent girls, pathways to future empowerment vary considerably. Some adolescent girls may develop skills, resources, and agency, leading to better job prospects as adults. For others, the path to empowerment may be steeper because of life transitions like dropping out of school, early marriage, or childbearing.

This report introduces an adapted framework for understanding adolescent girls' empowerment, emphasizing four key components:

- **Human capital fundamentals:** Education and health provide the bedrock for adolescent girls' future economic success.
- **Enabling resources:** These include knowledge and skills, financial capital, physical and digital capital, social capital, and time available for productive activities.
- **Agency:** Girls must be able to exert their voices, set goals, and make decisions.
- **Context:** This includes fragility, conflict, and violence; statutory laws; formal institutions; social norms and religion; labor market opportunities; and household context.

Together, these four components of adolescent girls' empowerment combine and interact to make up a fifth component, long-term **economic achievements**, such as income and participation in age-appropriate paid work (table ES.1).

TABLE ES.1 Components of Adolescent Girls' Empowerment Influence Their Long-Term Economic Achievements

Component	Indicator	Specific measures for indicator
Human capital fundamentals	Educational progress	Educational enrollment, attainment, and attendance; grade progression; literacy skills; numeracy skills
	Health	Survival/mortality; sexual and reproductive health rights; mental health; nutrition
Enabling resources	Knowledge and skills	Life skills (including socioemotional skills); financial literacy
	Financial capital	Access to economic resources: bank accounts, loans; economic assets: savings
	Physical and digital capital	Household assets; personal assets; access to digital spaces; cell phones
	Social capital	Peer networks; access to safe spaces
	Time	Time for engaging in productive activity
Agency	Goal setting	Aspirations for education, work, marriage, and childbearing
	Sense of agency	Self-efficacy; self-esteem; locus of control; gender attitudes
	Control	Control over decision-making and time use
Context	Fragility, conflict, and violence	Prevalence and duration of conflict and violence
	Statutory laws/legal framework	Laws relating to gender, resources, work, minimum age for marriage, minimum age for work, gender-based violence, and access to identification documents
	Formal institutions	Presence and characteristics of other formal institutions: schools; health; vocational, legal, and financial services (including banks and rotating savings and credit associations)
	Norms and religion	Expectations regarding gender roles, resource access and use, work, age of marriage, and gender-based violence; religious beliefs
	Labor market opportunities	Sector-specific access to jobs; quality of available job opportunities
	Household context	Parental and household members' gender attitudes; parental aspirations for girls' education and work; relationship dynamics in households (cooperation among household members, discussions among household members on various topics, etc.); household structure and composition
Economic achievement	Labor market outcomes	Job quality; income; paid work; formal or informal sector; salaried or self-employment; age-appropriate work

Source: Original table for this report.
Note: AG = agency; CO = context; EA = economic achievement; EN = enabling resources; HC = human capital fundamentals.

The conceptual framework presented in the report differs from existing frameworks in the African context (for example, Calder and Huda 2013; Jones et al. 2019; Moll 2018), not only in emphasizing components such as context and enabling resources, but also in considering the fact that girls may follow diverse paths to empowerment, whether a particular girl's path may be pursuing education exclusively without getting married or having children, or an alternative path that navigates transitions such as school dropout, early marriage, and childbearing. For a discussion of the challenges in measuring adolescent girls' empowerment and potential solutions, refer to box ES.1.

BOX ES.1 Measuring Adolescent Girls' Empowerment: Challenges and Path Forward

Why does measuring adolescent girls' empowerment matter?

Measuring adolescent girls' empowerment is crucial for informed policy and program design but remains challenging. Existing frameworks primarily focus on women's empowerment, and empowerment-specific measurement guidance for adolescent girls is limited. Measurement gaps in surveys include a lack of questions on digital capital, on agency aspects like control over time use, and on job quality. Additionally, surveys show little variation in question types across demographic groups, limiting understanding of subgroup nuances.

Key measurement challenges

1. **Lack of theoretical framework:** The absence of a clear theoretical framework for measurement of adolescent girls' empowerment leads to inconsistent measures across studies and surveys.

2. **Limited differentiation:** Measurement tools do not adequately differentiate among diverse demographic groups, making it hard to understand disparities.

3. **Survey variation:** Surveys vary significantly in wording and aspects measured, making comparisons regarding adolescent girls' empowerment difficult.

The path forward

These measurement challenges highlight the need for comprehensive and standardized measurement of adolescent girls' empowerment through three critical next steps.

1. **Prioritizing conceptualization:** Develop a clear and standardized conceptual framework for adolescent girls' empowerment. Ensure inclusivity by consulting with diverse stakeholders and practitioners to accommodate the varied needs and aspirations of adolescent girls.

2. **Coordinating efforts:** Standardize and harmonize key measures of adolescent girls' empowerment to enhance comparability and reliability, drawing inspiration from relevant successful practices for measuring women's economic empowerment.

3. **Developing new measures:** Create new tools, including community-level instruments, to cover underrepresented dimensions of adolescent girls' empowerment.

Each component of empowerment will evolve during adolescence, preparing girls to be economically prosperous in adulthood (figure ES.2). However, the evolution of these components and their relative prominence at different ages depend on girls' initial endowment in each component at the beginning of adolescence (age 10) and the various transitions they experience as they progress through adolescence.

The key components of adolescent girls' empowerment also differ by demographic group. To illustrate this diversity of experiences and their relationship with the components of empowerment, the report presents five profiles of adolescent girls residing in various parts of Africa, each represented by a distinct line in figure ES.2.

FIGURE ES.2   Adolescent Girls Can Follow Alternative Pathways toward Empowerment in Adulthood

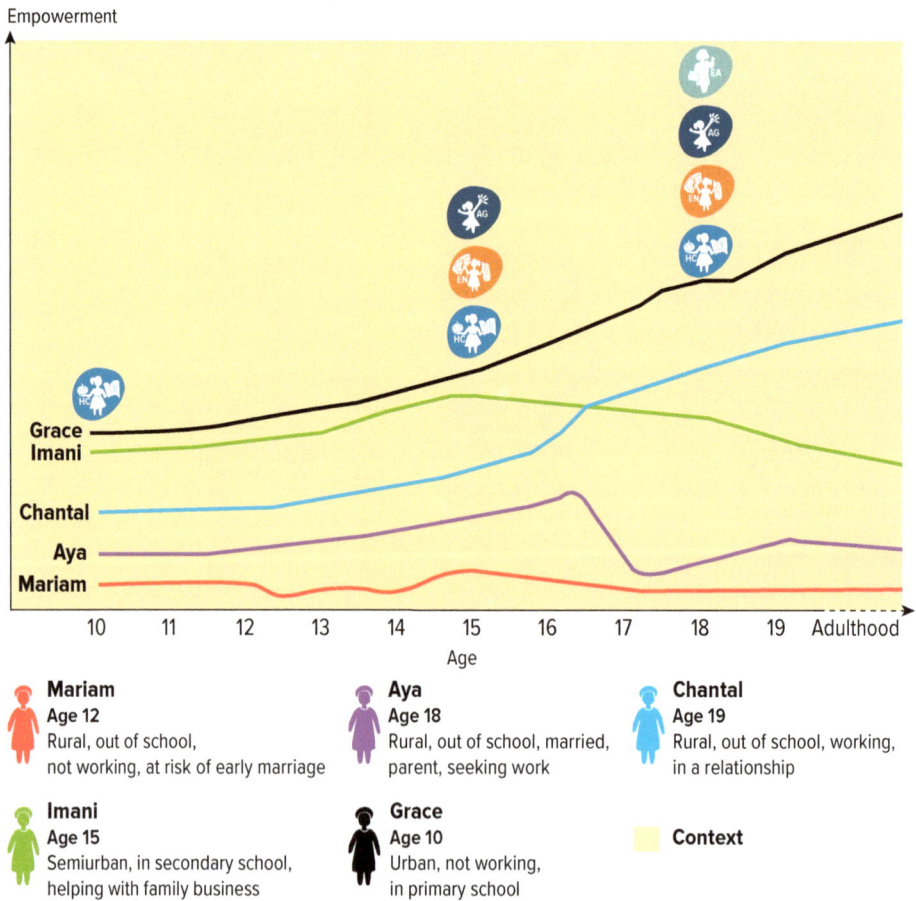

Source: Original figure for this report.

Note: AG = agency; EA = economic achievement; EN = enabling resources; HC = human capital fundamentals. Refer to table ES.1 for additional information about each component.

The framework employed in this report demonstrates that girls' pathways to empowerment in adulthood vary depending on their starting point in adolescence and the timing of interventions (figure ES.3). Throughout the report, this framework serves as a guide for evaluating the design and effectiveness of programs and policies, with a recognition that no single intervention will adequately meet the needs of all adolescent girls in Africa.

While not explicitly part of the framework, two cross-cutting experiences that interact with pathways to empowerment are important to consider for a more holistic view of adolescent girls' empowerment: gender-based violence and disabilities. Experiences of gender-based violence or harmful practices perpetrated at home, in school, in public spaces, within marriage,

FIGURE ES.3 Appropriately Designed Interventions to Support Adolescent Girls Can Boost Their Empowerment at Any Age, Whether They Are Still in School or Already Out of School, Are Married or Not, or Do or Do Not Have Children

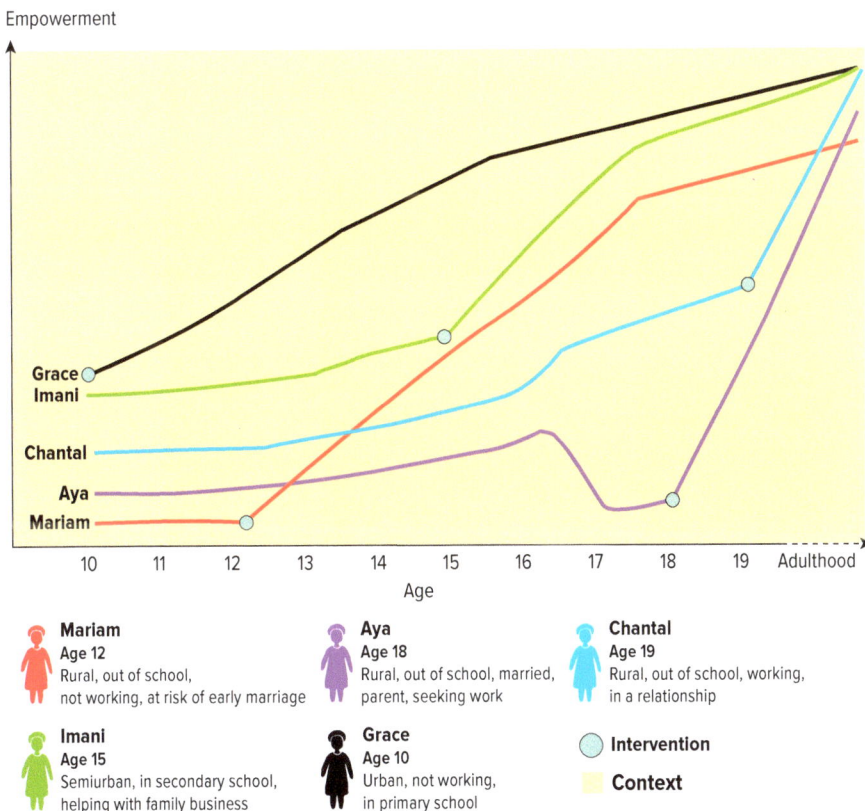

Source: Original figure for this report.

or in the workplace can affect multiple aspects of empowerment, including school attendance and performance, girls' sense of agency, and their ability to make decisions that affect their well-being. Girls often face a higher risk of violence during adolescence—more than at any other time in their lives. However, they may be less likely to report experiences of violence, given potential threats to their personal or family reputation. These risks of gender-based violence, combined with more limited access to services and support for survivors, present an important barrier to empowerment for adolescent girls. Physical and mental disabilities may also affect girls' ability to fulfill their educational and economic goals and minimize agency depending on the presence of societal norms and resources related to disabilities.

How Diverse Are Adolescent Girls' Experiences in Africa, and How Does the Diversity Matter for Their Prosperity?

A common policy aspiration in African countries is to ensure that adolescent girls remain in school, delay childbearing, and delay marriage. School enrollment rates for younger adolescent girls (ages 10 to 14) have reached more than 80 percent in many of these countries. However, by the time they get to older adolescence, less than half of 15- to 19-year-old girls are still exclusively in school, without having gotten married or having had children (figure ES.4).

Whereas regional trends in schooling and work have generally been positive, regional trends in marriage and childbearing have been mixed. Over the past 20 years, the percentage of 15- to 19-year-old girls in school increased in most African countries. Most African countries, but not all, also saw a decline in the share of girls who are out of school and exclusively working. Marriage rates generally fell across countries over this time frame. However, some countries saw increases, including Madagascar, Niger, Tanzania, and Zimbabwe. Additionally, the percentage of adolescent girls with children largely declined, except in a few countries, including Burundi and Zambia. In Comoros, Tanzania, and Zimbabwe, both rates of marriage and having children among adolescent girls increased over the past 20 years.

Adolescent girls' experiences vary not only across countries, but also within them, partly reflecting the countries' cultural, social, legal, and economic environments. Although country-level indicators provide valuable insights, they tend to mask subnational variation. Within individual countries, variations in outcomes such as rates of school enrollment, marriage, and childbearing, as well as gender attitudes, can be just as substantial as variations across countries. For a deeper exploration of the complexity of adolescent girls' empowerment and insights from impact evaluation surveys across African countries, refer to box ES.2.

FIGURE ES.4 Over Half of 15- to 19-Year-Old Girls in Africa Are Out of School or Married or Have a Child

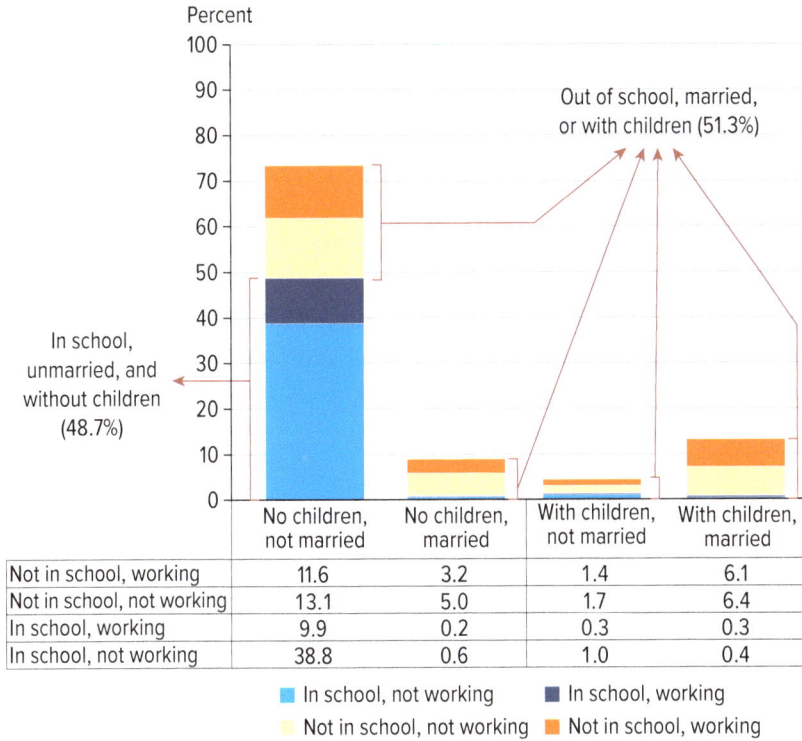

	No children, not married	No children, married	With children, not married	With children, married
Not in school, working	11.6	3.2	1.4	6.1
Not in school, not working	13.1	5.0	1.7	6.4
In school, working	9.9	0.2	0.3	0.3
In school, not working	38.8	0.6	1.0	0.4

Legend:
- In school, not working
- In school, working
- Not in school, not working
- Not in school, working

Source: Original figure for this report, based on data from USAID's Demographic and Health Surveys, accessed March 17, 2024, https://www.dhsprogram.com.

While recognizing the diversity of experiences within countries, this report categorizes countries into five distinct groups, each characterized by common features that reflect the intersections among rates of schooling, work, marriage, and childbearing (figure ES.5). Notably, these country categories correlate with the prevalence of gender-related laws in each type of context, which suggests the importance of the legal context in shaping adolescent girls' experiences (table ES.2). These five categories provide an instructive tool for understanding patterns in the experiences of adolescent girls and offer insight into approaches for supporting empowerment.

BOX ES.2 Exploring the Complexity of Adolescent Girls' Empowerment: Insights from Impact Evaluation Surveys in Africa

Why is a holistic approach necessary to effectively empower adolescent girls?

Empowering adolescent girls in Africa requires recognizing that empowerment is inherently multidimensional. Although interventions focusing on education and health are crucial for laying the foundation of success in adulthood, they are not sufficient to improve all dimensions of empowerment. Additionally, life transitions such as marriage and childbearing often significantly hinder girls' acquisition of human capital and agency, further constraining their ability to realize their full potential.

Key insights from selected African countries

This report uses data from impact evaluations of programs targeting adolescent girls across 11 countries in Africa to shed light on the complex interrelationships among various dimensions of empowerment and how these dimensions manifest themselves across different life stages:

1. **Multidimensional empowerment:** Empowerment among adolescent girls is multidimensional. Girls may exhibit empowerment in one domain while lacking it in another. Recognizing these variations is essential for designing effective empowerment programs.

2. **Weak correlations between empowerment dimensions:** There are generally weak correlations between human capital fundamentals (education and health) and other dimensions of empowerment, suggesting a need for holistic interventions that go beyond basic education and health to effectively enhance empowerment.

3. **Impact of life transitions and contextual factors:** Life transitions, like marriage and childbearing, and contextual factors deeply affect girls' empowerment. Married girls and young mothers face substantial challenges in maintaining their educational pursuits and pursuing their career aspirations, although some manage to retain or even enhance certain resources and achievements.

The path forward

These findings carry significant implications for shaping policies and programs aimed at empowering girls in Africa. The key points underscored by the analysis include the following:

1. **Broadening empowerment strategies:** Policies and programs should extend beyond just education and health to encompass a broader spectrum of empowerment strategies, prioritizing comprehensive support, including skills development and social protection.

2. **Tailored interventions:** Tailoring interventions to the specific needs of different demographic groups of girls, especially vulnerable ones such as young mothers balancing work or schooling with childcare responsibilities, is essential for effective empowerment.

3. **Harnessing digital tools:** Leveraging digital technologies can be a powerful means for reaching and supporting adolescent girls. However, it is crucial to ensure that girls have the necessary resources and skills to make the most of these opportunities.

4. **Continuous evaluation:** Constant monitoring and evaluation are vital to understand the evolving challenges and opportunities faced by adolescent girls in Africa, ensuring that policies and programs remain responsive and effective.

FIGURE ES.5 There Are Systematic Cross-Country Differences in Adolescent Girls' Experiences

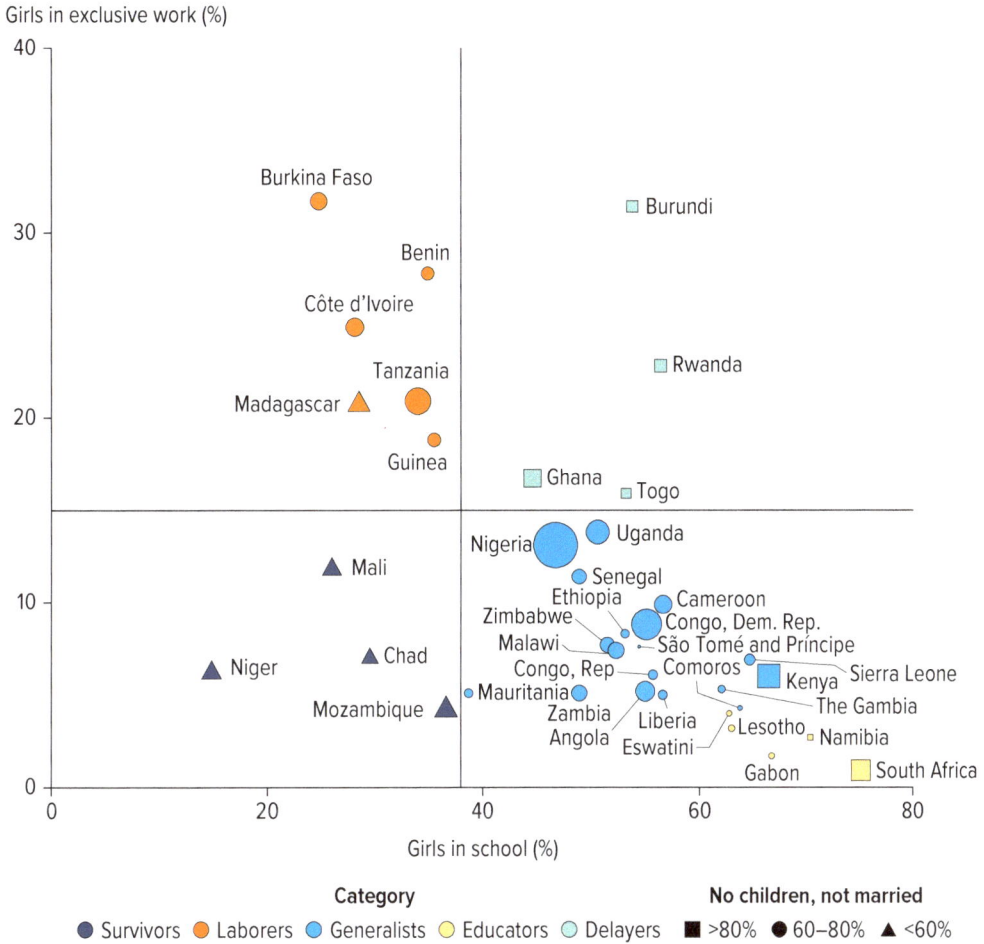

Source: Original figure for this report, based on data from USAID's Demographic and Health Surveys, accessed March 17, 2024, https://www.dhsprogram.com.

Note: Figure shows percentages of 15- to 19-year-old unmarried girls with no children who are enrolled in school (horizontal axis) and are exclusively working (vertical axis). The size of each country marker reflects country population size.

TABLE ES.2 Cross-Country Differences in Adolescent Girls' Experiences Correlate with Countries' Legal Environments

Country category	Key country characteristics	Relevant country laws
Marriage and childbearing delayers	The most successful at delaying marriage and childbearing among adolescent girls. Relatively high levels of schooling and work among adolescent girls.	All countries in this category have laws ensuring that a woman can get a job, a bank account, and national identification documents in the same way as a man.
Educators	Highest levels of school enrollment among adolescent girls, yet relatively low levels of employment, even for girls who are out of school.	All countries in this category have laws promoting education (free postprimary schooling and marriage ages above 18).
Generalists	Moderate levels among adolescent girls in regard to all characteristics: marriage and fertility delay, schooling, and work.	Countries in this category have a mix of legal environments and are not leaders in any domain of gender legal reforms.
Laborers	Highest levels of work among adolescent girls, with relatively low levels of schooling and moderate rates of marriage and childbearing.	Countries in this category are more likely to have employment-related laws (for example, ensuring women can get a job in the same way as men, equal pay for equal work, 14 weeks of paid leave for mothers) and laws prohibiting gender discrimination in credit access.
Survivors	Highest levels of vulnerability among adolescent girls. All countries in this category are low-income countries classified as fragility, conflict, or violence settings by the World Bank, with the highest rates of marriage and childbearing among adolescent girls, the lowest levels of schooling, and a high share who are not in work or schooling.	All countries in this category have laws that women and men can access national identification documents in the same way, presenting a foundation for access to social services.

Source: Original table for this report, based on data from USAID's Demographic and Health Surveys, accessed March 17, 2024, https://www.dhsprogram.com, and World Bank 2020.

What Do We Know about What Works to Build Human Capital Fundamentals and Enhance Economic Success for Adolescent Girls?

A strong foundation in human capital is crucial for achieving success in today's world and ensuring a smooth transition to a productive and healthy adulthood. Adolescence is a period in which girls experience rapid physical, emotional, social, and cognitive changes. Making investments in education and health during girls' adolescent years a priority can profoundly influence girls' adulthood and even shape the trajectory of the next generation. Such investments align with the promotion of a life path in which adolescent girls can educate themselves, adopt healthy lifestyles, and delay family formation. For girls pursuing alternative life paths, human capital fundamentals also play a crucial role in skills development and broader capital accumulation. However, it is essential to recognize that improving girls' human capital fundamentals doesn't automatically guarantee a successful transition into productive, safe, and dignified employment or a significant reduction in gender gaps in economic achievement in adulthood. Several factors, including marriage, childbearing, gender roles, and norms related to women's employment and household dynamics, also come into play (see, for example, Carvalho and Evans 2022; Elder and Kring 2016; Klasen 2019).

To empower adolescent girls to realize their economic potential and thrive in adulthood, it is crucial to expand beyond establishing human capital fundamentals. This involves promoting enabling resources, including socioemotional skills, financial literacy, and access to networks; fostering agency; and creating an environment conducive to their economic achievements. This report reviews the evidence on interventions addressing each of these areas and categorizes them as follows: (1) effective: at least three rigorous studies show the intervention has positive and statistically significant effects; (2) promising: one or two rigorous studies show the intervention has positive and statistically significant effects; (3) mixed: rigorous studies yield a mix of positive and negative statistically significant effects for the intervention or show it has no statistically significant effects; (4) no effect: at least two rigorous studies show the intervention has no statistically significant effects; (5) unknown or little evidence: fewer than two rigorous studies investigate the intervention and assess its effects (table ES.3).

TABLE ES.3 Evidence-Based Interventions Can Build Pathways to Prosperity

Intervention	Improving human capital fundamentals	Enhancing economic success
In-kind transfers for schooling	Effective	Effective
Comprehensive economic empowerment programs	Unknown	Effective
School fee reduction or elimination	Effective	Promising
School feeding	Effective	Promising
Improving quality of instruction	Effective	Unknown
Health services	Effective	Unknown
Sexual and reproductive health education	Effective	Unknown
Cash transfers	Effective	Mixed
Employment opportunities for women	Promising	Promising
Engaging boys, parents, and community	Promising	Promising
Information on return to education or on training	Promising	Promising
Child marriage ban	Promising	Unknown
Edutainment programs	Promising	Unknown
Inheritance law reform	Promising	Unknown
School construction	Promising	Unknown
Girls' group empowerment programs	Mixed	Mixed
Other life skills training, mentoring, and empowerment programs	Mixed	Mixed
Financial inclusion programs	Unknown	Mixed
Traditional vocational and business skills training	Unknown	Mixed

Source: Original table for this report.

The successful implementation of these interventions requires careful attention to design and execution. A notable example is the increasing adoption of girls' groups, or "safe spaces," as platforms to reach adolescent girls, especially those out of school. However, the evidence on their impact on adolescent girls' outcomes is mixed, calling for careful consideration of the key factors necessary to ensure their successful implementation. Box ES.3 provides detailed insights into the critical elements for effectively designing and implementing safe spaces programs.

BOX ES.3 Key Considerations for Successful Implementation of Safe Spaces

Since the mid-2010s, the girls' groups—"safe spaces"—approach has gained prominence in programming for adolescent girls, supported by a growing evidence base and practical guidance tools.

Key insights on safe spaces

Safe spaces are often referred to as a type of program for adolescent girls, but they should be viewed as a flexible platform for delivering a wide range of interventions. Safe spaces typically include three core features: a group of girls, regular meetings at a designated location, and a mentor who leads the group. Importantly, safe spaces are not limited to specific thematic areas and are adaptable to address diverse needs. They can also be implemented alongside additional interventions that engage girls' households, schools, and communities.

Critical factors for successful implementation

Implementers and experts have reached a consensus on critical factors for successful safe spaces implementation along the program delivery chain, as shown in table BES.3.1.

TABLE BES.3.1 Each Step in the Program Delivery Chain Necessitates Critical Factors for Successful Implementation

Step in program delivery chain	Critical factors
Community outreach	Involving the community during program preparation is essential for building ownership and trust in the program. Effective outreach methods include organizing family days, celebrations, and home visits by mentors. Leveraging peer networks and influential community members can encourage participation, and tailoring messaging to respect local customs is crucial.
Recruiting and supporting mentors	Mentors are critical to program quality, and their preferred qualifications depend on the context. Positive mentor performance is associated with characteristics such as being female, coming from the same communities as beneficiaries, speaking the local language, and having basic literacy and good social and leadership skills. Mentors need training, ongoing supervision, and support.
Targeting	Achieving change requires working with a critical mass of girls in a given area. Making it a priority to reach more girls in the same community before expanding to additional communities is important.
Recruiting girls	Outreach efforts should be inclusive and tailored to reach vulnerable, younger, out-of-school, and at-risk girls. Strategies like door-to-door recruitment and surveys or censuses can help identify potential beneficiaries and their specific needs.

(continued)

BOX ES.3 Key Considerations for Successful Implementation of Safe Spaces *(continued)*

TABLE BES.3.1 Each Step in the Program Delivery Chain Necessitates Critical Factors for Successful Implementation *(continued)*

Step in program delivery chain	Critical factors
Finding a location	Locations of safe spaces should be identified in consultation with communities, ensuring they are easily accessible, are private, and meet basic needs. Investing in making the spaces pleasant environments is essential.
Forming groups	Consideration should be given to segmenting groups based on characteristics like age, marital status, and educational enrollment status. Special considerations are needed for working with migrants or refugees and local populations in the same communities, and girls with disabilities should be included.
Defining content	Curriculums should align with participants' aspirations and address key challenges. Topics should be sequenced carefully, starting with foundational topics like life skills and basic literacy.
Delivering services	Program intensity is crucial; meetings should be regular and frequent. Sessions should be long enough to cover training and allow for feedback. Various participatory techniques can be used, and material should avoid reinforcing gender stereotypes.
Engaging with key stakeholders	Identifying key stakeholders and potential champions in the community can be helpful. Parallel safe spaces can be set up to provide information and training to strategic stakeholders like parents and boys, although this approach carries some risks.
Monitoring and evaluation	Access to good monitoring data and understanding program success and challenges are essential. Purposeful monitoring, evaluation, and learning measures should provide actionable information. Qualitative feedback mechanisms can improve program quality.
Scaling up	Challenges related to scaling up include program cost, implementing capacity, mentor availability, coordination with similar programs, and embedding within a national system.

Source: Original table for this report.

Beyond the design of interventions themselves, it is imperative to pay attention to political economy factors that can impede program and policy development and implementation and legal reforms. Key considerations include securing government support, underscoring the economic benefits of adolescent girls' empowerment initiatives, engaging with influential community leaders, and fostering regional coordination and collaboration.

The achievement of successful legal reforms, such as those targeting child marriage, relies on these considerations as well as on building extensive coalitions of partners and active engagement with the legal community.

How Should the Path Forward Be Forged?

The path forward in the journey to empower adolescent girls for success in Africa is clear and multifaceted. This report outlines six primary areas for policy and targeted programmatic action:

1. **Building human capital fundamentals through improved health and education.** Establishing core education and health resources during adolescence matters not only for its intrinsic value, but also for enhancing girls' agency and their accumulation of other resources. Strategies should aim to reduce households' out-of-pocket schooling costs through proven strategies like fee elimination, school feeding, and cash transfers to boost school enrollment and learning; expand access through school construction and transport; promote the use of promising strategies such as comprehensive interventions that combine sexual and reproductive health education with youth-friendly services and micronutrient supplementation to further improve girls' health and education outcomes; and leverage the mutually reinforcing connection between building a robust human capital foundation and delaying marriage and childbearing to yield multiplicative effects.

2. **Complementing human capital investments with interventions that provide girls with essential resources, agency, and a supportive environment conducive to their success.** Empowering adolescent girls for success goes beyond establishing human capital fundamentals. Strategies should foster integration of market-aligned vocational training, business support, life skills training, and other employment support into comprehensive economic empowerment programs to boost girls' employment and income, especially for those who are out of school; support investment in promising approaches aiming to expand and improve the services and opportunities to which girls have access, including employment opportunities for women; promote adoption of a nuanced approach to interventions like cash transfers and girls' clubs, adapting their design to local needs to enhance effectiveness and cost-efficiency at scale; and encourage customization of interventions to address contextual factors such as relevant legal frameworks, labor market structures, fragility and conflict, and community and household contexts, to ensure sustainable improvements in girls' empowerment outcomes.

3. **Tailoring interventions to address the diverse circumstances and needs of girls, putting a priority on the most vulnerable.** Strategies should identify and assign priority to various groups of girls, particularly the most vulnerable ones, including those from the poorest households, rural areas with limited resources, or areas affected by violence, bearing in mind that definitions of vulnerability may extend to many other circumstances and characteristics, such as ethnicity, religion, or disabilities. Girls managing dual roles of working and being in school, or working and taking care of children, require tailored programs to support their needs for continuing education, accessing childcare, and earning income. Young mothers and married girls face unique obstacles to continuing their education and need support to enhance their human capital fundamentals and accumulate other resources.

4. **Adopting a holistic approach in the design of interventions.** Policies should anticipate potential challenges that may arise at different stages of program development and implementation. Factors such as program costs, implementation capacity, and alignment with existing initiatives must be carefully considered. Additionally, leveraging digital tools and platforms can be beneficial for reaching girls who are out of school, marry early, or reside in rural areas, given evidence of expanding digital access across different countries, with different demographics, and across different socioeconomic groups. Technological innovations can also lower costs, given the challenges of tight fiscal space.

5. **Addressing data and evidence gaps.** Strategies should encourage development and testing measures in areas in which measurement is lacking, such as aspects of context, digital capital, and job quality, and promote generation of evidence and design of programs that allow an assessment of not only what works, but what works for whom, in particular for married adolescents and girls with children, who have often been overlooked. Policies should also make a priority of measuring program quality from the outset, using detailed indicators for assessing implementation effectiveness. Additional insights about cost-effectiveness are needed to understand the trade-offs among promising interventions. Effective avenues for scale-up are necessary to expand the scope of proven approaches.

6. **Mobilizing key stakeholders and fostering collaboration.** Strategies should aim to rally support from a diverse range of stakeholders, including community, national, and regional leaders; governmental bodies; the private sector; civil society; nongovernmental organizations; and other development partners. They should emphasize both the social and economic benefits of empowering adolescent girls, supported by a robust analytical framework, and facilitate collaboration among stakeholders to effectively implement evidence-based interventions, encompassing both programs and policy or legal reforms.

In contemplating the future of empowering adolescent girls for economic and overall success, it is essential to recognize that adolescent girls are a diverse group. Tailored approaches that consider diversity among them must be developed, and any efforts at scaling up should account for costs, capacity, and contextual factors, including those related to political economy, that may influence the effectiveness of interventions in different areas. Policy makers should ask themselves: What are the specific challenges confronted by, for instance, Aya, our 18-year-old married mother in a rural community? What resources and support does she require? Similarly, what does Imani, our 15-year-old in a semiurban setting, need to thrive? What are the most effective and cost-effective ways to put these girls and others like them, as well as others with different but equally valid needs, on a path to success? Box ES.4 summarizes the key innovations and contributions of this report to the ongoing dialogue on adolescent girls' empowerment in Africa.

The dialogue this report seeks to initiate should not revolve around whether policy makers act to improve girls' empowerment, but rather how they can effectively, equitably, and urgently do so. The cost of inaction is high. The time for change is now.

BOX ES.4 What Is New in This Report

Quantifying the return on investment

This report presents a compelling case for investing in adolescent girls in Africa by calculating the economic gains to be realized from crucial investment of this type. Incorporating estimates of effects of interventions to empower adolescent girls and associated implementation costs, it concretely demonstrates the potential for achieving a tenfold return from investments over the next 15 years.

Conceptual framework

Taking a comprehensive view, this report proposes a fresh conceptual framework that highlights a path toward the realization of empowerment for adolescent girls at different ages—pursuing education exclusively without marriage or childbearing. Additionally, it acknowledges alternative paths that reflect the reality that many adolescent girls in Africa have already dropped out of school, gotten married, started childbearing, or any combination of these.

New analysis

The report presents a novel overview of key facts about adolescent girls in Africa that matter for defining and measuring empowerment, drawing on data from a number of sources, including the Demographic and Health Surveys, the United Nations Children's Fund's Multiple Indicator Cluster Surveys, the World Bank's Global Financial Inclusion Index (Findex) database and Women, Business, and the Law database, and data from impact evaluation surveys of programs for

(continued)

BOX ES.4 What Is New In This Report *(continued)*

adolescent girls in Africa. It outlines the first data-driven categorization of countries by adolescent girls' empowerment status, providing an innovative tool for policy guidance.

Evidence reviews

Two chapters in the report present narrative reviews of existing evidence on the impacts of interventions to improve adolescent girls' human capital fundamentals and to enhance their empowerment. These reviews outline gaps in evidence regarding effective ways to support different groups of adolescent girls in Africa.

Spotlights

Four spotlights in the report provide further insight into key issues concerning adolescent girls' empowerment. The first illuminates gaps in the measurement of adolescent girls' empowerment. The second presents descriptive evidence from impact evaluations on vulnerable adolescent girls' empowerment. The third provides guidance on how to ensure quality implementation of safe spaces. The fourth discusses the political economy of adolescent girls' empowerment.

Policy guidance

The report concludes with evidence-based recommendations for policy makers, practitioners, and researchers with the intention that these recommendations will drive further dialogue and collaboration to improve the lives of adolescent girls in Africa and beyond.

Qualitative insights

Throughout, the report draws on qualitative insights from extensive consultations with adolescent girls, policy makers, and practitioners.

Note

1. Throughout the report, "Africa" refers to the 48 countries included in the World Bank's regional classification for Sub-Saharan Africa. For details, see https://datahelpdesk.worldbank.org/knowledgebase/articles/906519-world-bank -country-and-lending-groups.

References

Calder, Rebecca, and Karishma Huda. 2013. "Adolescent Girls, Economic Opportunities Study, Rwanda." Development Pathways, London.

Carvalho, Shelby, and David K. Evans. 2022. *Girls' Education and Women's Equality: How to Get More out of the World's Most Promising Investment.* Washington, DC: Center for Global Development.

Elder, Sara D., and Sriani Kring. 2016. *Young and Female—A Double Strike? Gender Analysis of School-to-Work Transition Surveys in 32 Developing Countries.* Work4Youth Publications. Geneva: International Labour Office.

Jones, Nicola, Sarah Baird, Joan Hicks, Megan Devonald, Eric Neumeister, Elizabeth Presler-Marshall, Abreham Iyasu, and Workneh Yadete. 2019. *Adolescent Economic Empowerment in Ethiopia.* Baseline Report Series. London: Gender and Adolescence: Global Evidence.

Klasen, Stephan. 2019. "What Explains Uneven Female Labor Force Participation Levels and Trends in Developing Countries?" *World Bank Research Observer* 34 (2): 161–97. https://doi.org/10.1093/wbro/lkz005.

Moll, Amanda Lane. 2018. "Adolescent Economic Empowerment in a Kenyan Urban Rural Context." PhD dissertation, Georgia State University, Atlanta.

Petroni, Suzanne, Mara Steinhaus, Natacha Stevanovic Fenn, Kirsten Stoebenau, and Amy Gregowski. 2017. "New Findings on Child Marriage in Sub-Saharan Africa." *Annals of Global Health* 83 (5–6): 781–90. https://doi.org/10.1016/j.aogh.2017 .09.001.

Rossouw, Laura, Michael Kevane, Estelle Koussoubé, and Kehinde Ajayi. 2024. "Lost Potential: The Cost of Inaction of Adolescent Girls' Empowerment." Background paper for this report. World Bank, Washington, DC.

UNICEF (United Nations Children's Fund). 2022. "Child Marriage in West and Central Africa: A Statistical Overview and Reflections on Ending the Practice." UNICEF, New York. https://data.unicef.org/resources/child-marriage-in-west -and-central-africa-a-statistical-overview-and-reflections-on-ending-the-practice/.

UNICEF (United Nations Children's Fund). 2023. "Is an End to Child Marriage within Reach? Latest Trends and Future Prospects: 2023 Update." UNICEF, New York.

United Nations Department of Economic and Social Affairs, Population Division. 2024. World Population Prospects 2024. Custom data acquired via data portal, accessed August 22, 2024. https://population.un.org/wpp/.

Wodon, Quentin, Chata Male, Ada Nayihouba, Adenike Onagoruwa, Aboudrahyme Savadogo, Ali Yedan, Jeff Edmeades, et al. 2017. "Economic Impacts of Child Marriage: Global Synthesis Report." World Bank and International Center for Research on Women, Washington, DC.

World Bank. 2020. *Women, Business and the Law 2020.* Washington, DC: World Bank. https://openknowledge.worldbank.org/server/api/core/bitstreams/6c2b5974 -9a3b-5249-995b-2b22e5fd7909/content.

Abbreviations

AGEP	Adolescent Girls' Empowerment Program
AGI	Adolescent Girls Initiative
AGILE	Adolescent Girls Initiative for Learning and Empowerment
AIDS	acquired immune deficiency syndrome
CGD	Center for Global Development
DHS	Demographic and Health Surveys
ELA	Empowerment and Livelihood for Adolescents
FCV	fragility, conflict, and violence
Findex	Financial Inclusion Index
GBV	gender-based violence
HIV	human immunodeficiency virus
KGS	Keeping Girls in School
PASS	Promoting Safe Sex Among Adolescents in Tanzania
SDGs	Sustainable Development Goals
SSA	Sub-Saharan Africa
SWEDD	Sahel Women's Empowerment and Demographic Dividend
UFGE	Umbrella Facility for Gender Equality
UNDESA	United Nations Department of Economic and Social Affairs
UNICEF	United Nations Children's Fund
WBL	*Women, Business and the Law*

All dollar amounts are US dollars unless otherwise indicated.

Introduction

Estelle Koussoubé, Kehinde Ajayi and Fatima Zahra

Key Messages

- Africa has the world's largest youth population, with adolescent girls playing a pivotal role in shaping the region's future.
- Investing in adolescent girls' empowerment is not just a moral obligation, but a smart economic decision, with potential returns exceeding 10 times the initial investment.
- Adolescent girls in Africa face disproportionate obstacles, including high risks of child marriage and early childbearing and limited access to education and employment opportunities.

The Path to Africa's Prosperity Lies in Investing in Its Adolescent Girls

Adolescent girls in Africa represent a pivotal demographic group with the potential to transform the continent's social and economic landscape. This report delves into the complex challenges Africa's adolescent girls face and highlights the transformative impact of targeted investments in their lives. By examining effective policies, analyzing successful programs, and offering evidence-based recommendations, this report aims to illuminate pathways to empower adolescent girls across Africa. To anchor this report's analysis in real-world experiences, this report begins with the story of Malindi—an adolescent girl whose life exemplifies both the profound challenges and the remarkable potential of Africa's adolescent girls.

Malindi is 19 years old and currently in twelfth grade. She has been a beneficiary of the Keeping Girls in School (KGS) Education Program in Zambia since eighth grade, which has played a critical role in enabling her

---

A reproducibility package is available for this book in the Reproducible Research Repository at https://reproducibility.worldbank.org.

1

to continue her education. Malindi is an engaged student, and in tenth and eleventh grades, she was the vice president of the girls' club established by the program. She speaks enthusiastically about the club:

> We were talking about [in the club] how to take care of ourselves and what words to use when talking to our friends, even if they upset us. We also talked about the dangers of early marriages. We even wanted to make plays that show the consequences of early marriage, and the challenges and consequences of pregnancies. . . . We also talked about cleaning our environment, and also to behave as pupils.

In eleventh grade, she became pregnant but was able to take maternity leave for two months when she gave birth. With the support of the education program, she was able to return to school. She explains how the program helped her during her pregnancy, particularly highlighting the role of the guidance and counseling teacher, which Malindi explained made a significant difference:

> She [the guidance and counseling teacher] advised me that if you get educated, especially now that you have a baby, you will have a good future, and your child will live a good life. . . . She would also encourage me to stay on KGS as I would see the benefits in the future. She encouraged me to continue with school and not be discouraged by anything until I finish my education and go to college. The guidance and counseling teachers really assist us, especially us girls with children; otherwise, we wouldn't have managed to be in school. . . .

> We are grateful for the help they [the program] give us because [without it] we wouldn't manage to get an education. Like in my case, my family is poor. My young sister stopped coming to school because my father couldn't pay the user fee. That is how she got married.

This is just one example of the challenges faced by girls in Africa, and how tailored initiatives that consider their unique experiences can create a substantial positive influence in their lives, setting them on a path toward economic success. The example also offers insight into the fact that adolescent girls constitute a diverse group with distinct experiences, underscoring the importance of considering these differences in any attempt to effectively reach and support all of them. These are key points that this report will emphasize.

Africa boasts the largest youth population of any region in the world, holding the key to its own prosperity: investing in the untapped economic potential of its adolescents, particularly girls.[1] In 2021, a staggering 42 percent of the population in Africa was below the age of 15 (UNDESA 2024a), and nearly half of those living in poverty fell within this age group (Beegle and Christiaensen 2019). In 2023, approximately 145 million adolescent girls (ages 10 to 19) lived in the region, making up more than one-fifth of the world's adolescent girl population (figure I.1). This proportion is expected to increase to more than one-third by 2050, according to the Population Division of the United Nations Department of Economic and Social Affairs (UNDESA 2024a).

FIGURE I.1 By 2050, More Than One-Third of the World's Adolescent Girls Will Live in Africa

Population of adolescent girls (millions)   Percent

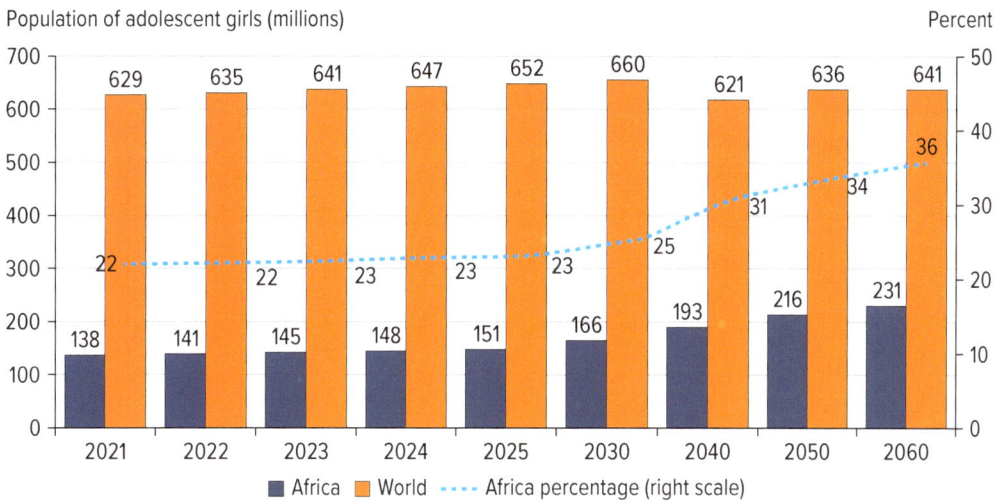

Source: Original figure for this report, based on data from UNDESA 2024a.
Note: Figure illustrates populations of females ages 10 to 19 (estimated for 2021–23 and projected for all other years). Projections use the medium scenario, representing central tendencies derived from means of fertility or mortality rates and median net migration, based on thousands of probabilistic trajectories accounting for demographic variability over time (UNDESA 2024b).

The number of adolescents in Africa and their pivotal role in shaping the region's future and global dynamics must be understood within the broader context of the complex nature of this life stage. Adolescence represents a critical transition marked by physical, psychological, social, and cultural changes. To unlock the full potential of Africa's youth, enabling them to thrive and contribute significantly to their economies, critical investments must be made, with a central focus on adolescents ages 10 to 19. These investments should promote these adolescents' empowerment (Weny, Snow, and Zhang 2017) while ensuring inclusivity. Developing innovative policies and programs aimed at enhancing the empowerment of adolescents is imperative in achieving the Sustainable Development Goals (SDGs), including those related to gender equality (SDG 5), poverty eradication (SDG 1), quality education (SDG 4), decent work and inclusive growth (SDG 8), and reducing inequality (SDG 10).

This report emphasizes that focusing on adolescent girls and their economic prosperity is a sensible choice for shaping Africa's future. Investments directed specifically toward adolescent girls have the potential to shift the trajectory of their lives and ensure that they enter adulthood empowered to thrive. However, it is crucial to recognize the diversity in adolescent girls' experiences and to adapt to the contexts that shape their unique paths.

Why Prioritize Pathways to Prosperity for Adolescent Girls in Africa?

Adolescent girls' empowerment is foundational to women's empowerment and holds the promise of long-term economic gains for Africa, especially amid economic challenges and forecasts of sluggish growth (World Bank 2023). A vision for a more prosperous future based on this premise can be realized when women and girls are included and equipped to achieve their full potential from adolescence onward.

Moreover, focusing on girls is imperative because they often face unique obstacles that set them on considerably different trajectories from their male peers. Africa has the highest risk of child marriage for girls in the world, with one in three girls marrying before the age of 18. Notably, West and Central Africa is home to 7 of the 10 countries with the highest prevalence of child marriage globally (UNICEF 2022). Moreover, 25 percent of young African women (ages 20 to 24) give birth before the age of 18 (UNICEF 2024). Additionally, an estimated one in four girls ages 15 to 19, compared with nearly one in seven boys, is not in school, employed, or in training (ILO 2020). These gender disparities are entrenched within systems that perpetuate gender inequality into adulthood, leaving young women with lower educational attainment and poorer employment outcomes than young men.

The situation becomes even more challenging when the impact of crises is taken into consideration. Recent events such as the COVID-19 pandemic, internal conflicts, and violent extremism, as well as shifts in the economic landscape, have the potential to exacerbate existing gender disparities, further disadvantaging girls (Lundberg and Wuermli 2012; Schady et al. 2023). For instance, recent studies have shown that the COVID-19 pandemic, while generally affecting girls and boys similarly in terms of education outcomes,[2] has led to an increased likelihood of child marriage and unintended pregnancies (Briggs et al. 2020; Dessy et al. 2021; Kadzamira et al. 2024; Zulaika et al. 2022). Incidents of gender-based violence and violence against children have also increased (Bhatia et al. 2021; Mbushi et al. 2022; Peterman et al. 2020). Furthermore, research indicates that women and girls, particularly those in informal employment, faced severe labor market consequences during the COVID-19 pandemic and experienced a slower recovery compared with their male counterparts. For instance, increased caregiving responsibilities due to school closures and economic fragility have compromised older adolescent girls' access to employment opportunities and their prospects of returning to work after job losses (Nieves, Gaddis, and Muller 2021; Torres et al. 2021; World Bank 2022).

Simultaneously, digital technology is reshaping African economies, providing opportunities to expand businesses in both the formal and informal sectors (Choi, Dutz, and Usman 2020). Yet the gender gap in digital skills and access to digital technologies may prevent girls from fully realizing related economic benefits and limit their ability to engage with programs designed to facilitate empowerment. A recent analysis of eight countries in Africa showed that girls have lower levels of digital skills compared with boys, even when girls have access to a computer at home (Amaro et al. 2020).

Given these multifaceted challenges and opportunities, investing in adolescent girls' empowerment emerges as not just a moral imperative, but also a smart economic decision. Each dollar invested in adolescent girls' empowerment can yield a return more than 10 times that in economic impact. The cost of inaction—that is, the cost of delaying or failing to implement suitable, effective programs and policies to empower adolescent girls (estimated over 15 years)—is substantial. The present value of increased income from scaling up adolescent girls' empowerment programs in Africa is estimated at approximately $2.4 trillion, and the total cost of investing in the next two generations of girls across all African countries amounts to approximately $200 billion. These two factors result in a net benefit-to-cost ratio of about 10 to 1, emphasizing the significant economic impact of investing in adolescent girls' empowerment (Rossouw et al. 2024).[3]

What Does This Report Do?

This report, motivated by the need to advance adolescent girls' empowerment in Africa, comprehensively examines policies and programs designed to foster the empowerment of adolescent girls ages 10 to 19, taking into account the significant diversity in their life experiences. The report presents new analyses and a comprehensive conceptual framework for understanding, measuring, and enhancing adolescent girls' empowerment. This approach embraces the diverse range of experiences among adolescent girls, offering a comprehensive perspective on their journey toward empowerment.

The work presented here builds upon earlier efforts that laid the groundwork for understanding and addressing the unique challenges adolescent girls face on their path to economic success in Africa. For instance, Lloyd (2005) emphasizes the need to consider both the productive and reproductive aspects of adolescent girls' experiences. The Adolescent Girls Initiative, supported by the World Bank from 2008 to 2015, made significant advances in exploring interventions to improve adolescent girls' transition from school to work in eight countries (Afghanistan, Haiti, Jordan, the Lao People's Democratic Republic, Liberia, Nepal, Rwanda, and South Sudan), including three in Africa. Also, the Gender and Adolescence: Global Evidence Consortium[4] has played a pivotal role in expanding the concept of adolescent girls' empowerment. It defines six "capability domains" relevant for adolescent girls as they go through this phase of their lives: education and learning, bodily integrity (including freedom from sexual and gender-based violence and child marriage), physical and reproductive health and nutrition, psychosocial well-being, voice and agency, and economic empowerment (GAGE Consortium 2017).

Additionally, this report builds on insights and lessons from the rich history of many African societies that emphasize traditional practices that have historically supported the empowerment of adolescent girls. For example, among the Ijebu in Nigeria, the practice of organizing young people into age sets around the time of adolescence provided a platform for cultivating educational training and nurturing social capital (Williams and Ogunkoya 2021). Inheritance has also played a significant role in building assets for girls in specific societies. Adolescent girls in many African societies traditionally retained the right to inherit property from their family of birth, which was equal to their male siblings' share. This practice provided them with lifelong access to their families' resources as a means of production, along with social identity and support (Oyěwùmí 1997).

Similarly, several recent reviews enhanced understanding of what works in programs and policies aimed at fostering adolescent girls' empowerment in Africa. For instance, Evans, Mendez Acosta, and Yuan (2024) focus on the impact of large-scale programs and policies on final education outcomes, addressing questions related to how education systems can help achieve gender equality in education at scale. Additionally, reviews like those by Stavropoulou (2018) and Haberland et al. (2021) often delve into specific types of interventions aimed at empowering adolescent girls economically. Bergstrom and Özler (2023) provide a comprehensive narrative review of interventions targeting adolescent well-being in low- and middle-income countries, focusing on those that aim to increase educational attainment, delay childbearing, or delay marriage (or any combination of the three). Despite these valuable contributions, a broader consensus is still required to inform evidence-based recommendations for future programs and policies aimed at creating pathways to prosperity for adolescent girls. This report offers a unique contribution by providing a comprehensive understanding of the topic. The analysis in this report examines evidence across all domains of empowerment, as defined in the report's conceptual framework.

The report has four core chapters and four "spotlights" inserted between these chapters to shed light on different aspects related to adolescent girls' empowerment.[5] Chapter 1 sets the stage by introducing a conceptual framework for the realization of empowerment for adolescent girls at different ages. Simultaneously, it explores alternative paths, recognizing the reality that many adolescent girls must navigate diverse trajectories. Chapter 2 turns to an analysis of trends and subnational differences (within and across countries) and profiles the experiences of adolescent girls in various demographic groups, based on their schooling, work, marriage, and childbearing status. Chapter 3 reviews the evidence regarding interventions aimed at improving adolescent girls' human capital fundamentals, namely, education and health. Chapter 4 provides an overview of recent evidence regarding interventions aimed at improving other crucial domains of empowerment, including enhancing resources and agency, while examining the context in which adolescent girls live. Both chapters 3 and 4 outline evidence-based approaches for supporting girls in Africa.

In addition to the core chapters, the report illuminates four key areas through spotlight sections. Spotlight 1 sheds light on the challenges involved in measuring adolescent girls' empowerment. Spotlight 2 explores the multidimensionality of adolescent girls' empowerment. Spotlight 3 presents key considerations for quality implementation of "girls' groups" programs, and finally, spotlight 4 explores the political economy of adolescent girls' empowerment.

Chapter 5 concludes with evidence-based recommendations for researchers, policy makers, and practitioners. These recommendations are aimed at fostering continued dialogue and collaboration, with the overarching goal of enhancing the lives of adolescent girls not only in Africa, but also in other contexts.

Annex IA. Calculating the Cost of Inaction

Introduction

This annex calculates a range of values for the "cost of inaction" in the policy area of adolescent girls' empowerment in Africa. Inaction means that suitable, effective programs and policies to empower adolescent girls that could be implemented in 2025 might instead be delayed until 2040. The cost of 15 years of inaction, then, is the difference in benefits, net of costs, for adolescent girls ages 10 to 19 in 2025 and each subsequent cohort reaching adolescence by 2040. In 2022, there were about 139 million adolescent girls in 48 African countries, and in the coming 15 years another 150 million girls, at least, will become adolescents. The potential gains from empowerment are thus very large.

The benefits for adolescent girls are measured as the increase in their "private" lifetime earnings, since the broader concept of well-being is difficult to quantify at present, as are the indirect impacts on extended families. Adolescent girls may go on to play a role in supporting not only themselves, but also their extended families. An earlier World Bank report (Milazzo and Van de Walle 2015) showed that households in Africa are increasingly likely to be headed by women. Combined with the fact that women are often the primary caregivers to their immediate and extended families, there is increasing reliance on girls and women, relative to male family members, as the important providers in their households (Gambe et al. 2023), affecting the lives and opportunities of all household members. It is therefore important to note the difference in the private and social returns to investing in adolescent girls. Private returns are the improved well-being for the girls themselves, whereas social returns include, among other effects, the extended impact on the well-being of their families. This annex focuses on the private returns to empowerment.

The approach employed has five steps. The first step is to build a conceptual model of key determinants of the outcome of higher earnings (as a lower bound for well-being). This model considers several interrelated factors: education attainment, age at marriage, fertility decisions, migration choices, occupational selections, labor force participation, and life expectancy. The second is to populate the model's parameters using estimates from the available social science research literature for African countries. For example, Mincer earnings equations are used to estimate the current returns to education for women in Africa. Estimating the likely wage profiles of girls is key to translating the values from the model into lifetime earnings.

The third step is to draw from the distribution of parameters and calculate the difference in earnings between an inaction scenario and an empowerment scenario. The calculation is replicated many times, and the average of the calculations reported. The fourth step entails calculating the potential costs of implementing suitable, effective programs and policies to empower adolescent girls. The fifth and final step involves calculating the benefits minus costs and comparing the results to other cost-benefit calculations for other large-scale interventions aimed at improving well-being.

The following procedure is employed to calculate the cost of inaction:

- For each of the 48 countries in Africa, a data set of 30 adolescent girls of each age, 10 to 16, in 2025 is simulated (it is assumed that 17- to 19-year-olds cannot be treated, at scale), plus 30 adolescent girls age 10 in 2026, plus 30 age 10 in 2027, and so on, with the last "potentially untreated" cohort age 10 in 2040, so that a total "sample" or "draw" for each simulation round is 660 adolescent girls. The assumption is that cohorts who are age 10 in 2041 and after will be "treated," that is, they will all benefit from empowerment programs.

- Each girl in the simulation sample is randomly assigned an initial level of primary education, a variable indicating whether she is still enrolled in school, and an urban-rural designation, with probabilities given by the most recent Demographic and Health Survey for that country—or for an average of all survey countries, for countries with no Demographic and Health Survey data. It is assumed that for each age cohort, there is a modest increase over time in mean primary school attainment, at both the extensive margin (more girls in school) and intensive margin (more attainment for those who enroll), for each new birth cohort after the initial group of girls. Chapter 2, with its profiles of adolescents in Africa, discusses in depth many of these distributions from the Demographic and Health Surveys.

- Each girl is randomly assigned an initial empowerment or agency score, correlated with urban-rural residence and primary education level.

- Each girl is assigned an empowerment treatment effect, indicating how much her agency score rises as a result of empowerment interventions for adolescent girls. It is assumed that all girls in the country are treated and the interventions have the same positive effect.

- Whether the girl is married as an adolescent and the number of children she has as an adolescent are drawn from a joint distribution that depends on education, agency, and urban-rural residence.

- Both are reduced if the girl receives treatment in an empowerment program.

- Secondary school attainment is modeled as depending on whether the girl marries before turning 19, how many children she has before 19, agency, urban-rural residence, and whether she was still enrolled in school as an adolescent. A separate education effect is presumed to come from adolescent girls' empowerment programs.

- The likelihood of migration from a rural to an urban area is drawn from a probability distribution that depends on age at marriage, age at first childbirth, secondary education attainment, agency, and urban-rural status.

- Fertility, occupational choice (formal or microenterprise), and longevity are drawn from a probability distribution that depends on age at marriage, age at first childbirth, level of education, empowerment, and urban-rural status.

- Annual earnings are determined by Mincer equations that vary with education, experience, and urban-rural status. Currently, for robustness, parameters are applied from seven different Mincer earnings equations (country-specific estimates, continent-wide estimates, separate estimates for urban and rural, separate estimates for high- and low-income wage earners, and estimates for men applied to women wage earners). In future simulations, earnings might depend on occupational choice (formal employment, small or medium enterprise, or low-productivity informal).

- A small exogenous mortality rate is assumed, for each country, that determines whether a girl in the sample might die before completing her expected working life.

- The present discounted value of lifetime earnings is calculated, using a discount rate of 3 percent.

- The average individual present discounted value of earnings is calculated by estimating the number of present, and likely future over the subsequent 10 years, adolescent girls of each age in each country.

- The total national increase in the present discounted value of earnings is computed as the difference between action and inaction.

- Costs are estimated for programs and policies for each country, under certain scaling assumptions.

- The cost of inaction for each country is calculated as the present value of the net benefit of empowerment programs minus the costs of interventions.

Although the analysis sheds light on the potential economic impact of empowering adolescent girls, it is important to understand its methodological context. The approach employed, which focuses on private monetary returns, provides a conservative estimate that likely understates the full benefits, including broader social and nonmonetary gains. The methodology uses historical earnings profiles and simplified modeling assumptions that, while providing a solid foundation, may not fully capture the complex dynamics of changing economic conditions. Future research could improve this model by incorporating general equilibrium effects and feedback loops. Although the parameter estimates, drawn from existing studies, offer a strong starting point, refining these estimates with more long-term data and evaluating larger-scale interventions will enhance their applicability across diverse contexts. These considerations highlight the need for ongoing research to provide a better understanding of the true cost of inaction and the substantial impact of investing in adolescent girls' empowerment.

Simulation Intermediate Output

Since many of the parameters in the model are probabilities and are random draws from reasonable ranges of possible values, the model is simulated 50 times for each parameter selection (seven Mincer equations, three education effects, and three agency effects from adolescent girls' empowerment programs) to determine the mean net total present value, as well as the range of variation.

Table IA.1 reports mean values across the 3,150 simulations. Each simulation includes 660 simulated observations from each of 48 countries. Countries are grouped by income category according to their 2020 real gross domestic product per capita at purchasing-power parity, as given in the World Bank's World Development Indicators for that year.

TABLE IA.1 Mean Values, Across Simulations, for Key Variables for Individual Women in Different Countries Vary as Expected by Country Income Level

Country income level	Share of women marrying early (percent)	Number of children	Final years of schooling	Age at death	Probability of having a formal job	Probability of migrating
Low income	24.50	5.27	8.30	66.24	0.19	0.032
Lower-middle income	19.10	4.29	10.00	65.44	0.20	0.028
Upper-middle income	13.50	3.36	12.20	64.55	0.22	0.022
High income	16.20	2.41	13.58	62.49	0.24	0.023

Source: Original table for this report.
Note: The table shows mean values of variables calculated for each income classification group by taking the average of all girls in the simulations (unweighted by the actual population sizes of countries) who are members of that income group.

The table presents the share of women marrying early, the number of children born to each woman, her final level of education attainment in years of schooling, whether the woman holds a formal sector job, whether the woman migrates to an urban area if she is a rural resident, and her average age at death. The values are roughly in line with actual values and vary in the expected way by country income group. For example, the number of children a woman has declines with country income level, her level of education attainment rises, and the probability she has a formal job also rises.

Economic Gains from Adolescent Empowerment

Figure IA.1 presents the potential economic impact of adolescent girls' empowerment interventions across African countries from 2025 to 2040. Each bar represents a country's mean increase in the present discounted value of lifetime earnings for adolescent girls who could benefit from these interventions. The calculations are based on multiple simulations, each of which draws initial conditions and parameters from probability distributions for each girl. The height of each bar shows the country-specific mean across all simulations. Error bars indicate the range of possible outcomes based on variations in parameter values and initial conditions. The cumulative height of all bars, totaling $2,402 billion, represents the estimated Africa-wide economic gain if these empowerment interventions are implemented.

The calculations in figure IA.1 exclude simulations with "large effect" scenarios; that is, the bar for each country is a conservative estimate, in that it uses the smallest assumed education and agency effect from the assumed adolescent girls' empowerment program implemented in every country. The estimate is also conservative because it addresses only a few effects of empowerment. A more comprehensive strategy that targets multiple outcomes could produce even larger effects. Chapters 3 and 4 present a comprehensive discussion of policies and programs targeting the various dimensions of empowerment. These include policies that increase girls' access to schooling, improve their sexual and reproductive health, and delay marriage and childbearing.

FIGURE IA.1 Simulated Total Net Increased Lifetime Earnings from Adolescent Girls' Empowerment Vary by Country, with an Estimated Africa-wide Total Gain of $2,402 Billion

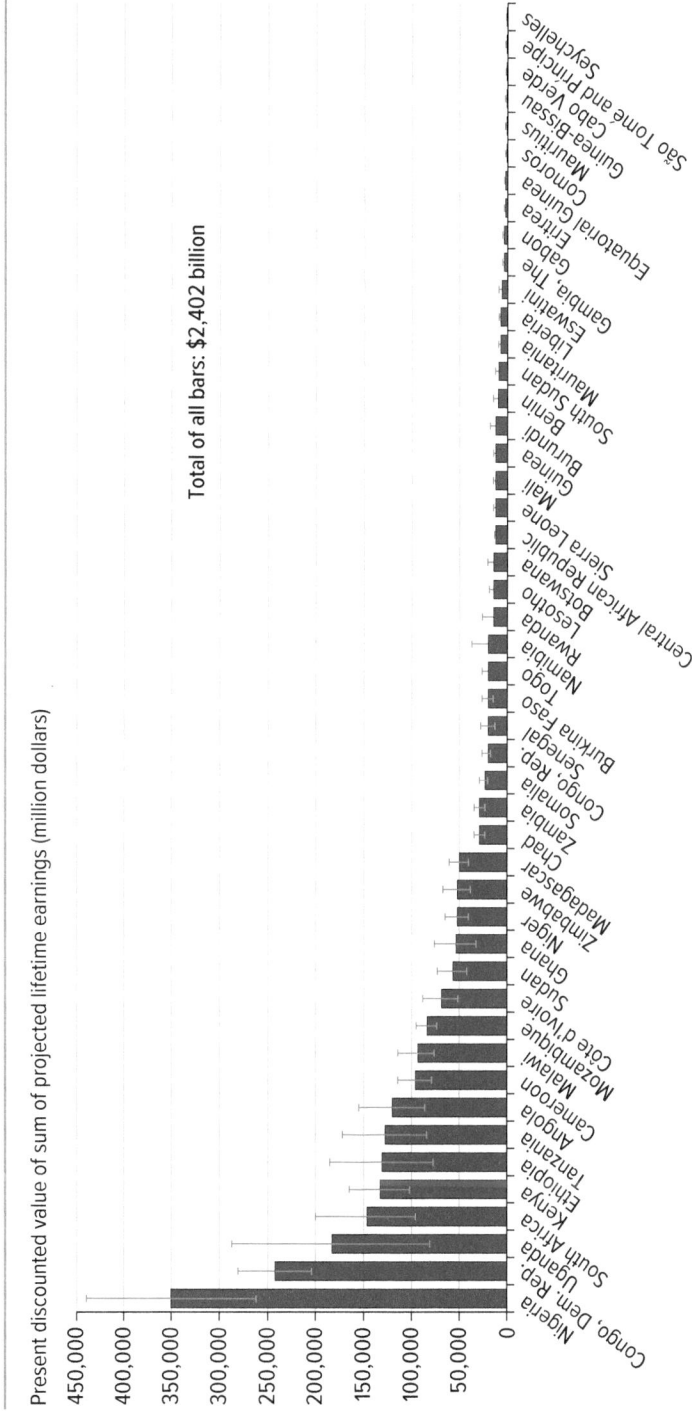

Source: Original figure for this report.

Note: The height of each bar represents the mean present discounted value of increased lifetime earnings resulting from adolescent girls' empowerment programs in each country, calculated from multiple simulations. Error bars indicate the standard error of this estimated mean, calculated from multiple simulations.

To provide insights into how much different assumed effects contribute to aggregate increases in the present value of earnings for women, the total increase in earnings for each of the simulations is calculated; figure IA.2 shows a histogram of the total summed effects. As the figure shows, there is considerable variation in potential outcomes depending on the magnitude of program effects.

FIGURE IA.2   Distribution of Simulated Total Net Increased Lifetime Earnings from Adolescent Girls' Empowerment Shows Considerable Variation Across All African Countries

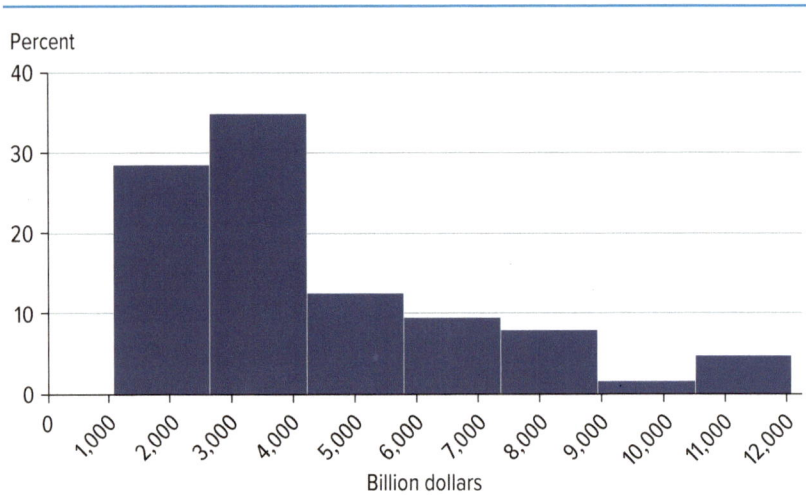

Source: Original figure for this report.

Cost of Investing in Adolescent Girls' Empowerment

An array of interventions, policies, and programs will likely lead to significant empowerment of adolescent girls, setting off a chain of changes in decisions about schooling, marriage, fertility, labor force participation, and health choices. Although potentially transformative, these interventions come with substantial costs, including program staffing, materials, and policy implementation expenses, among other costs.

The cost estimates in this analysis are based on the Adolescent Girl Initiative program in Kenya (Austrian et al. 2022). This program was costed over a two-year period from 2016 to 2017, and the costing included microcosting of the line items for each of four intervention arms targeting the empowerment of adolescent girls: violence prevention, education (including a conditional cash transfer, school fee subsidy, and schooling kit, conditional on enrollment and attendance), health (including safe spaces for girls where health and life skills topics were discussed), and wealth creation (which included financial education and saving tools). For more comprehensive information on these interventions, refer to Austrian et al. (2020), Austrian et al. (2021), and Austrian et al. (2022).

Table IA.2 presents estimates of the unit cost per girl per year for country groups according to income level. These costs differ for girls in primary and secondary school, as well as for those residing in urban or rural areas.

TABLE IA.2 Estimates of Direct Economic Cost of Empowerment Programs Vary by School Level and Urban-rural Location

(2022 dollars)

Country income level	Urban primary	Rural primary	Urban secondary	Rural secondary
Low income	180.89	335.24	216.51	374.64
	(10.99)	(28.62)	(12.89)	(30.61)
Lower-middle income	258.96	520.52	334.13	611.76
	(13.54)	(33.47)	(21.52)	(32.89)
Upper-middle income	464.31	1048.39	727.90	1361.21
	(43.56)	(106.07)	(99.29)	(115.30)
High income	820.61	1810.55	1668.85	2793.31
	(156.50)	(499.40)	(126.37)	(229.15)

Source: Original table for this report.
Note: Standard errors are provided in parentheses. Cost estimates are from Austrian et al. (2022) and are scaled to country-specific settings.

The Kenya cost estimates provided in the table are adjusted for each country context. Extrapolating from a single country intervention to all African countries included in the analysis, however, is not ideal. Evans and Popova (2016) suggest that costs might differ substantially from country to country. For instance, they find that transportation costs per school in rural Kenya are 27 times higher than those in urban India. Similarly, they find that differing community teacher salaries across countries can result in an 88 percent variation in cost-effectiveness estimates.

The annual cost per year per girl is next multiplied by the number of girls per year benefiting from the empowerment program. All costs incurred after 2025 are discounted to their present value using a discount rate of 3 percent (Hollingworth et al. 2023). Figure IA.3 displays the present value of offering each adolescent girl in the 20 birth cohorts in every African country the opportunity to participate in an empowerment program. The total cost, summed across all countries, is about $198 billion.

FIGURE IA.3 Projected Present Discounted Value of Costs of Empowerment Programs for Adolescent Girls Totals Approximately $198 Billion Across All African Countries

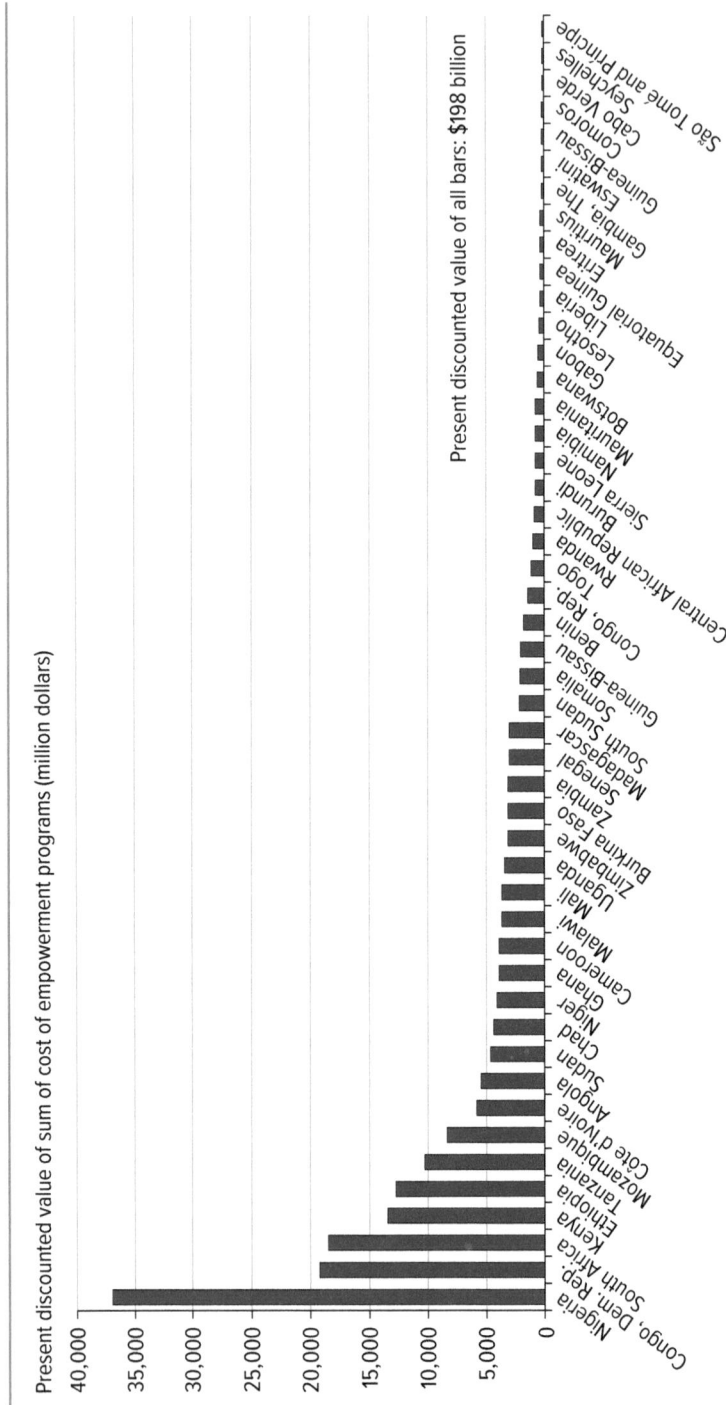

Source: Original figure for this report.

Note: The height of each bar represents the present value of having each adolescent girl for the 20 birth cohorts described in annex 1A be reached by an empowerment program.

Notes

1. Throughout this report, *Africa* refers to the 48 countries in Sub-Saharan Africa, based on the World Bank's regional classification.
2. Although learning losses for girls and boys have generally been similar, a review of studies suggests that the pandemic exacerbated factors contributing to school dropout rates for girls in specific areas, for example, rural areas in Kenya and areas where child marriages are more prevalent in Nigeria (Moscoviz and Evans 2022). Conversely, another study using representative data from six African countries suggests similar rates of school attendance for boys and girls (Kis et al. 2023).
3. Annex IA includes the detailed calculations.
4. The Gender and Adolescence: Global Evidence Consortium is a global study of 20,000 girls and boys in six countries, including Ethiopia and Rwanda in Africa.
5. Although this report aims to address adolescent girls' empowerment comprehensively, certain topics beyond its scope should be acknowledged. First, the focus here is solely on adolescent girls in Africa, given the unique obstacles they face, such as early marriage and childbearing during adolescence. Boys (in Africa and elsewhere) face distinct challenges in their journey to empowerment that warrant a deeper examination but are beyond the scope of this report. Second, this report exclusively focuses on adolescent girls' empowerment and does not encompass empowerment as a general concept or pertain to other domains like political empowerment. Third, this report does not provide detailed coverage of outcomes that are not a direct part of the components of empowerment but may be important parallel outcomes critical to girls' well-being, such as experiences of violence. Similarly, although certain key domains of empowerment such as adolescent girls' mental health have gained attention, especially since the COVID-19 pandemic, the existing evidence, though increasing, remains too scarce to enable meaningful conclusions to be drawn and therefore is not reviewed in this report. Lastly, while recognizing the social construction of gender and the importance of acknowledging multiple identities, this report employs a binary definition of gender for the purposes of analysis and discussion, owing to data availability and the predominant criteria used for empowerment programs in the region.

References

Amaro, Diogo, Lauren Pandolfelli, Ingrid Sanchez-Tapia, and Matt Brossard. 2020. "COVID-19 and Education: The Digital Gender Divide among Adolescents in Sub-Saharan Africa." *UNICEF Data Blog*, August 4, 2020. https://data.unicef.org /data-for-action/covid-19-and-education-the-digital-gender-divide-among -adolescents-in-sub-saharan-africa/.

Austrian, Karen, Erica Soler-Hampejsek, Jere R. Behrman, Jean Digitale, Natalie Jackson Hachonda, Maximillian Bweupe, and Paul C. Hewett. 2020. "The Impact of the Adolescent Girls Empowerment Program (AGEP) on Short and Long Term Social, Economic, Education and Fertility Outcomes: A Cluster Randomized Controlled Trial in Zambia." *BMC Public Health* 20 (1): 1–15.

Austrian, Karen, Erica Soler-Hampejsek, Beth Kangwana, Nicole Maddox, Maryama Diaw, Yohannes D. Wado, Benta Abuya, Eva Muluve, Faith Mbushi, and Hassan Mohammed. 2022. "Impacts of Multisectoral Cash Plus Programs on Marriage and Fertility after 4 Years in Pastoralist Kenya: A Randomized Trial." *Journal of Adolescent Health* 70 (6): 885–94.

Austrian, Karen, Erica Soler-Hampejsek, Beth Kangwana, Yohannes Dibaba Wado, Benta Abuya, and John A. Maluccio. 2021. "Impacts of Two-Year Multisectoral Cash Plus Programs on Young Adolescent Girls' Education, Health and Economic Outcomes: Adolescent Girls Initiative—Kenya (AGI-K) Randomized Trial." *BMC Public Health* 21: 2159. https://doi.org/10.1186/s12889-021 -12224-3.

Beegle, Kathleen, and Luc Christiaensen. 2019. *Accelerating Poverty Reduction in Africa.* Washington, DC: World Bank. https://doi.org/10.1596/978-1-4648-1232-3.

Bergstrom, Katy, and Berk Özler. 2023. "Improving the Well-Being of Adolescent Girls in Developing Countries." *World Bank Research Observer* 38 (2): 179–212. https://doi.org/10.1093/wbro/lkac007.

Bhatia, Amiya, Camilla Fabbri, Ilan Cerna-Turoff, Ellen Turner, Michelle Lokot, Ajwang Warria, Sumnima Tuladhar, et al. 2021. "Violence against Children during the COVID-19 Pandemic." *Bulletin of the World Health Organization* 99 (10): 730–38. https://doi.org/10.2471/BLT.20.283051.

Briggs, Hannah, Nicole Haberland, Sapna Desai, Thomas de Hoop, and Thoai Ngo. 2020. "The Impact of COVID-19 on Opportunities for Adolescent Girls and the Role of Girls' Groups." Brief, Evidence Consortium on Women's Groups, Washington, DC.

Choi, Jieun, Mark Dutz, and Zainab Usman. 2020. *The Future of Work in Africa: Harnessing the Potential of Digital Technologies for All.* Washington, DC: World Bank. https://hdl.handle.net/10986/32124.

Dessy, Sylvain, Horace Gninafon, Luca Tiberti, and Marco Tiberti. 2021. "COVID-19 and Children's School Resilience: Evidence from Nigeria." Working Paper 952, Global Labor Organization (GLO), Essen, Germany. https://www.econstor.eu /handle/10419/243100.

Evans, David K., Amina Mendez Acosta, and Fei Yuan. 2024. "Girls' Education at Scale." *World Bank Research Observer* 39 (1): 47–74. https://doi.org/10.1093/wbro /lkad002.

Evans, David K., and Anna Popova. 2016. "Cost-Effectiveness Analysis in Development: Accounting for Local Costs and Noisy Impacts." *World Development* 77: 262–76.

GAGE (Gender and Adolescence: Global Evidence) Consortium. 2017. *Gender and Adolescence: Why Understanding Adolescent Capabilities, Change Strategies and Contexts Matters.* London: GAGE.

Gambe, Rutendo G., Joseph Clark, Stephanie A. Meddick-Dyson, Blessing O. Ukoha-Kalu, Gertrude N. Nyaaba, and Fliss E. M. Murtagh. 2023. "The Roles and Experiences of Informal Carers Providing Care to People with Advanced Cancer in Africa—A Systematic Review and Critical Interpretive Analysis." *PLOS Global Public Health* 3 (4): e0001785.

Haberland, Nicole, Thomas de Hoop, Sapna Desai, Sarah Engebretsen, and Thoai Ngo. 2021. "Adolescent Girls' and Young Women's Economic Empowerment Programs: Emerging Insights from a Review of Reviews." Working Paper 03, Evidence Consortium on Women's Groups, Washington, DC. https://doi.org/10.31899 /pgy17.1031.

Hollingworth, S. A., G. Leaupepe, J. Nonvignon, A. P. Fenny, E. A. Odame, and F. Ruiz. 2023. "Economic Evaluations of Non-communicable Diseases Conducted in Sub-Saharan Africa: A Critical Review of Data Sources." *Cost Effectiveness and Resource Allocation* 21 (1): 57.

ILO (International Labour Office). 2020. *Global Employment Trends for Youth 2020: Technology and the Future of Jobs*. Geneva: ILO.

Kadzamira, Esme, Jacob Mazalale, Elizabeth Meke, Isaac Vyamcharo Mwale, Fidelis Jimu, Laura Moscoviz, and Jack Rossiter. 2024. "What Happened to Student Participation after Two Rounds of School Closures in Malawi—and How Have Schools Responded?" *Center for Global Development* (blog), November 24, 2024. https://www.cgdev.org/blog/what-happened-student-participation-after-two -rounds-school-closures-malawi-and-how-have.

Kis, Anna B., Claire Boxho, Isis Gaddis, Estelle Koussoubé, and Léa Rouanet. 2023. "The Gendered Impacts of COVID-19 on Adolescents' School Attendance in Sub-Saharan Africa." Policy Research Working Paper 10472, World Bank, Washington, DC. https://doi.org/10.1596/1813-9450-10472.

Lloyd, Cynthia B., ed. 2005. *Growing Up Global: The Changing Transitions to Adulthood in Developing Countries*. Washington, DC: National Academies Press. https://doi .org/10.17226/11174.

Lundberg, Mattias, and Alice Wuermli. 2012. *Children and Youth in Crisis: Protecting and Promoting Human Development in Times of Economic Shocks*. Washington, DC: World Bank.

Mbushi, Faith, Natalie Wyss, Emily EunYoung Cho, Karen Austrian, Eva Ireri Muluve, Laura Muthoni, and Beth Kangwana. 2022. "Gendered Effects of COVID-19 School Closures: Kenya Case Study." GIRL Center Research Brief 11, Population Council, New York.

Milazzo, A., and D. Van de Walle. 2015. "Women Left Behind? Poverty and Headship in Africa." Policy Research Working Paper 7331, World Bank, Washington, DC.

Moscoviz, Laura, and David K. Evans. 2022. "Learning Loss and Student Dropouts during the COVID-19 Pandemic: A Review of the Evidence Two Years after Schools Shut Down." Working Paper 609, Center for Global Development, Washington, DC.

Nieves, Carmen de Paz, Isis Gaddis, and Miriam Muller. 2021. "Gender and COVID-19: What Have We Learnt, One Year Later?" Policy Research Working Paper 9709, World Bank, Washington, DC.

Oyěwùmí, Oyèrónkẹ́. 1997. *The Invention of Women: Making an African Sense of Western Gender Discourses.* Minneapolis: University of Minnesota Press.

Peterman, Amber, Alina Potts, Megan O'Donnell, Kelly Thompson, Niyati Shah, Sabine Oertelt-Prigione, and Nicole Van Gelder. 2020. "Pandemics and Violence against Women and Children." Working Paper 528, Center for Global Development, Washington, DC.

Rossouw, Laura, Michael Kevane, Estelle Koussoubé, and Kehinde Ajayi. 2024. "Lost Potential: The Cost of Inaction of Adolescent Girls' Empowerment." Background paper for *Pathways to Prosperity for Adolescent Girls in Africa.* Unpublished, World Bank, Washington, DC.

Schady, Norbert, Alaka Holla, Shwetlena Sabarwal, and Joana Silva. 2023. *Collapse and Recovery: How the COVID-19 Pandemic Eroded Human Capital and What to Do about It.* Washington, DC: World Bank.

Stavropoulou, Maria. 2018. *Interventions Promoting Adolescent Girls' Economic Capabilities: What Works? A Rapid Evidence Review.* London: Overseas Development Institute. https://www.econstor.eu/handle/10419/193656.

Torres, Jesica, Franklin Maduko, Isis Gaddis, Leonardo Iacovone, and Kathleen Beegle. 2021. "The Impact of the COVID-19 Pandemic on Women-Led Businesses." Policy Research Working Paper 9817, World Bank, Washington, DC. http://documents .worldbank.org/curated/en/808641635211295483/The-Impact-of-the-COVID-19 -Pandemic-on-Women-Led-Businesses.

UNDESA (United Nations Department of Economic and Social Affairs). 2024a. World Population Prospects 2024. Custom data acquired via data portal, accessed August 22, 2024. https://population.un.org/wpp/.

UNDESA (United Nations Department of Economic and Social Affairs). 2024b. "World Population Prospects 2024: Methodology of the United Nations Population Estimates and Projections." UNDESA/POP/2024/DC 10. Advance unedited version. https://population.un.org/wpp/Publications/Files/WPP2024 _Methodology_Advance_Unedited.pdf.

UNICEF (United Nations Children's Fund). 2022. "Child Marriage in West and Central Africa: A Statistical Overview and Reflections on Ending the Practice." UNICEF, New York. https://data.unicef.org/resources/child-marriage-in-west -and-central-africa-a-statistical-overview-and-reflections-on-ending-the-practice/.

UNICEF (United Nations Children's Fund). 2024. "Early Childbearing Can Have Severe Consequences for Adolescent Girls." UNICEF, New York. https://data .unicef.org/topic/child-health/adolescent-health/.

Weny, Kathrin, Rachel Snow, and Sainan Zhang. 2017. "The Demographic Dividend Atlas for Africa: Tracking the Potential for a Demographic Dividend." United Nations Population Fund, New York.

Williams, Catherine, and Niyi Ogunkoya. 2021. "Women and the Age-Group System among the Ijebu of Southwestern Nigeria." *Yoruba Studies Review* 1 (December): 123–36. https://doi.org/10.32473/ysr.v1i1.130018.

World Bank. 2022. "Assessing the Damage: Early Evidence on Impacts of the COVID-19 Crisis on Girls and Women in Africa." World Bank, Washington, DC. https://hdl.handle.net/10986/37347.

World Bank. 2023. *Delivering Growth to People through Better Jobs*. Africa's Pulse, No. 28 (October 2023). Washington, DC: World Bank. https://doi.org/10.1596/978-1-4648-2043-4.

Zulaika, Garazi, Miriam Bulbarelli, Elizabeth Nyothach, Annemieke van Eijk, Linda Mason, Eunice Fwaya, David Obor, et al. 2022. "Impact of COVID-19 Lockdowns on Adolescent Pregnancy and School Dropout among Secondary Schoolgirls in Kenya." *BMJ Global Health* 7 (1): e007666. https://doi.org/10.1136/bmjgh-2021-007666.

CHAPTER 1

What Does Adolescent Girls' Empowerment Mean?

Fatima Zahra, Kehinde Ajayi,
Henrietta Asiamah and Estelle Koussoubé

Key Messages

- Adolescent girls differ from women across multiple dimensions, which highlights the need for an alternative conceptualization of empowerment that acknowledges these differences.

- For some adolescent girls, the aspirational goal of empowerment is to obtain the skills, resources, and agency necessary to be autonomous and prosperous during adulthood.

- For others, the pathway to empowerment and prosperity may be steeper because of life transitions like dropping out of school, getting married, and having children, which have an impact on how they obtain skills, resources, and agency.

- Four key components of adolescent girls' empowerment (human capital fundamentals, enabling resources, agency, and context) interact to influence a fifth component: their long-term economic achievements.

- Appropriately designed interventions to support adolescent girls can boost their empowerment at any age, whether they are on a path of staying in school, delaying marriage, delaying childbearing, or facing different circumstances.

This Report Presents a New Framework to Conceptualize Adolescent Girls' Empowerment

Adolescent girls differ from women across multiple dimensions of empowerment. Women's empowerment frameworks have laid the foundation for conceptualizing the dimensions of empowerment, which include resources, agency, and achievements (Dandona 2015; Kabeer 1999; Mosedale 2005). However, adolescent girls differ in critical ways within and across these dimensions. Relative to women, girls' access to some resources,

A reproducibility package is available for this book in the Reproducible Research Repository at https://reproducibility.worldbank.org.

such as financial institutions or sexual and reproductive health services, is constrained by age and other factors. Cognitively, girls develop the ability to set goals and engage in complex decision-making as they age, an ability that women typically possess to a greater extent. Moreover, paid work, a common indicator of economic achievement for women, constitutes child labor for younger adolescent girls and may be detrimental to their accumulation of human capital. Therefore, what it means to be empowered is different for girls and women.

Even among adolescent girls, pathways to empowerment and prosperity will vary. Some adolescent girls may have the opportunity to grow their skills, resources, and agency and consequently have access to better-quality jobs as adults. However, other adolescent girls—when faced with poverty, gender norms, and other barriers—may leave school and assume adult roles, such as getting married and having children early. These transitions may affect their ability to acquire skills and resources, exercise agency, and access paid work, making their pathways to empowerment and prosperity distinct from those of girls who do not experience these transitions. Whether they are on a path of pursuing education exclusively without getting married or having children, or on a divergent path toward empowerment, it is important to recognize and address the varying obstacles and opportunities faced by adolescent girls.

Based on these considerations, this chapter introduces an adapted framework for adolescent girls' empowerment, with key components including human capital fundamentals, enabling resources, agency, context, and economic achievements (table 1.1). These components build on previous conceptual frameworks for adolescent girls' empowerment, particularly in the African context (Calder and Huda 2013; Jones et al. 2019; Moll 2018), which have considered education and skills training to be central to adolescent girls' empowerment. These previous frameworks also emphasize the importance of resources such as market-appropriate skills, savings, and income-generating opportunities; highlight agency as critical to the process of adolescent girls' empowerment; and are explicit about including norms and institutions as a component that shapes adolescent girls' empowerment. However, previous frameworks do not distinguish among adolescent girls' experiences across critical life transitions. The framework presented in this report, by contrast, incorporates the diversity of adolescent girls' experiences, allowing a deeper examination of adolescent girls' empowerment from a conceptual and policy perspective.

TABLE 1.1 Components of Adolescent Girls' Empowerment Influence Their Long-Term Economic Achievements

Component	Indicator	Specific measures for indicator
Human capital fundamentals	Educational progress	Educational enrollment, attainment, and attendance; grade progression; literacy skills; numeracy skills
	Health	Survival/mortality; sexual and reproductive health rights; mental health; nutrition
Enabling resources	Knowledge and skills	Life skills (including socioemotional skills); financial literacy
	Financial capital	Access to economic resources: bank accounts, loans; economic assets: savings
	Physical and digital capital	Household assets; personal assets; access to digital spaces; cell phones
	Social capital	Peer networks; access to safe spaces
	Time	Time for engaging in productive activity
Agency	Goal setting	Aspirations for education, work, marriage, and childbearing
	Sense of agency	Self-efficacy; self-esteem; locus of control; gender attitudes
	Control	Control over decision-making and time use
Context	Fragility, conflict, and violence	Prevalence and duration of conflict and violence
	Statutory laws/legal framework	Laws relating to gender, resources, work, minimum age for marriage, minimum age for work, gender-based violence, and access to identification documents
	Formal institutions	Presence and characteristics of other formal institutions: schools; health; vocational, legal, and financial services (including banks and rotating savings and credit associations)
	Norms and religion	Expectations regarding gender roles, resource access and use, work, age of marriage, and gender-based violence; religious beliefs
	Labor market opportunities	Sector-specific access to jobs; quality of available job opportunities
	Household context	Parental and household members' gender attitudes; parental aspirations for girls' education and work; relationship dynamics in households (cooperation among household members, discussions among household members on various topics, and so on); household structure and composition
Economic achievement	Labor market outcomes	Job quality; income; paid work; formal or informal sector; salaried or self-employment; age-appropriate work

Source: Original table for this report.

This New Framework Outlines Five Core Components of Adolescent Girls' Empowerment

The framework developed for this report, illustrated in figure 1.1, shows that each component of adolescent girls' empowerment evolves during adolescence, preparing girls to be prosperous in adulthood. However, the evolution of these components and their relative prominence at different ages depends on girls' initial endowment in each component at the beginning of adolescence (age 10) and the various transitions they experience over time. This diversity of experiences and their relationship with the components of adolescent girls' empowerment is highlighted through five profiles, which are represented with five distinct lines in the figure. This section describes the components of adolescent girls' empowerment, and the following section elaborates on the five profiles.

FIGURE 1.1 Adolescent Girls Follow Different Paths Toward Empowerment in Adulthood

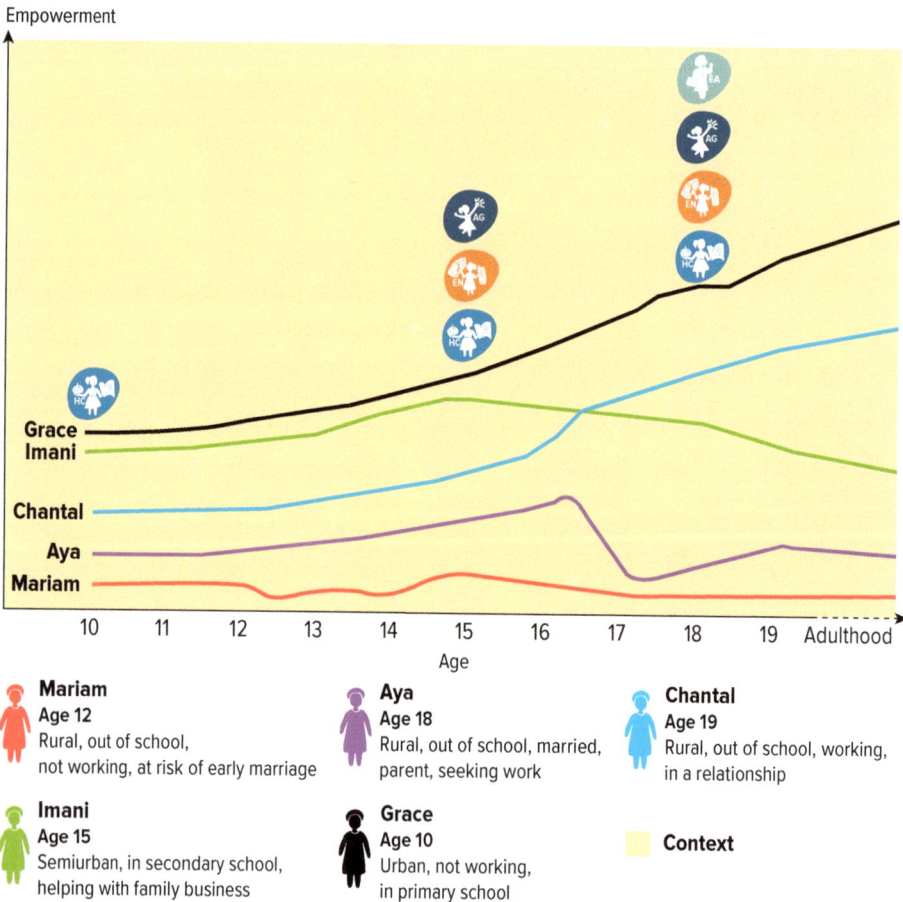

Mariam
Age 12
Rural, out of school, not working, at risk of early marriage

Aya
Age 18
Rural, out of school, married, parent, seeking work

Chantal
Age 19
Rural, out of school, working, in a relationship

Imani
Age 15
Semiurban, in secondary school, helping with family business

Grace
Age 10
Urban, not working, in primary school

Context

Source: Original figure for this report.
Note: AG = agency; EA = economic achievement; EN = enabling resources; HC = human capital fundamentals. Refer to table 1.1 for additional information about each factor.

Adolescent Girls' Empowerment Consists of Five Core Components

Human capital fundamentals are a core component of girls' empowerment. They include educational progress and health, both of which are critical to labor market outcomes in adulthood, including better earnings (Branson and Leibbrandt 2013; Hanushek et al. 2017). The importance of resources in the area of human capital fundamentals, education in particular, aligns with findings from consultations with adolescent girls in various settings. These resources serve as the foundation for an individual's future economic success, as they not only constitute resources on their own but also influence the accumulation of other essential resources and agency.

Enabling resources relevant to the process of adolescent girls' empowerment include knowledge and skills, physical and digital capital, financial capital, social capital, and time. Beyond human capital fundamentals, complementary knowledge and skills (such as financial literacy, socioemotional skills, and other life skills) are critical resources for enabling economic success. Examples of girls' physical and digital capital include household assets, personal assets, and access to and ownership of digital technology. Social capital encompasses peer groups and other beneficial relationships with specific members within an adolescent girl's community or social network. Lastly, time refers to the time available for productive activity or any other activities that adolescent girls deem to be empowering. Although these examples are not exhaustive, they are grounded in prior conceptual and empirical work on adolescent girls' empowerment (Calder and Huda 2013; Jones et al. 2019; Moll 2018). In addition, with regard to each type of resource, both access to the resource and a girl's existing stock of that resource must be considered. For instance, financial capital can include access both to financial resources such as loans through banks and to savings accumulated through girls' income or other sources as well.

Agency comprises girls' ability to exert their voices, set goals, make choices, and act upon these choices. This includes their educational, occupational, marital, or childbearing aspirations (Hitlin and Johnson 2015) and decision-making with regard to various aspects of their lives (Zimmerman et al. 2019), such as how they use their time or whether they can continue going to school or access public spaces. Girls who have a sense of agency have confidence in their ability to assert control over their lives; this sense of agency is often measured through self-efficacy, locus of control, or similar constructs (Sidle 2019).

Context includes elements of adolescent girls' environments—including laws, norms, and religion; labor market opportunities; formal and informal institutions; household context; and fragility, conflict, and violence—that may either enable or constrain their empowerment. Norms can be domain specific, including those related to girls' work, resources, or age, as well as marriage or gender-based violence. Laws encompass both customs and formal laws, including those regarding access to resources (for example, whether pregnant girls can attend school or whether girls can operate financial accounts, work, or register businesses). Formal and informal institutions include those providing services in girls' environments, such as schools, health care facilities, and financial services. In addition, household context comprises parents' or adult caregivers' preferences, attitudes, and behaviors, along with the structure and dynamics of the households in which girls live. These elements of the environment are also affected by local labor market opportunities and the broader political environment, as in the case of settings affected by fragility, conflict, and violence. In the framework employed in this report, context represents the canvas upon which other components of empowerment rest and is therefore presented as a yellow background (figure 1.1). Context influences the resources to which girls have access, their ability to set goals and exercise agency, and the types of job opportunities that allow them to achieve their economic goals.

Together, these four components of adolescent girls' empowerment interact to influence their long-term **economic achievements**, such as income and participation in age-appropriate paid work. For instance, financial literacy may enable girls to make decisions about how they invest or use their savings. In addition, the presence of secondary schools and of prominent women working outside of gender-stereotypical occupations in a community may influence girls' aspirations. Lastly, digital literacy and access to digital technology may enable girls to access better-quality jobs beyond their immediate community. Although the interactions between the components of adolescent girls' empowerment are complex, these examples of the potential implications of financial literacy, digital inclusion, access to education, and exposure to role models illustrate how components of adolescent girls' empowerment might interact with each other in practice. Additionally, cross-cutting factors (such as experiences of gender-based violence or disabilities) can also substantially influence pathways to adolescent girls' empowerment (box 1.1).

BOX 1.1 Adolescent Girls' Empowerment and Cross-Cutting Experiences

Although not explicitly part of the framework employed in this report, there are some cross-cutting experiences that interact with pathways to empowerment and are important to consider for a more holistic view of adolescent girls' empowerment. This box highlights two of these experiences.

(continued)

BOX 1.1 Adolescent Girls' Empowerment and Cross-Cutting Experiences
(continued)

First, experiences of gender-based violence and harmful practices perpetrated at home, in school, in public spaces, within marriage, or at the workplace can affect multiple aspects of girls' empowerment, including their school attendance and performance (Psaki, Mensch, and Soler-Hampejsek 2017), their sense of agency, and their ability to make decisions that affect their well-being. Girls are often more at risk of violence during adolescence than at any other time in their lives. However, they may be less likely to report experiences of violence, given potential threats to their personal or family reputation. These risks associated with gender-based violence, combined with more limited access to services and support for survivors, present an important barrier to empowerment for adolescent girls.

Second, physical and mental disabilities may affect girls' ability to fulfill their educational (Mizunoya, Mitra, and Yamasaki 2018) and economic goals and minimize their agency, depending on societal norms and available resources related to disabilities. Disabilities may also affect whether girls marry and their experiences with marriage and motherhood.

Adolescent Girls Follow Diverging Pathways to Empowerment

The key components of adolescent girls' empowerment also differ by demographic group and geographies. This section begins with stylized, data-informed descriptions of the lives of five girls residing in various parts of Africa (table 1.2). It also reviews how well-timed interventions and services can positively alter their paths toward empowerment. The examples presented are intended to be illustrative and are not an exhaustive overview of the pathways to empowerment for distinct groups of girls. (Chapter 2 presents details on the experiences of adolescent girls in each country.)

TABLE 1.2 Five Stylized Profiles of Adolescent Girls in Africa Illustrate Diverging Pathways to Empowerment

Name	Age	General description
Grace	10	Urban, in primary school, not working for pay
Mariam	12	Rural, out of school, not working for pay, at risk of early marriage
Imani	15	Semiurban, in secondary school, helping with family business
Aya	18	Rural, out of school, married, parent, seeking work for pay
Chantal	19	Rural, out of school, working for pay, in a relationship

Source: Original table for this report.

Grace is a 10-year-old student (figure 1.2). Her primary school is in the capital city of her country. She studies hard and is inspired by her favorite teacher. She wants to become a teacher when she grows up. After school, she is mostly busy with household chores, looking after her younger siblings, and cooking meals with her mother. Her mother completed secondary school, but because of household responsibilities, does not have time for a formal job. Grace is the oldest of the four children in her family, and her parents would like her to stay in school so that she can find a decent job and support the rest of the family. She lives in an urban, middle-class community with few job opportunities and in an environment with strong gender norms that assign responsibilities for household chores and care work primarily to girls and women.

In the framework introduced in the previous section (figure 1.1), Grace is on a path toward fulfilling common policy aspirations. She is in school at age 10, and on this trajectory, she will continue to make educational progress throughout adolescence and will be allowed to invest time in establishing strong human capital fundamentals. Along the way, she will gather enabling resources such as digital literacy skills and social capital by building networks

FIGURE 1.2 The Pathway to Empowerment for Grace Diverges With and Without Intervention

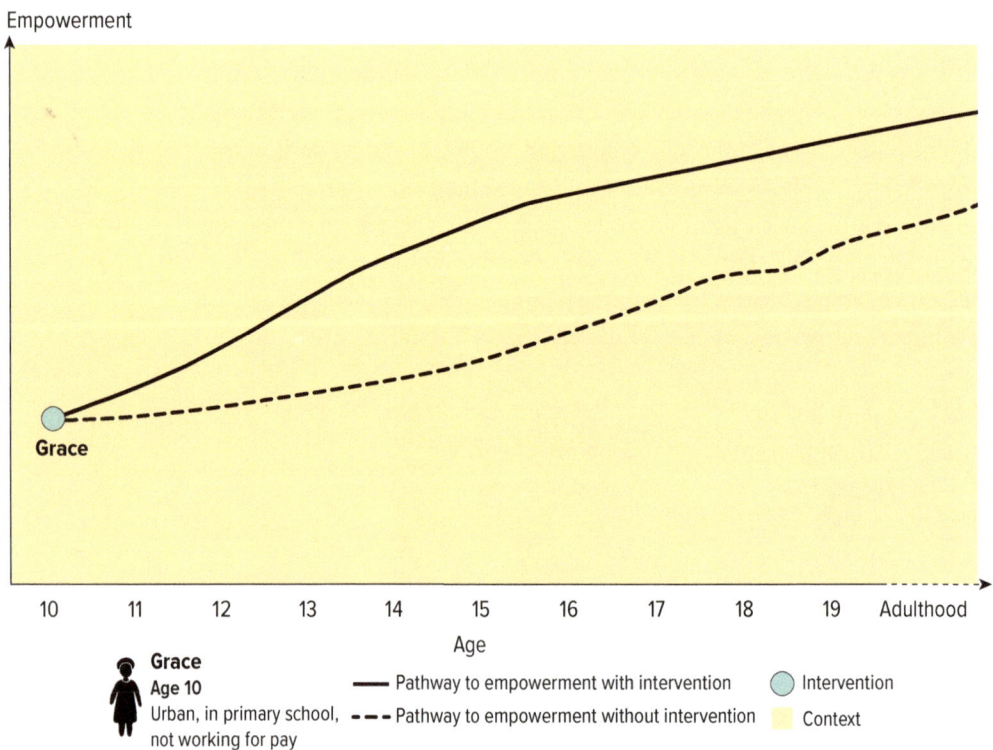

Source: Original figure for this report.

with friends and mentors. Since she lives in an urban area and her family supports her aspirations, she will be able to access services and household resources. When she is ready to look for a job, the availability of good-quality jobs may be a critical factor in her transition to work and her ability to achieve her economic goals.

As indicated by the solid circle (which represents an intervention) along the graph line in figure 1.2, Grace may still benefit from interventions that enhance other resources to which she may not readily have access—for instance, life skills training, mentoring, or job training to aid her transition between school and work, or access to a savings account and financial literacy. Grace's story shows that empowerment is a process that begins when girls are young and evolves through adolescence. Even when girls remain in school and have a supportive home environment, they may require other resources and contextual enablers to achieve their desired economic outcomes when they are older.

Mariam is a 12-year-old girl living in a rural area (figure 1.3). She has been out of school since the age of 10, when violent conflict broke out in her community.

FIGURE 1.3 The Pathway to Empowerment for Mariam Diverges With and Without Intervention

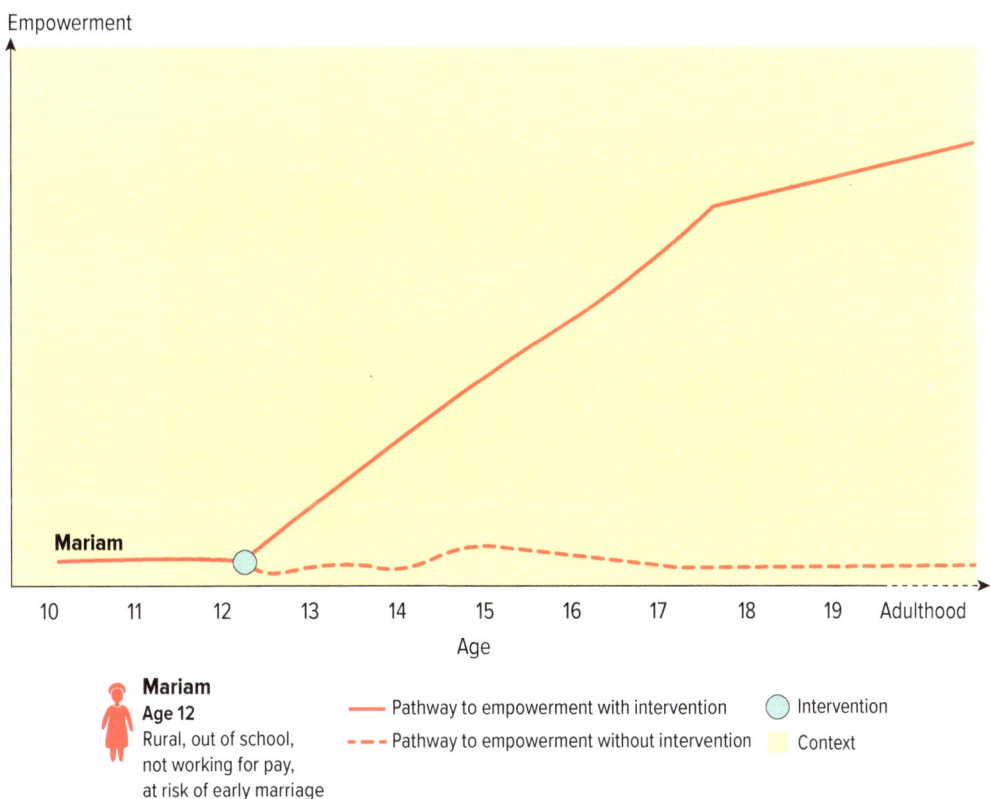

Source: Original figure for this report.

She does not talk about what she saw during the conflict but has expressed that she is afraid to leave her family. She is not working for pay and stays at home attending to household chores. Her parents are considering sending her away to live with an extended family member in the closest city as a domestic worker, so that she can make some money to support them. She has also started to receive marriage proposals.

Mariam's context drives the human capital, enabling resources, and agency she can develop over adolescence. The violence around her restricts her ability to continue school, constrains her family's access to resources, removes any sense of control and agency, and can spur her involvement in precarious work. She is at risk of early marriage and thus early childbearing, which may solidify the cycle of poverty. Mariam's story demonstrates the critical importance of context in girls' ability to accumulate the necessary skills and agency to be prosperous in adulthood.

For girls like Mariam, intervening early, perhaps with cash transfers to facilitate a return to school and programs that help enhance multiple resources, including safety through safe spaces, may be beneficial. Given their challenging start to adolescence, it is important to recognize that pathways to future empowerment for these girls may remain heavily dependent on lasting safety and an increase in the availability of resources and opportunities for employment.

Imani is a 15-year-old girl living in a semiurban area (figure 1.4). She recently completed primary school and has transitioned to secondary school but must now travel an hour every day to get to the closest secondary school in her district. She attends school when she can but sometimes cannot make the journey if she cannot afford the transport fare. Before and after school, she has started helping her mother sell food in the local market. She has also started selling used clothing to her friends to help pay for her school fees, and she is hoping to be able to find a place as a boarding student so that she can live close to school. The criteria for accessing a boarding school in her district include school attendance and student achievement, with no consideration for household income. Many of her friends dropped out after primary school and are struggling to find work.

Imani, now entering her late teens, has established a solid educational foundation but faces challenges in continuing her schooling as a result of her limited financial means. Her need to work for pay or sell clothes could limit the time she can devote to her studies, even though she has high educational aspirations and believes in her academic abilities. Moreover, the cost of transportation and the policies around support for boarding school present additional hurdles in achieving her aspirations.

FIGURE 1.4 The Pathway to Empowerment for Imani Diverges With and Without Intervention

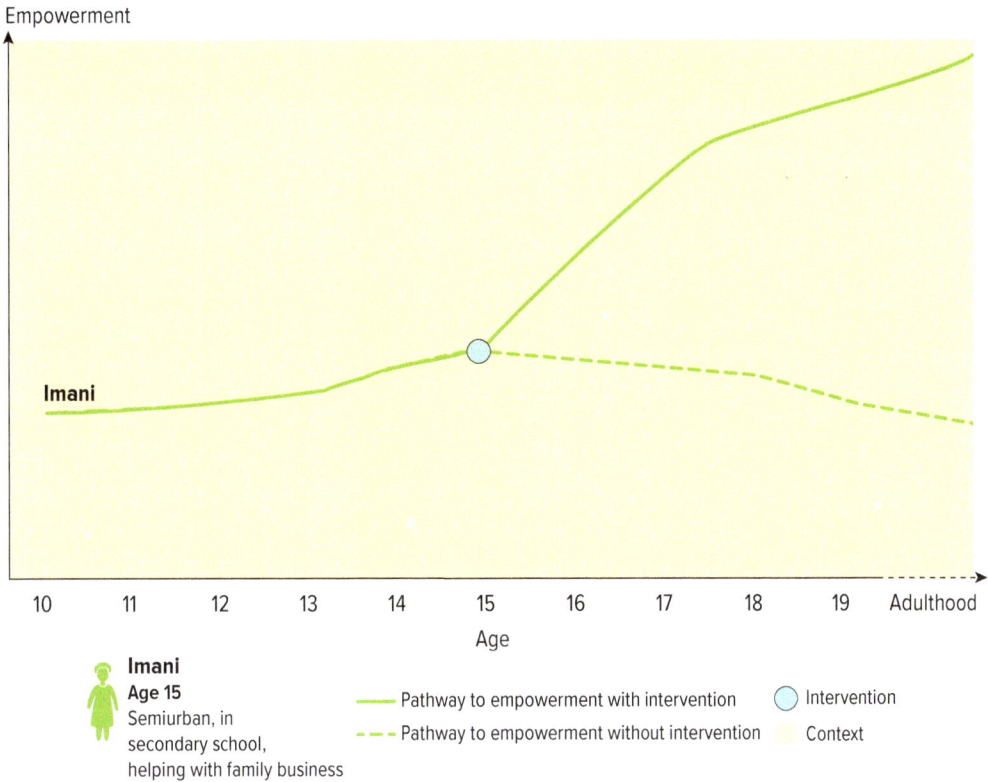

Source: Original figure for this report.

For girls who are in similar circumstances to Imani's, support for continuing education may be a critical intervention to ensure they can complete secondary school. In addition, providing vocational training after secondary school, as well as tailored mentoring and empowerment programs, may be beneficial to their future success in the labor market.

Aya is an 18-year-old married mother of a 2-year-old girl and lives in a rural area (figure 1.5). She dropped out of school at age 16 when she got pregnant and later married her child's father as a second wife, at age 17. Her husband is much older and travels a lot. She occasionally gets money from him but wants her own source of income, especially now that her child is getting older. She was selected to receive cash transfers through a government social safety net program but is getting to the end of the six-month program. She is, however, eligible for a government-subsidized childcare facility that could be beneficial for her and her child, since she moved away from her village after marriage and has limited caregiving support. Girls in her village are not allowed to return to school after they become pregnant, and access to reproductive health care is limited. The women who work in her community are usually self-employed.

FIGURE 1.5 The Pathway to Empowerment for Aya Diverges With and Without Intervention

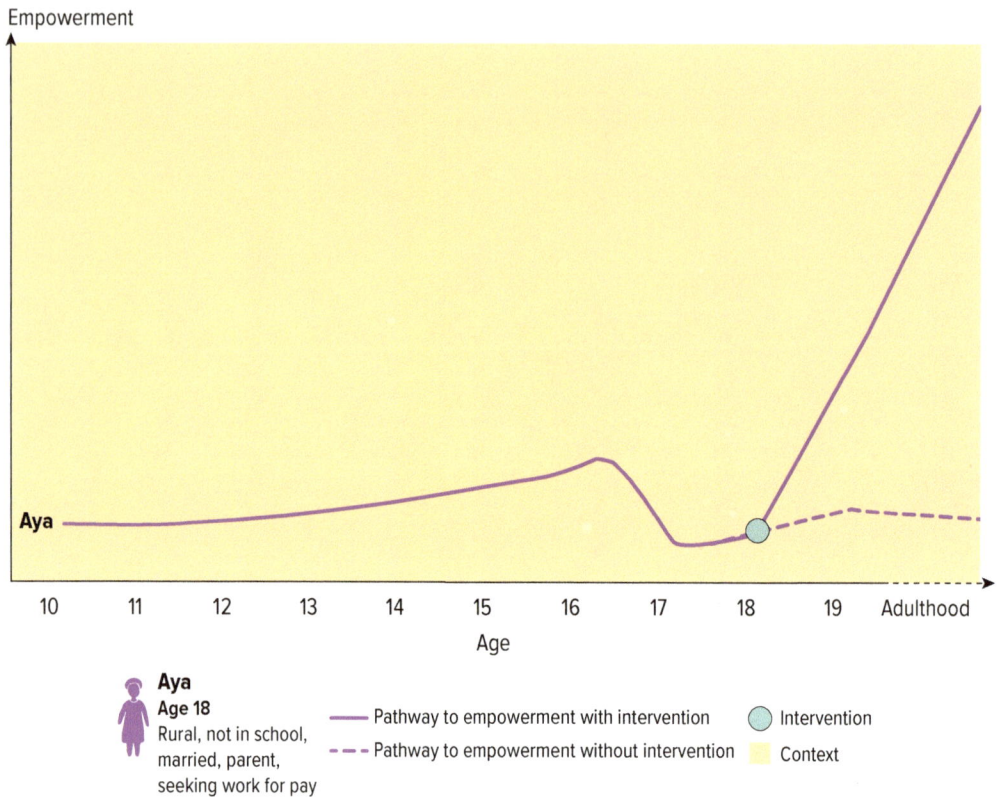

Source: Original figure for this report.

Aya is in the final years of her adolescence and has already experienced critical transitions, including leaving school on account of pregnancy, marriage, and childbearing, which, along with social norms, restrict her ability to return to school and the time she is able to invest in acquiring any other resources. Access to government programs like cash transfers has allowed greater financial freedom and flexibility for some girls, but Aya's occupational aspirations depend on access to support for childcare, gendered norms regarding work and childbearing, and the labor market opportunities available to her. Receiving additional support may increase her sense of agency in making decisions that are best for her and her family.

For older girls like Aya, who are in situations in which they must juggle many responsibilities and their return to school is unlikely, the provision of resources and skills that are directly linked to improving their access to work is critical. Such interventions may include comprehensive economic empowerment programs that combine vocational training with grants, on-the-job training, or ongoing mentoring; extended support for childcare and parenting; and access to bank accounts.

Chantal is a 19-year-old girl living in a rural area (figure 1.6). She completed secondary school when she was 18 and shortly afterward began working as a contract worker on a farm, where the hours are long and most of the employees are men. She is part of a rotating savings and credit association with some of her coworkers at the farm. She has been thinking about starting a home-based enterprise so she has time to manage household tasks and attend information technology courses that will help her make more money. She has a boyfriend, with whom she has been in a relationship for two years. He repeatedly asks her for money to support his carpentry business. She also has her own mobile phone and a national identification card.

Chantal has entered adulthood with the necessary educational resources and agency to help her start her first job, and she is trying to increase her earnings

FIGURE 1.6 The Pathway to Empowerment for Chantal Diverges With and Without Intervention

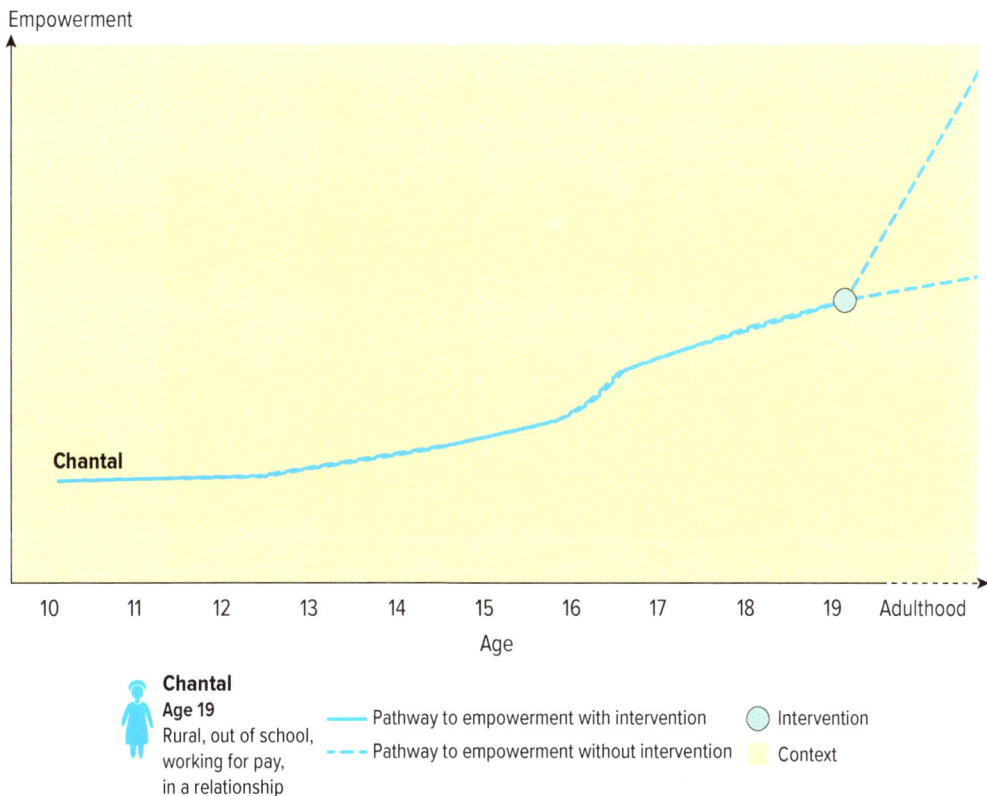

Chantal
Age 19
Rural, out of school, working for pay, in a relationship

—— Pathway to empowerment with intervention
‐ ‐ ‐ Pathway to empowerment without intervention

○ Intervention
▢ Context

Source: Original figure for this report.

by acquiring skills in an industry that may provide access to higher pay and better job quality. She has high occupational aspirations and a strong sense of agency in her ability to make changes that will help her move closer to the life she desires for herself and her partner.

Equipped with a foundation that has helped them invest in the requisite human capital fundamentals, along with enabling resources, agency, and the context necessary to fulfill labor market aspirations, girls like Chantal will benefit most from additional economic empowerment interventions and employment opportunities that are tailored to their goals and needs.

This Framework Provides a Guide for Understanding and Supporting Adolescent Girls' Empowerment

The framework employed in this chapter (and throughout this report) shows that girls' pathways to empowerment in adulthood vary, depending on how and where they begin adolescence and the point in their lives at which they require support from intervention programs. Discussions with adolescent girls have validated the components of the framework (box 1.2).

BOX 1.2   Empowerment as Perceived by Adolescent Girls in Benin and Kenya

This report draws on workshops conducted with adolescent girls from a range of contexts and backgrounds. The workshops were conducted in Nairobi, Kenya, and two rural communities, Atomey and Perma, situated in the south and north of Benin, respectively. These communities differ in terms of the available economic opportunities, their accessibility, and the quality of the communities' infrastructure. The aim in conducting the workshops was to gain insights into how adolescent girls view empowerment and whether the components in the framework employed in this report align with these views. Diverse settings were intentionally chosen to enable the researchers to understand the influence of context on girls' views of empowerment. To adequately capture the diversity of girls' experiences, girls participating in these workshops were divided into three groups: girls ages 10 to 14 who were in school and living with their parents; girls ages 15 to 19 who were unmarried and without children, some of whom were working; and girls ages 15 to 19 who were married or unmarried mothers, some of whom were also working. Below are key workshop findings.

Kenya

- All girls perceived education as vital to future success and to being able to access jobs that have higher pay.
- Older girls defined power as the ability to earn money and be self-driven and independent. For most girls, regardless of age, being respectful, obedient, humble, and helpful to their

(continued)

BOX 1.2 Empowerment as Perceived by Adolescent Girls in Benin and Kenya *(continued)*

families and community were common traits used to describe someone their age who would be considered a role model.

- Views of dating and relationships varied considerably between girls without children (regardless of age) and adolescent mothers.
  - For the former, partners were largely seen as a source of support, with similar ambitions for education and employment.
  - By contrast, adolescent mothers said girls who become pregnant when young may be left with unsupportive partners and struggle to meet their own and their children's needs. These mothers further highlighted their own stress and poor mental health, but also their resilience in trying to find work, save, and become more independent over time.
- Most girls described inadequate educational support and facilities, food insecurity, poverty, and lack of familial support as key challenges in being able to fulfill their goals. Among adolescent mothers, lack of education was cited as an additional challenge.
- Context was key in girls' descriptions of types of jobs girls with or without education would be able to access. In addition to the support of family, friends, and mentors, whom most girls cited as important sources of support and advice, adolescent mothers also underscored the role of institutions like the government and nongovernmental organizations in helping them find work.

Benin

- "A powerful girl is a girl who excels in school," says a 10-year-old unmarried schoolgirl in Atomey. In both Atomey and Perma, education was perceived as critical to the accumulation of personal and business assets, as well as to success in future economic activities. In addition, doing well at school, obtaining a high school degree, and sending children to good schools were viewed as powerful on their own. These views may have been influenced by nongovernmental organizations in Atomey and proximity to an urban center, including the associated economic opportunities, in Perma.
- "A powerful girl is a girl who becomes what she wants to be," says a 15-year-old unmarried secondary school student in Atomey. The characteristics perceived as embodying power varied by girls' circumstances, though some were common to all. Girls described a powerful girl as someone who is ambitious, is fearless, desires success, is self-determined, is independent, is zealous in the pursuit of a career, and has good financial management skills. Such a girl would not depend on her husband for support and would have her own income-generating activity, control over her income, and the requisite skills to grow her business. In addition, work was not seen as incompatible with success in school, especially in Perma, where it was viewed as a means of covering small expenses while in school.
- Furthermore, girls described an empowered girl and young woman as someone who is obedient, respectful, serious, submissive, and committed to her domestic chores as well as her work outside the home, thus upholding traditional gender norms.

(continued)

BOX 1.2 Empowerment as Perceived by Adolescent Girls in Benin and Kenya *(continued)*

- Girls in both communities described a lack of skills and information, specifically financial literacy and business skills; a lack of financial and physical capital, agency, and time; and low aspirations as key challenges in being able to fulfill their goals. They also discussed other challenges such as witchcraft and jealousy. Lastly, they mentioned early pregnancy as an impediment to reaching present and future economic goals.

- Girls emphasized the significance of social capital, community support, and, more specifically, support from role models and individuals involved in the activities they aspire to conduct. They further highlighted the importance of good communication skills and empathetic behaviors to gain this support.

FIGURE 1.7 Appropriately Designed Interventions to Support Adolescent Girls Can Boost Their Empowerment at Any Age, Whether They Are Still in School or Already Out of School, Are Married or Unmarried, or Have or Do Not Have Children

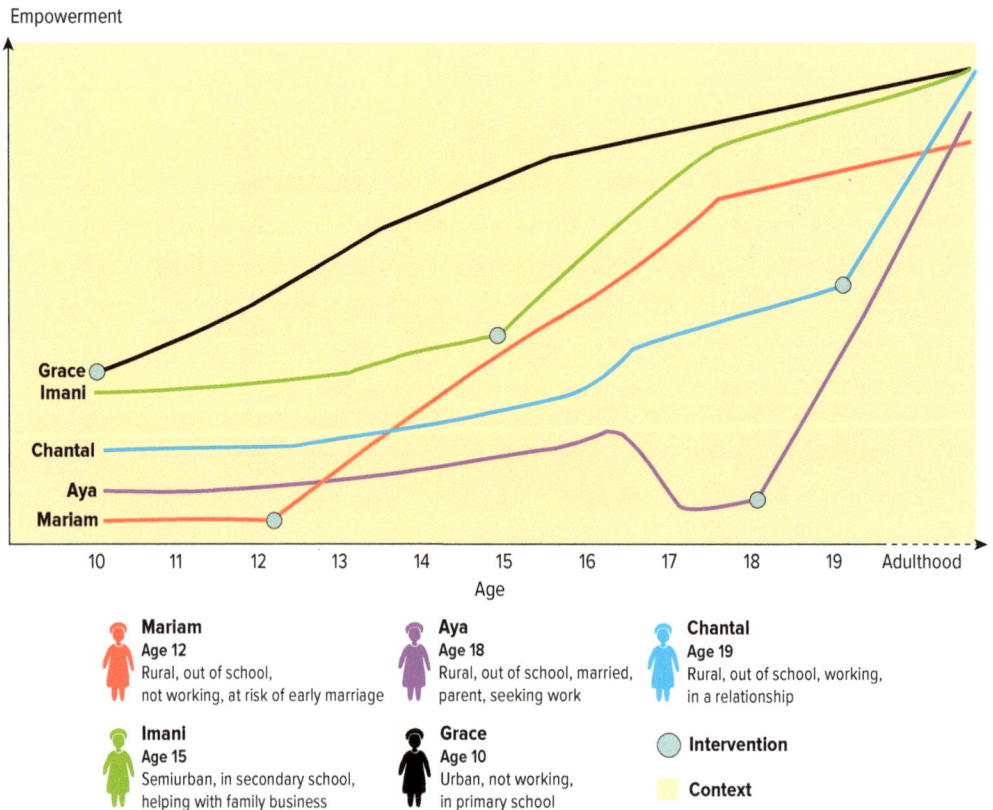

Source: Original figure for this report.

Appropriately designed interventions to support adolescent girls can boost their empowerment at any age, whether they are still in school, unmarried, and without a child, or facing different circumstances (figure 1.7). The rest of this report uses this framework as a guide for evaluating the design and effectiveness of programs and policies for empowering adolescent girls, recognizing that no single empowerment program or intervention will adequately meet the needs of all adolescent girls in Africa. Additionally, developing and applying measures that accurately capture girls' experiences and progress is crucial (spotlight 1).

References

Branson, N., and Murray Leibbrandt. 2013. "Educational Attainment and Labour Market Outcomes in South Africa, 1994–2010." Economics Department Working Paper 1021, Organisation for Economic Co-operation and Development, Paris.

Calder, Rebecca, and Karishma Huda. 2013. "Adolescent Girls' Economic Opportunities Study, Rwanda." Development Pathways, London.

Dandona, A. 2015. "Empowerment of Women: A Conceptual Framework." *International Journal of Indian Psychology* 2 (3): 35–45.

Hanushek, Eric A., Guido Schwerdt, Ludger Woessmann, and Lei Zhang. 2017. "General Education, Vocational Education, and Labor-Market Outcomes over the Lifecycle." *Journal of Human Resources* 52 (1): 48–87.

Hitlin, Steven, and Monica Kirkpatrick Johnson. 2015. "Reconceptualizing Agency within the Life Course: The Power of Looking Ahead." *American Journal of Sociology* 120 (5): 1429–72.

Jones, Nicola, Sarah Baird, Joan Hicks, Megan Devonald, Eric Neumeister, Elizabeth Presler-Marshall, Abreham Iyasu, and Workneh Yadete. 2019. *Adolescent Economic Empowerment in Ethiopia*. London: Gender and Adolescence: Global Evidence.

Kabeer, N. 1999. "Resources, Agency, Achievements: Reflections on the Measurement of Women's Empowerment." *Development and Change* 30 (3): 435–64.

Mizunoya, Suguru, Sophie Mitra, and Izumi Yamasaki. 2018. "Disability and School Attendance in 15 Low- and Middle-Income Countries." *World Development* 104: 388–403.

Moll, Amanda L. 2018. "Adolescent Economic Empowerment in a Kenyan Urban Rural Context." PhD diss., Georgia State University, Atlanta.

Mosedale, Sarah. 2005. "Assessing Women's Empowerment: Towards a Conceptual Framework." *Journal of International Development* 17 (2): 243–57.

Psaki, Stephanie R., Barbara S. Mensch, and Erica Soler-Hampejsek. 2017. "Associations between Violence in School and at Home and Education Outcomes in Rural Malawi: A Longitudinal Analysis." *Comparative Education Review* 61 (2): 354–90.

Sidle, Aubryn A. 2019. "Action on Agency: A Theoretical Framework for Defining and Operationalizing Agency in Girls' Life Skills Programs." Gendered Perspectives on International Development Working Paper 313, Michigan State University, East Lansing, MI.

Zimmerman, Linnea A., Mengmeng Li, Caroline Moreau, Siswanto Wilopo, and Robert Blum. 2019. "Measuring Agency as a Dimension of Empowerment among Young Adolescents Globally: Findings from the Global Early Adolescent Study." *Social Science and Medicine—Population Health* 8: 100454.

SPOTLIGHT 1
The Challenges of Measuring Girls' Empowerment

Henrietta Asiamah, Estelle Koussoubé and Fatima Zahra

Key Messages

- Significant measurement gaps exist in assessing context and diverse capital types that are essential components and indicators of adolescent girls' empowerment, particularly digital resources.
- Widespread variation in the wording of questions and in aspects of adolescent girls' empowerment captured across different surveys hampers comparison and synthesis, requiring further effort to standardize core measures.
- Tools for measuring adolescent girls' empowerment typically do not differ based on demographic groups and life transitions, highlighting the need for developing new measures that reflect disparities in empowerment experiences among girls.

The Importance of Measuring Progress in Adolescent Girls' Empowerment

Investing in adolescent girls' empowerment is increasingly recognized by policy makers and practitioners as a key driver for economic growth and development in Africa. However, measuring progress toward this goal remains a challenge.

The measurement of adolescent girls' empowerment is important because it helps identify the specific needs and challenges faced by various groups of adolescent girls and informs the development of effective policies and programs to support their empowerment. It also allows tracking of progress and assessment of the impact of interventions aimed at promoting adolescent girls' empowerment, which is critical for evidence-based decision-making and resource allocation by policy makers and practitioners.

Whereas there is a vast literature on measuring empowerment for women (for example, Buvinic et al. 2020; Donald et al. 2020; and Glennerster, Walsh, and Diaz-Martin 2018),[1] guidance on measuring adolescent

A reproducibility package is available for this book in the Reproducible Research Repository at https://reproducibility.worldbank.org.

girls' empowerment remains limited, particularly in the case of younger adolescents. Given the critical importance of adolescent girls' empowerment, it is essential to develop and apply measures that accurately capture girls' experiences and progress. It is also important to recognize that adolescent girls' empowerment differs from women's empowerment and that different aspects of the components of adolescent girls' empowerment may be more relevant to measure for some groups of adolescent girls than for others.

This spotlight examines survey tools from recent impact evaluations of programs aimed at improving girls' empowerment outcomes. The objective is to identify gaps in the measurement of key empowerment outcomes and provide guidance to researchers and other stakeholders regarding the measurement of adolescent girls' empowerment. This analysis focuses on these specific surveys, instead of large-scale surveys like the Demographic and Health Surveys and United Nations Children's Fund's Multiple Indicator Cluster Surveys, for two main reasons. First, the components of empowerment covered in these two surveys predominantly emphasize empowerment as it applies to women, without differentiation between older adolescent girls and women. Second, these large-scale surveys cover limited components, such as education and time use, for younger adolescents. Thus, identifying measurement gaps through surveys tailored specifically to adolescent girls' empowerment programs allows for a clearer examination of these gaps compared with using surveys that aim to measure human development or reproductive health more broadly.

To identify gaps in the measurement of girls' empowerment outcomes, this report examines survey tools, including adolescent girls' questionnaires, household questionnaires, and community questionnaires where available, from 10 impact evaluation studies conducted by the World Bank's Africa Gender Innovation Lab and the Population Council in collaboration with other partners. These studies focus on programs aimed at empowering adolescent girls in Africa. Table S1A.1 in annex S1A provides a brief description of these studies, including information on the interventions undertaken by the programs under study. For each study, the annex maps the empowerment indicators measured in the surveys across the components outlined in the report's conceptual framework (presented in chapter 1).[2] This mapping exercise offers a deeper understanding of gaps in measuring adolescent girls' empowerment, as it permits an examination of whether key empowerment indicators and measures identified in the conceptual framework were included in the surveys, how they were measured, and for which subpopulations (for example, younger versus older adolescent girls or married versus unmarried girls). It also allows the specific questions used to measure these indicators to be reviewed. Although the report does not aim to discuss the strengths and limitations of each question extensively, this analysis permits the variation in measures within and across surveys to be assessed.

Gaps in the Measurement of Adolescent Girls' Empowerment from Recent Survey Tools

Broad Gaps

After the survey tools and specific questions used in the surveys are mapped, this analysis reveals significant gaps in the measures of empowerment captured by these tools and questions, compared with the key components and indicators highlighted in this report's conceptual framework. These gaps are particularly pronounced within the context, resources, and economic achievement components.

As expected, given the nature of the studies analyzed—that is, impact evaluations designed to assess the effectiveness of specific programs and interventions—a significant measurement gap is found to exist across all surveys in regard to the context component. For instance, none of the surveys examined included any questions related to statutory laws or legal frameworks. However, although it is understandable that these surveys did not collect data on laws that would have little variation for analytical purposes, only one survey captured information on the availability and characteristics of services and facilities that are essential for adolescent girls' empowerment, such as schools, health facilities, facilities for training in technical skills, legal services, financial services, and labor market opportunities. Furthermore, only two surveys measured the prevalence or duration of conflict and local violence, which are crucial contextual factors affecting adolescent girls' empowerment.

When indicators of adolescent girls' empowerment are examined (figure S1.1), it is found that questions on access to digital capital and knowledge related to digital skills, both of which are important for current and future livelihood opportunities, were also limited to two to four surveys. The analysis also finds that questions on control over time use as an indicator of agency were covered in only one survey. Additionally, only four surveys included questions about job quality, and none included questions about age-appropriate work.[3] While specific measures such as earnings, time spent at work, and being engaged in paid work are often used to capture economic achievement, it is worth noting that not all types of work are associated with increased empowerment. For instance, precarious jobs, jobs with long working hours and low pay, and risky jobs are not considered desirable forms of employment. Measuring job quality and age-appropriate work is therefore key to offering a more comprehensive understanding of adolescent girls' empowerment. This can help inform the design of programs and policies to create favorable working conditions

FIGURE S1.1 Survey Tools Capture Indicators of Adolescent Girls' Empowerment

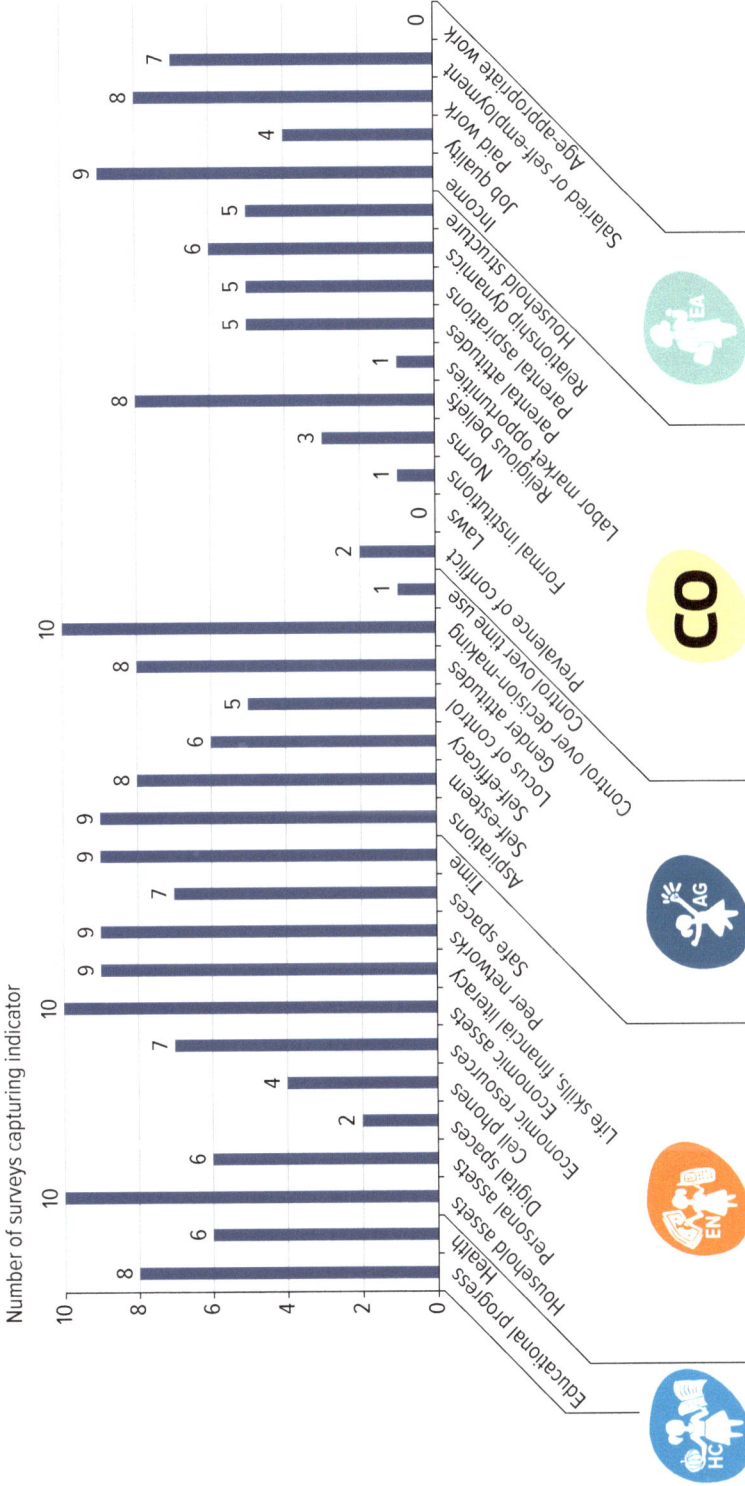

Source: Original figure for this report.

Note: AG = agency; CO = context; EA = economic achievement; EN = enabling resources; HC = human capital fundamentals.

Specific Gaps

Table S1.1 provides a detailed overview of the gaps in measures associated with each indicator of adolescent girls' empowerment, as defined in the conceptual framework. It focuses on three factors:

1. Is an indicator poorly covered (defined here as being measured in fewer than seven of the surveys examined)?[4]

2. Do the questions used across surveys capture different aspects of an indicator (for example, do questions measure aspects such as cell phone ownership or cell phone usage)?

3. Are questions related to the same aspect of an indicator asked in different ways (for example, are questions about time spent on work asked with reference to different recall periods)?

TABLE S1.1 Measurement of Adolescent Girls' Empowerment Using Existing Survey Tools Has Numerous Gaps

Components and indicators	Is the indicator poorly covered (that is, included in fewer than seven surveys)?	Do questions cover different aspects across surveys?	Are there major differences in question wording?
Human capital fundamentals			
Educational progress (attainment, enrollment, grade repetition, attendance)	No	Yes	Yes
Health (sexual and reproductive health, mental health, nutrition)	Yes	Yes	Yes
Physical and digital capital			
Household assets	No	No	No
Personal assets	Yes	No	No
Access to digital spaces and cell phones	Yes	Yes	No
Financial capital			
Access to economic resources (bank accounts, loans)	No	Yes	No
Economic assets (savings)	No	Yes	No
Knowledge and skills			
Life skills and financial literacy	No	Yes	No
Social capital			
Peer networks	No	Yes	No
Access to safe spaces	No	Yes	No

(continued)

TABLE S1.1 Measurement of Adolescent Girls' Empowerment Using Existing Survey Tools Has Numerous Gaps *(continued)*

Components and indicators	Is the indicator poorly covered (that is, included in fewer than seven surveys)?	Do questions cover different aspects across surveys?	Are there major differences in question wording?
Time			
Time for productive activity	No	No	Yes
Goal setting			
Aspirations for education, work, marriage, and childbearing	No	Yes	No
Sense of agency			
Self-efficacy, self-esteem, and locus of control	No	No	Yes
Gender attitudes	No	Yes	Yes
Control			
Control over decision-making	No	No	Yes
Control over time use	Yes	No	No
Fragility, conflict, and violence			
Prevalence of conflict	Yes	No	No
Statutory and customary laws			
Laws on gender, resources, work, age, and acceptability of violence	Yes	N/A	N/A
Formal institutions			
Presence and characteristics of formal institutions, including schools and health, vocational, legal, and financial services	Yes	No	No
Norms and religion			
Norms on gender, access to and use of resources, work, age of marriage, and acceptability of violence	Yes	No	No
Religious beliefs	No	No	No
Labor market opportunities			
Sector-specific access to jobs	Yes	No	No
Quality of available job opportunities	Yes	No	No
Household context			
Parental and household members' gender attitudes	Yes	No	No
Parental aspirations for girls' education and work	Yes	No	No
Relationship dynamics in households: discussion and cooperation among household members	Yes	Yes	No
Household structure and composition	Yes	No	No

(continued)

TABLE S1.1 Measurement of Adolescent Girls' Empowerment Using Existing Survey Tools Has Numerous Gaps *(continued)*

Components and indicators	Is the indicator poorly covered (that is, included in fewer than seven surveys)?	Do questions cover different aspects across surveys?	Are there major differences in question wording?
Labor market outcomes			
Income	No	Yes	No
Job quality	Yes	No	No
Paid work	No	No	Yes
Salaried or self-employment	No	No	Yes
Age-appropriate work	Yes	No	No

Source: Original table for this report.

In most cases, questions cover different aspects of specific indicators, making comparisons of specific measures across surveys difficult. Moreover, the statements used to construct subjective and composite measures, such as those related to self-efficacy, locus of control, and gender attitudes, show major differences across surveys. Although some level of variation is to be expected—especially in regard to composite measures—given the different survey contexts, this variation may also reflect other aspects of instrument development. These aspects may include unfamiliarity with existing measurement tools and a lack of consensus on how to measure certain empowerment outcomes, including control over time use and job quality, as well as a lack of validated tools that can be used for creating new surveys. Additionally, attempts to reduce the survey length, to the detriment of capturing certain components of empowerment, could contribute to this variation. Moreover, the absence of a clear theory of change or conceptual framework when survey tools are being designed could explain why some specific indicators are not well covered.

Gaps by Demographic Groups

Across all components and indicators covered in the surveys, very little variation is found in the types of questions asked of girls across different demographic groups, including younger (ages 10 to 14) and older (ages 15 to 19) girls, girls in and out of school, married and unmarried girls, girls with and without children, and girls who reside in rural and urban areas. Specifically, some surveys administered questions about sexual and reproductive health only to older adolescent girls. Similarly, some surveys restricted questions about reproductive health to married girls or girls known to be in relationships. Girls who were not enrolled in school were asked questions about their reasons for dropping out, their intentions in regard to returning to school, and their educational attainment, whereas girls enrolled in school were asked about absenteeism and school performance in some surveys. No differences are noted in questions across empowerment components based on childbearing status or location. It is important to note, however, that not all surveys represented different groups of girls, and therefore comparisons are limited to surveys in which both subgroups within a particular demographic group (for example, younger versus older girls) were present. The lack of significant variation in question type across different demographic groups suggests a potential limitation in conceptualizing and capturing the specific nuances and experiences of diverse subgroups of girls.

Advancing the Measurement of Adolescent Girls' Empowerment is Feasible and Should Prioritize Addressing Existing Gaps

This spotlight illuminates the challenges involved in measuring adolescent girls' empowerment and highlights several key findings. It finds that surveys tend to focus on specific components and indicators of empowerment, such as human capital, sense of agency, social capital, labor market outcomes, and control. However, there is variation in the selection and coverage of indicators within these components, making comparisons across studies challenging. Furthermore, the spotlight identifies significant gaps in the measurement of indicators of empowerment, particularly in areas such as context and digital capital and certain aspects of economic achievement. The lack of standardized questions and the variation in the statements used for subjective and composite measures further complicate comparability and synthesis of analytical results.

To address these challenges, it is crucial to focus on conceptualization, improved standardization, and harmonization of some key measures and approaches. Prioritization within these efforts is also necessary. Notably, significant progress has been made in developing validated measures for women's empowerment, exemplified by initiatives such as the World Bank's Measures for Advancing Gender Equality initiative and the International Food Policy Research Institute's Women's Empowerment in Agriculture Index, among others. Key components of adolescent girls' empowerment such as agency—including indicators related to goal setting and sense of agency—and context, including household context, can leverage progress made in women's empowerment measurement. There is a substantial conceptual overlap between women's empowerment and adolescent girls' empowerment in these domains. However, certain aspects of agency for adolescent girls, such as control over decision-making and economic achievements, differ significantly from those in women's empowerment. These areas warrant prioritization in efforts toward conceptual refinement and the development of new measures. Efforts should also ensure that frameworks and measures can capture the differences in girls' empowerment outcomes based on their demographic characteristics and circumstances.

Furthermore, there is a need for the development of measurement tools capable of capturing components of empowerment that are not well covered by the existing tools. This includes developing community-level instruments that allow the examination of context-related indicators of adolescent girls' empowerment in areas in which there is little overlap with similar women's empowerment measures. Clear guidelines for researchers and other stakeholders, guided by strong conceptual frameworks, are required to increase the comparability and reliability of findings.

It is recommended that these guidelines be prepared through a thorough consultation process with multiple stakeholders to produce a comprehensive compendium of measures that have broad support within the field. Although not all measures may be included in all surveys, given considerations regarding the budget and the time burden on respondents, having a repository of measures to choose from would contribute to enhancing understanding of the factors influencing adolescent girls' empowerment and facilitate the design of targeted interventions that effectively support the diverse needs and aspirations of adolescent girls.

Annex S1A. Impact Evaluations of 10 Programs Aiming at Improving Adolescent Girls' Empowerment in Africa

Table S1A.1 provides a brief description of the 10 impact evaluations analyzed in this spotlight.

TABLE S1A.1 Impact Evaluations of Programs Aiming at Improving Adolescent Girls' Empowerment in Africa

Program (Citation)	Program objective	Program description and outcomes measured	Age range	Country	Rurality/urbanicity
Economic Empowerment of Adolescent Girls and Young Women (Adoho et al. 2014)	Increase the employment and income of young women by providing livelihood and life skills training and facilitating their transition to productive work.	• Trained girls in business development skills, job skills, or both, targeted to sectors with high demand for workers; consisted of six months of classroom training followed by six months of placement and support. • Outcomes measured included economic outcomes (employment, earnings, and savings and investment behaviors), indicators of social empowerment (including mobility, decision-making, and self-confidence), and household-level indicators (such as food security and attitudes of the household head toward gender norms).	16–27	Liberia	Urban and rural
Rwanda Adolescent Girls Initiative (Botea, Chakravarty, and Haddock 2015)	Improve employment, incomes, and empowerment of disadvantaged adolescent girls and young women and test two integrated models for promoting this goal.	• Provided vocational training to girls in culinary skills, arts and crafts, food processing, and agriculture. The training was offered in nine vocational training centers across four districts. • Outcomes measured included participation in nonfarm employment, participation in wage employment or internships, cash income from an income-generating activity, having a savings account, and the amount saved.	16–24	Rwanda	Urban and rural

(continued)

TABLE S1A.1 Impact Evaluations of Programs Aiming at Improving Adolescent Girls' Empowerment in Africa *(continued)*

Program (Citation)	Program objective	Program description and outcomes measured	Age range	Country	Rurality/urbanicity
Sisters of Success (Koroknay-Palicz, Montalvao, and Seban 2017)	Foster girls' adoption of healthy behaviors, building their confidence and self-esteem, knowing and exercising their rights, developing savings and financial literacy habits, and increasing their community participation and involvement, and help them work toward their own personal development goals.	• Matched mentors randomly with girls; the mentors followed a precise curriculum targeting various aspects of girls' development. • Outcomes measured included girls' likelihood of dropping out of school; risky sexual behavior and likelihood of becoming pregnant as minors; voice and influence; occupational choice; earnings and savings; attitudes and aspirations; access to resources (time, money, and social support); life skills; peer influences and access to role models; and self-efficacy, self-confidence, and self-esteem.	12–15	Liberia	Urban
Adolescent Girls Empowerment Program (Austrian et al. 2020)	Build the health, social, and economic assets of vulnerable girls; reduce child marriage and unintended pregnancy.	• Provided weekly girls' group meetings led by mentors on health, life skills, and financial education over two years. Additional program components included a health voucher for general wellness and reproductive health services and an adolescent-friendly savings account. • Outcomes measured included self-esteem, social networks, attitudes and behaviors related to gender, work and saving activity, nutrition status, literacy and numeracy skills, cognitive function, sexual and reproductive health knowledge, and sexual behavior.	10–19	Zambia	Urban and rural
Empowerment and Livelihood for Adolescents (Bandiera et al. 2020)	Empower adolescent girls against economic and sexual and reproductive health challenges.	• Provided life skills training to build knowledge and reduce risky behaviors and vocational training to enable girls to establish small-scale enterprises. • Outcomes measured included HIV- and pregnancy-related knowledge, establishment of small-scale enterprises, likelihood of girls being engaged in income-generating activities, and participation of girls in self-employment.	14–20	Uganda	Urban and rural

(continued)

TABLE S1A.1 Impact Evaluations of Programs Aiming at Improving Adolescent Girls' Empowerment in Africa *(continued)*

Program (Citation)	Program objective	Program description and outcomes measured	Age range	Country	Rurality/urbanicity
Girl Empower (Özler et al. 2020)	Equip adolescent girls with the skills to make healthy, strategic life choices and to stay safe from sexual abuse.	• Invited adolescent girls to join local mentorship groups led by trained mentors to learn about life skills and financial literacy and to open savings accounts with seed money. • Outcomes measured included the incidence of sexual violence, school enrollment and completion, delayed marriage and fertility, self-esteem, self-confidence, self-efficacy, financial and health knowledge, and gender attitudes.	13–14	Liberia	Rural
Adolescent Girls Initiative—Kenya Equip (Austrian et al. 2021)	Improve adolescent girls' education, health, and economic outcomes.	• Delivered multisectoral interventions, including community dialogues on the role and value of girls, a conditional cash transfer for education, weekly group meetings for girls with health and life skills training, and financial literacy training and incentives for savings activities. • Outcomes measured included the experience of violence, gender-equitable attitudes, grade attainment, knowledge and behaviors related to sexual and reproductive health, knowledge and behaviors related to finance and income generation, and decision-making skills.	11–15	Kenya	Urban and rural

(continued)

TABLE S1A.1 Impact Evaluations of Programs Aiming at Improving Adolescent Girls' Empowerment in Africa *(continued)*

Program (Citation)	Program objective	Program description and outcomes measured	Age range	Country	Rurality/urbanicity
Promoting Safe Sex Among Adolescents in Tanzania (Shah et al. 2022)	Motivate girls' adoption of safe behaviors to improve their sexual and reproductive health outcomes.	• Leveraged ELA clubs, where adolescent girls were offered life skills and sexual and reproductive health education; offered a goal-setting intervention in which girls were asked to commit to remaining free of HIV and sexually transmitted infections and to develop three specific strategies to accomplish this goal. Additionally, offered girls' male partners a soccer intervention that educated and inspired young men to make better sexual and reproductive health choices. • Outcomes measured included female reports of intimate-partner violence, reported sexual activity, pregnancies, and knowledge of contraception methods; health behaviors (including drinking, smoking, socializing, and self-reported mental and physical health); and economic behaviors (including savings and employment status, along with other behavioral indicators, including risk taking and optimism).	12–24	Tanzania	Urban and rural
Kenya Micro-Franchising (Brudevold-Newman et al. 2023)	Promote female entrepreneurship.	• Provided business-specific training, capital, supply chain links, life skills training, and ongoing mentoring; offered women an unrestricted one-off cash transfer without any additional services. • Outcomes measured included the likelihood of being self-employed and improvement in income levels and overall well-being (living conditions index, food security index, current well-being, and future well-being).	18–19	Kenya	Urban

(continued)

TABLE S1A.1 Impact Evaluations of Programs Aiming at Improving Adolescent Girls' Empowerment in Africa *(continued)*

Program (Citation)	Program objective	Program description and outcomes measured	Age range	Country	Rurality/urbanicity
Sahel Women's Empowerment and Demographic Dividend (Boulhane et al. 2024)	Empower girls and women at the individual, community, and societal levels.	• Provided adolescent girls safe spaces where they could gain life skills and receive sexual and reproductive health information. • Outcomes measured included participation in an income-generating activity, aspirations, fertility, marriage, self-esteem and self-efficacy, gender attitudes, decision-making, and sexual and reproductive health knowledge and behavior.	10–19	Côte d'Ivoire	Urban and rural

Source: Original table for this report.

Note: ELA = Empowerment and Livelihood for Adolescents; HIV = human immunodeficiency virus.

Notes

1. The increase in measurement efforts has been bolstered by the launch of initiatives such as the Women's Empowerment in Agriculture Index, launched by the International Food Policy Research Institute; the Oxford Poverty and Human Development Initiative; and the US Agency for International Development's Feed the Future. Additionally, the World Bank's Measures for Advancing Gender Equality initiative, in collaboration with the International Food Policy Research Institute, the International Rescue Committee, and researchers at Oxford University, as well as the Center for Global Development and Data2X's Women's Economic Empowerment Measurement Learning Collaborative and the Evidence-based Measures of Empowerment for Research on Gender Equality initiative at the University of California San Diego, have contributed to this effort.

2. The report's conceptual framework identifies a number of key components that collectively contribute to adolescent girls' empowerment: human capital fundamentals, which include educational progress and health; enabling resources, which focus on knowledge and skills development, financial capital, physical and digital capital, social capital, and time allocation; agency, which includes aspects like goal setting, sense of agency, and control; context, which includes fragility, conflict, and violence, statutory laws and legal frameworks, formal institutions, norms and religion, labor market opportunities, and household context; and economic achievement, which focuses on labor market outcomes.

3. The International Labour Organization's Minimum Age Convention (Convention 138) sets the minimum working age in member states that have ratified the convention at 15 years for ordinary work (13 years for light work). Developing countries have the option of setting an age of 14 years for ordinary work and 12 years for light work. Light work is defined as work not likely to be harmful to children's health or development that does not prejudice children's attendance at school, their participation in vocational orientation or training programs approved by the competent authority, or their capacity to benefit from the instruction received. For hazardous work, the minimum age is set at 18.

4. If a lower threshold is employed for an indicator's being well covered (five rather than seven surveys), important gaps in terms of indicator coverage are still identified.

References

Adoho, Franck, Shubha Chakravarty, Dala T. Korkoyah Jr., Mattias Lundberg, and Afia Tasneem. 2014. "The Impact of an Adolescent Girls Employment Program: The EPAG Project in Liberia." Policy Research Working Paper 6832, World Bank, Washington, DC. https://openknowledge.worldbank.org/handle/10986/17718.

Austrian, Karen, Erica Soler-Hampejsek, Jere R. Behrman, Jean Digitale, Natalie Jackson Hachonda, Maximillian Bweupe, and Paul C. Hewett. 2020. "The Impact of the Adolescent Girls Empowerment Program (AGEP) on Short and Long Term Social, Economic, Education and Fertility Outcomes: A Cluster Randomized Controlled Trial in Zambia." *BMC Public Health* 20 (1): 349.

Austrian, Karen, Erica Soler-Hampejsek, Beth Kangwana, Yohannes Dibaba Wado, Benta Abuya, and John A. Maluccio. 2021. "Impacts of Two-Year Multisectoral Cash Plus Programs on Young Adolescent Girls' Education, Health and Economic Outcomes: Adolescent Girls Initiative–Kenya (AGI-K) Randomized Trial." *BMC Public Health* 21 (1): 2159. https://doi.org/10.1186/s12889-021 -12224-3.

Bandiera, Oriana, Niklas Buehren, Robin Burgess, Markus Goldstein, Selim Gulesci, Imran Rasul, and Munshi Sulaiman. 2020. "Women's Empowerment in Action: Evidence from a Randomized Control Trial in Africa." *American Economic Journal: Applied Economics* 12 (1): 210–59.

Botea, Ioana, Shubha Chakravarty, and Sarah Haddock. 2015. "The Adolescent Girls Initiative in Rwanda: Final Evaluation Report." World Bank, Washington, DC.

Boulhane, Othmane, Claire Boxho, Désiré Kanga, Estelle Koussoubé, and Léa Rouanet. 2024. "Empowering Adolescent Girls through Safe Spaces and Accompanying Measures in Côte d'Ivoire." Policy Research Working Paper 10721, World Bank, Washington, DC.

Brudevold-Newman, Andrew, Maddalena Honorati, Pamela Jakiela, Owen Ozier, and Gerald Ipapa. 2023. "A Firm of One's Own: Experimental Evidence on Credit Constraints and Occupational Choice." Working Paper 646, Center for Global Development, Washington, DC. https://www.cgdev.org/sites/default /files/firm-ones-own-experimental-evidence-credit-constraints-and -occupational-choice.pdf.

Buvinic, Mayra, Megan O'Donnell, James C. Knowles, and Shelby Bourgault. 2020. *Measuring Women's Economic Empowerment: A Compendium of Selected Tools.* Washington, DC: Data2x and the Center for Global Development.

Donald, Aletheia, Gayatri Koolwal, Jeannie Annan, Kathryn Falb, and Markus Goldstein. 2020. "Measuring Women's Agency." *Feminist Economics* 26 (3): 200–26.

Glennerster, Rachel, Claire Walsh, and Lucia Diaz-Martin. 2018. "A Practical Guide to Measuring Women's and Girls' Empowerment in Impact Evaluations." Gender Sector, Abdul Latif Jameel Poverty Action Lab, Massachusetts Institute of Technology, Cambridge, MA.

Koroknay-Palicz, Tricia, Joao Montalvao, and Juliette Seban. 2017. "Sisters of Success: Measuring the Impact of Mentoring and Girls' Groups in Supporting Girls' Transition into Adolescence and Adulthood, in Liberia." Innovation for Poverty Action, New York.

Özler, Berk, Kelly Hallman, Marie-France Guimond, Elizabeth A. Kelvin, Marian Rogers, and Esther Karnley. 2020. "Girl Empower—A Gender Transformative Mentoring and Cash Transfer Intervention to Promote Adolescent Wellbeing: Impact Findings from a Cluster-Randomized Controlled Trial in Liberia." *Social Science and Medicine—Population Health* 10: 100527. https://doi.org/10.1016/j .ssmph.2019.100527.

Shah, Manisha, Jennifer Seager, Joao Montalvao, and Markus Goldstein. 2022. "Two Sides of Gender: Sex, Power, and Adolescence." Policy Research Working Paper 10072, World Bank, Washington, DC.

CHAPTER 2

What Do We Know about Adolescent Girls' Experiences in Africa?

Kehinde Ajayi and Vrinda Sharma

Key Messages

- Although school enrollment rates for younger adolescent girls (ages 10 to 14) have surpassed 80 percent in many African countries, over half of 15- to 19-year-old girls in Africa are out of school or married or have a child.

- Adolescent girls are more likely than adolescent boys to be married, have children, be out of school, and not be working. Girls also experience more drastic increases in marriage, childbearing, and school dropout rates than boys do as they transition from adolescence to adulthood.

- While school enrollment rates for girls have substantially increased in Africa over the past decade, regional trends in adolescent marriage and childbearing have been mixed.

- The distribution of adolescent girls' experiences varies across and within countries, partly reflecting these girls' cultural, social, legal, and economic environments. The differences in adolescent girls' experiences have important implications for levels of their empowerment as well as for the design of programs and policies to enhance it.

- Adolescent girls in settings involving fragility, conflict, and violence (FCV) are more likely to be married, have children, and be out of school compared with girls in non-FCV settings. They are also less likely to have a financial account.

Adolescent Girls Are a Diverse Group

A common policy aspiration is to ensure that adolescent girls remain in school, delay childbearing, and delay marriage.[1] In most African countries, school enrollment rates for younger adolescent girls (ages 10 to 14) have surpassed 80 percent. However, by the time they reach older adolescence, barely half of 15- to 19-year-old girls are still exclusively schooling, without getting married or having children (figure 2.1).

A reproducibility package is available for this book in the Reproducible Research Repository at https://reproducibility.worldbank.org.

FIGURE 2.1 Over Half of 15- to 19-Year-Old Girls in Africa Are Out of School or Married or Have Children

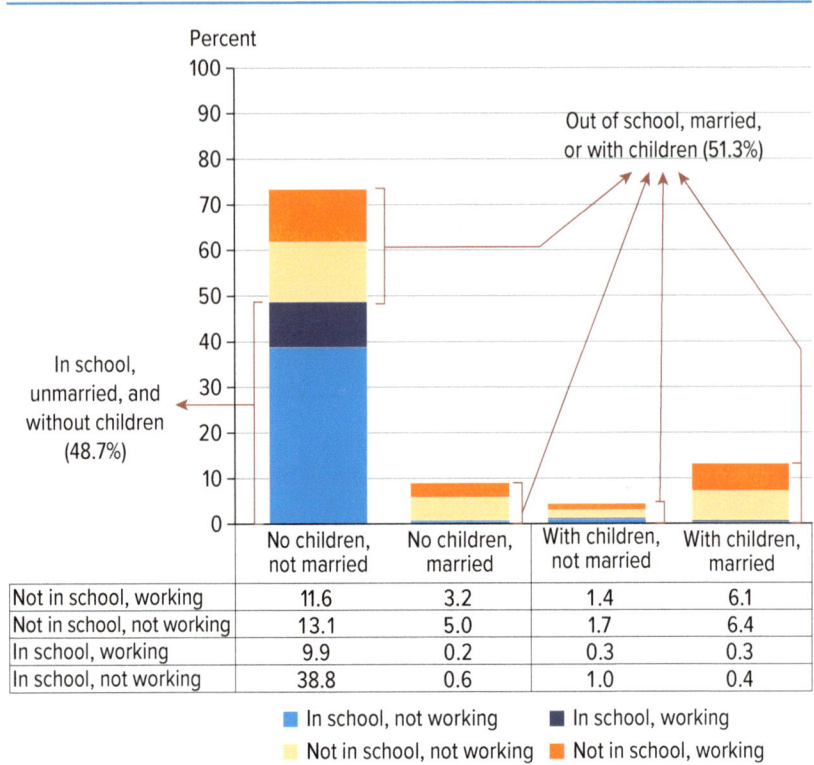

	No children, not married	No children, married	With children, not married	With children, married
Not in school, working	11.6	3.2	1.4	6.1
Not in school, not working	13.1	5.0	1.7	6.4
In school, working	9.9	0.2	0.3	0.3
In school, not working	38.8	0.6	1.0	0.4

Legend:
- ■ In school, not working
- ■ In school, working
- ■ Not in school, not working
- ■ Not in school, working

Source: Original figure for this report, based on data from the US Agency for International Development's Demographic and Health Surveys for adolescent girls ages 15 to 19, accessed March 17, 2024, https://www.dhsprogram.com.

Note: The Demographic and Health Surveys provide statistics on adolescent girls that are comparable across multiple countries, but with incomplete regional coverage. Data are available for 37 of the 48 countries in the region. This report used the most recent Demographic and Health Surveys samples available when analysis for the report began (Annex 2A reports the countries and years covered). The study population, adolescent girls, is segmented along four demographic dimensions: in or out of school, working or not working, with or without children, and married or unmarried, highlighting the intersections among these four experiences. Working is defined as being "currently employed" based on responses to the survey question. The Africa regional estimate uses denormalized weights.

In many countries, the typical 15- to 19-year-old girl is on a divergent path to adulthood. Adolescent girls ages 15 to 19 are almost equally split between attending and not attending school. Among the 48.7 percent who are still in school, unmarried, and not mothers, over one in five are already working. Thus, designing interventions for adolescents both in and out of school is critical to achieve comprehensive impacts. Furthermore, ensuring access to safe and dignified work is crucial for girls who are already working. Finally, adjusting interventions for impacts of childbearing and marriage is necessary for the more than 25 percent of older adolescent girls who are married, have children, or both.

Acknowledging these diverse pathways to adulthood is a key step toward designing tailored interventions to improve the well-being of adolescent girls with varying life circumstances. Identifying patterns in experiences generates insights for policy making. For example, for adolescent girls, marriage is more strongly associated with being out of school than is childbearing. Altogether, 4.4 percent of older adolescent girls in Africa have a child and are unmarried. Nearly 30 percent of these girls are still enrolled in school. By contrast, 9 percent of older adolescent girls in Africa are married without a child. Less than 10 percent of these girls are still enrolled in school. Among the 13.2 percent of 15- to 19-year-old girls in Africa who are married and have a child, only 5 percent are enrolled in school. Moreover, married adolescent girls are more likely than unmarried adolescent mothers to be out of school and not working. These correlations suggest that marriage and childbearing present differing obstacles to schooling and to empowerment.

Differences in Life Trajectories of Adolescent Girls and Boys Widen as They Age

Gender differences in life experiences are observable among young adolescents, and these differences increase with age. Although there are relatively small gender gaps in schooling among 10- to 14-year-olds in most African countries (with notable exceptions in some settings involving FCV, like Burkina Faso, Burundi, and the Republic of Congo), gender gaps in participation in household work and economic work persist (figure 2.2). Girls consistently perform housework at higher levels than boys (or in a few countries, levels equal to those of boys). By contrast, when it comes to participation in economic work, countries are almost evenly split among those with equal or close-to-equal participation, those with higher participation for boys, and those with higher participation for girls. The largest gender participation gaps are found in countries where girls are more likely to participate in economic work than boys (The Gambia and Lesotho).

FIGURE 2.2 Gender Gaps in Schooling Are Small for Young Adolescents, but Participation Gaps in Housework and Economic Work Persist

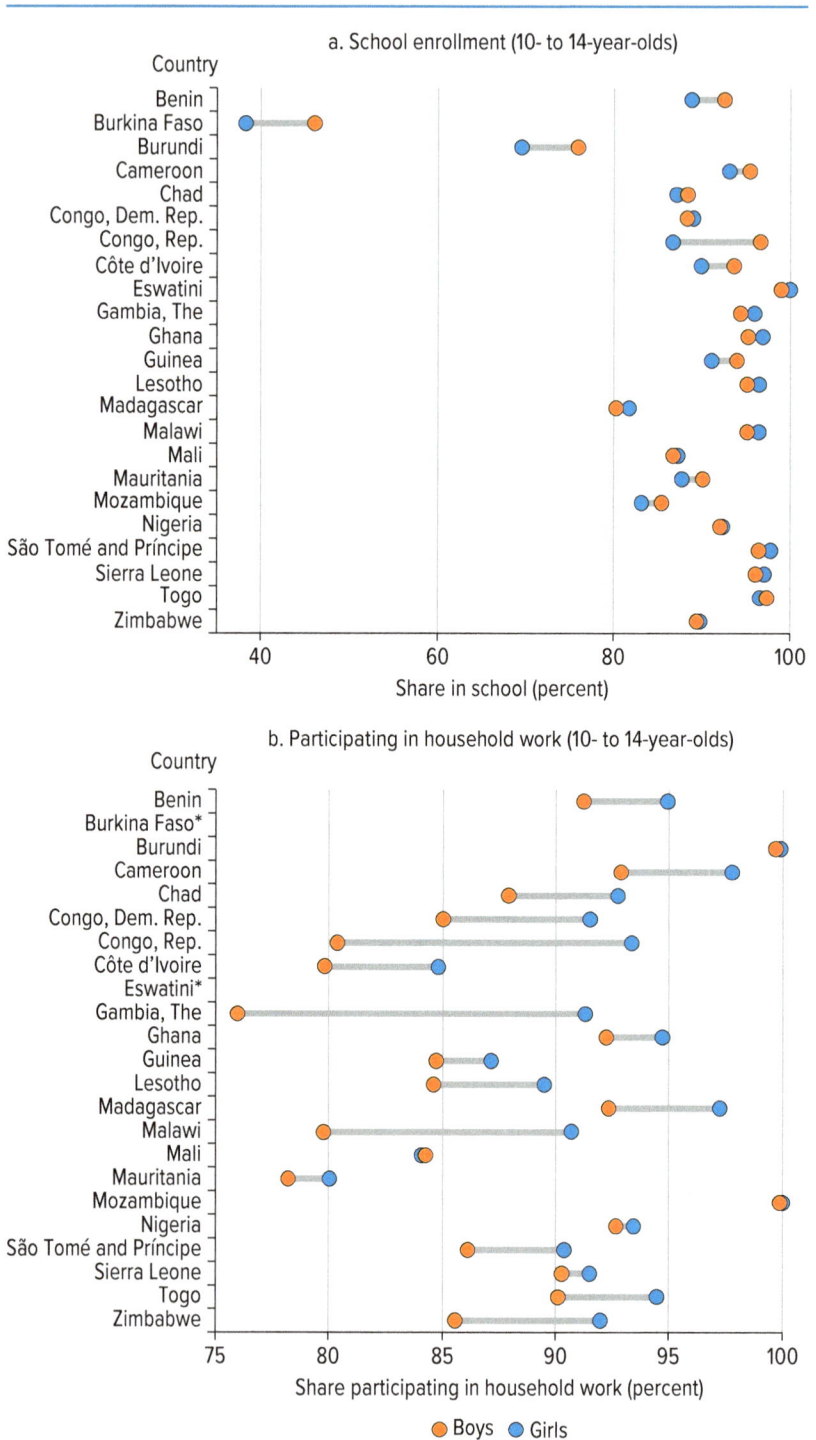

a. School enrollment (10- to 14-year-olds)

b. Participating in household work (10- to 14-year-olds)

● Boys ● Girls

(continued)

FIGURE 2.2 Gender Gaps in Schooling Are Small for Young Adolescents, but Participation Gaps in Housework and Economic Work Persist *(continued)*

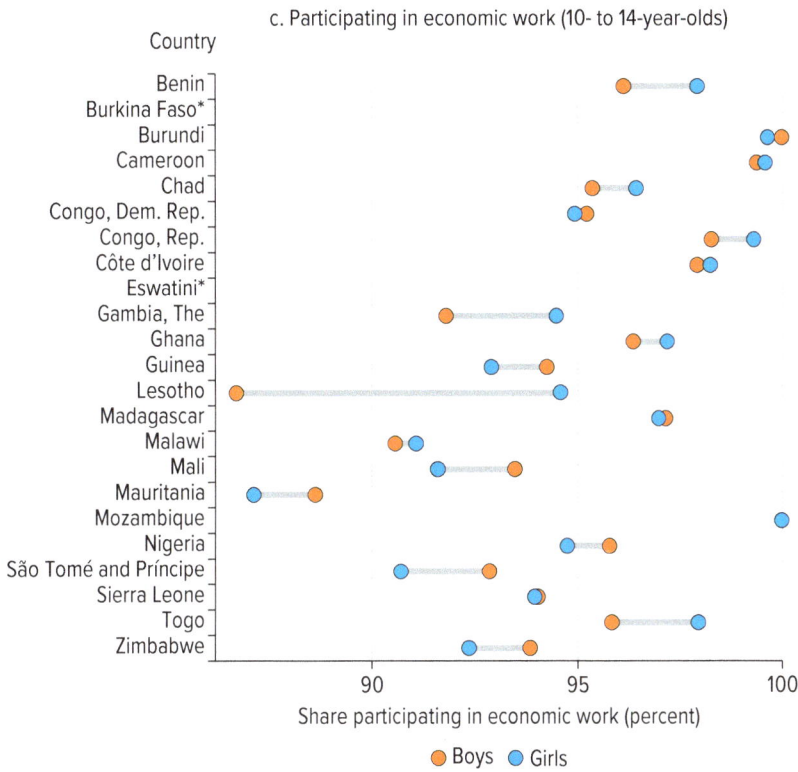

c. Participating in economic work (10- to 14-year-olds)

Source: Original figure for this report, based on data from the United Nations Children's Fund's Multiple Indicator Cluster Surveys, accessed November 28, 2023, https://mics.unicef.org/.
Note: Gray bars in the figure represent the difference between rates for boys and those for girls.
* = data not available.

Adolescent girls' experiences increasingly diverge from those of adolescent boys as they age. Older adolescent girls (ages 15 to 19) are more likely than adolescent boys to be married, to have children, or both (figure 2.3). About 22 percent of girls in this age group are married, compared with less than 2 percent of boys. This implies that adolescent girls are not marrying boys their age, which raises the question of the social and economic agency that girls may lose or gain through marriage to older men. Moreover, 26 percent of girls in this age group are neither working nor in school, whereas the comparable percentage for boys is about 9 percent (consistent with results in ILO [2020]).

FIGURE 2.3 The Transition from Adolescence to Adulthood Is Starker for Girls Than for Boys

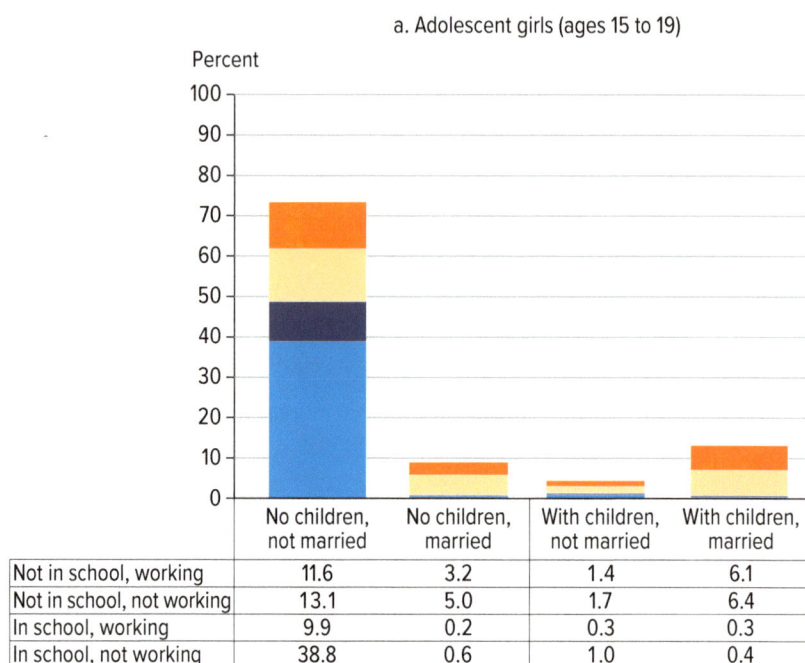

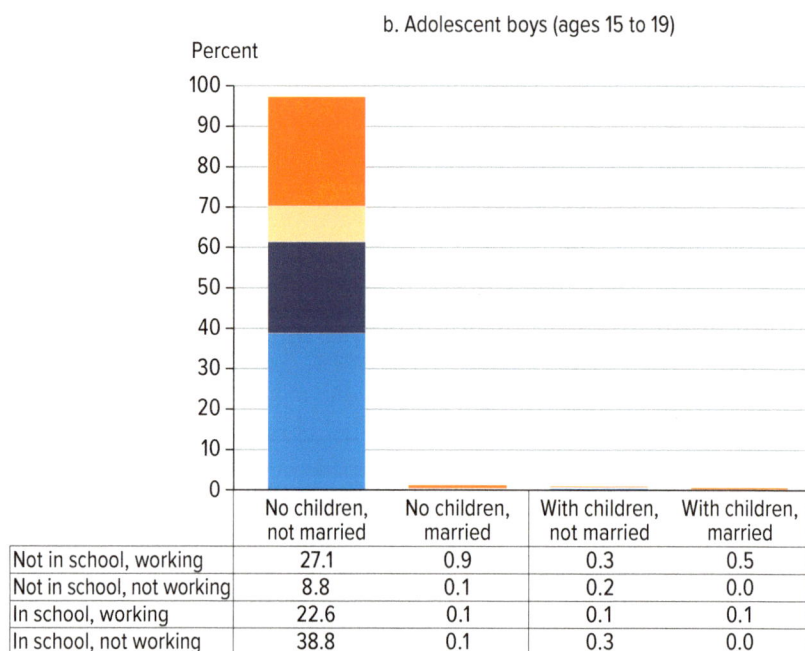

a. Adolescent girls (ages 15 to 19)

	No children, not married	No children, married	With children, not married	With children, married
Not in school, working	11.6	3.2	1.4	6.1
Not in school, not working	13.1	5.0	1.7	6.4
In school, working	9.9	0.2	0.3	0.3
In school, not working	38.8	0.6	1.0	0.4

b. Adolescent boys (ages 15 to 19)

	No children, not married	No children, married	With children, not married	With children, married
Not in school, working	27.1	0.9	0.3	0.5
Not in school, not working	8.8	0.1	0.2	0.0
In school, working	22.6	0.1	0.1	0.1
In school, not working	38.8	0.1	0.3	0.0

■ In school, not working   ■ In school, working
■ Not in school, not working   ■ Not in school, working

(continued)

FIGURE 2.3 The Transition from Adolescence to Adulthood Is Starker for
Girls Than for Boys *(continued)*

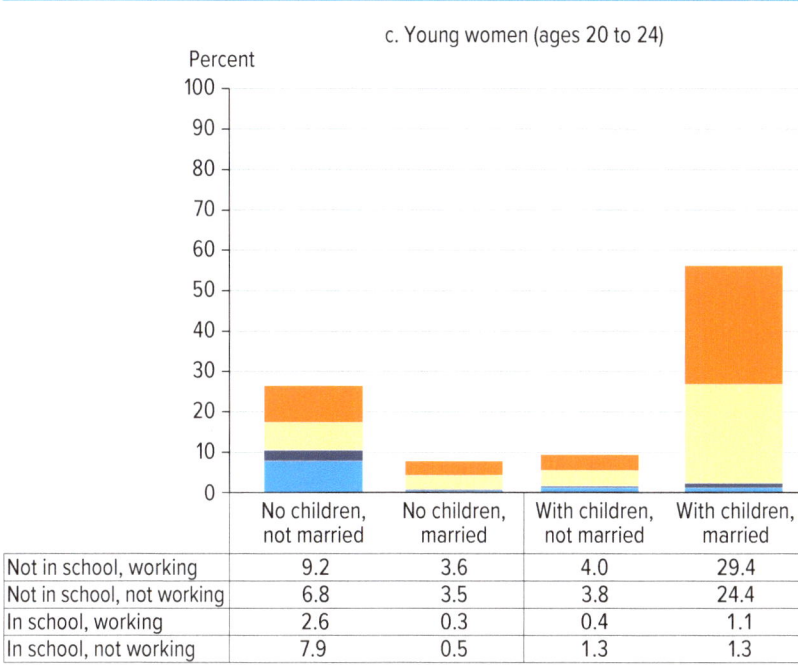

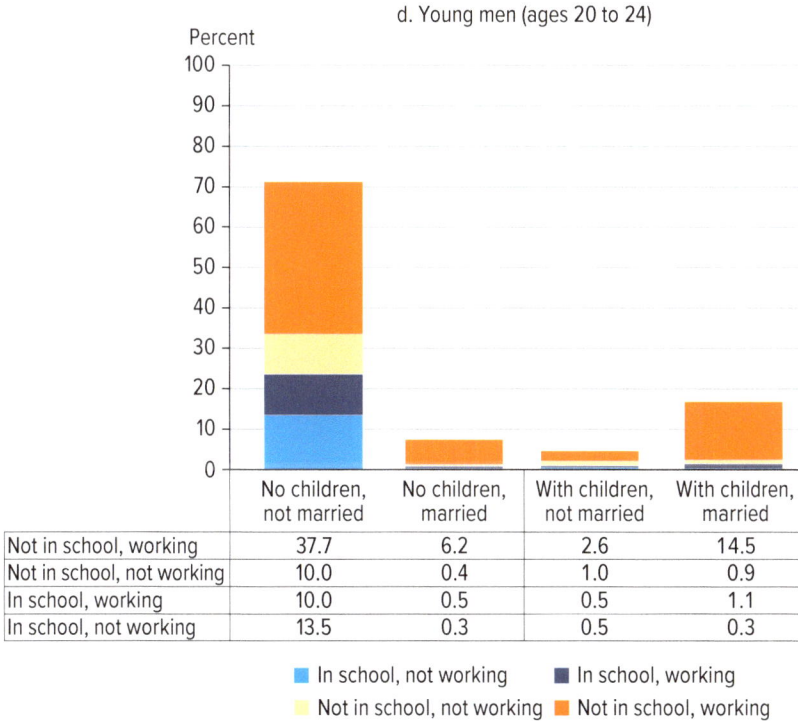

c. Young women (ages 20 to 24)

	No children, not married	No children, married	With children, not married	With children, married
Not in school, working	9.2	3.6	4.0	29.4
Not in school, not working	6.8	3.5	3.8	24.4
In school, working	2.6	0.3	0.4	1.1
In school, not working	7.9	0.5	1.3	1.3

d. Young men (ages 20 to 24)

	No children, not married	No children, married	With children, not married	With children, married
Not in school, working	37.7	6.2	2.6	14.5
Not in school, not working	10.0	0.4	1.0	0.9
In school, working	10.0	0.5	0.5	1.1
In school, not working	13.5	0.3	0.5	0.3

■ In school, not working   ■ In school, working
■ Not in school, not working   ■ Not in school, working

Source: Original figure for this report, based on data from the US Agency for International Development's Demographic and Health Surveys, accessed March 17, 2024, https://www.dhsprogram.com.

Similarly, the transition from older adolescence (ages 15 to 19) to young adulthood (ages 20 to 24) comes with a greater increase in marriage, childbearing, and school dropout rates for girls than for boys. Among young African women, 56 percent have a child and are married. Fewer than 16 percent remain in school. Young African men, on the other hand, are predominantly still unmarried and without children. Around 27 percent remain in school, and most of those out of school are working. Thus, African men are more likely to continue their education into their early adulthood or to transition from school into participating in the labor force. Young African women, however, do not go to school or participate in the labor force at rates equal to those of young men, weakening their future labor market prospects. These gender differences highlight the importance of focusing on gender-specific challenges facing adolescent girls in Africa.

While Regional Trends in Schooling and Exclusive Work Have Generally Been Positive, Trends in Marriage and Childbearing Have Been More Mixed

The current educational status of adolescent girls in Africa reflects substantial progress in school enrollment over the past two decades. Since 2000, most African countries have increased the percentage of 15- to 19-year-old girls in school (figure 2.4). Nigeria is the only African country without a statistically significant change in school enrollment between rounds of the US Agency for International Development's Demographic and Health Surveys. Low-income countries in Africa have seen the largest gains, with Rwanda increasing girls' school enrollment rates from less than 10 percent to 56 percent and Uganda increasing them from 23 percent to more than 50 percent in the span of two decades. Overall, these trajectories point to the fact that adolescent girls across the region are increasingly likely to remain in school. In a few countries (Côte d'Ivoire, Namibia, Nigeria, and Tanzania) school enrollment rates have increased or remained constant, and rates of girls who are out of school and working exclusively have increased. This implies a decline in the share of girls who are neither in school nor working in these countries.

FIGURE 2.4 School Enrollment Rates for 15- to 19-Year-Old Girls Have
Increased across the Region

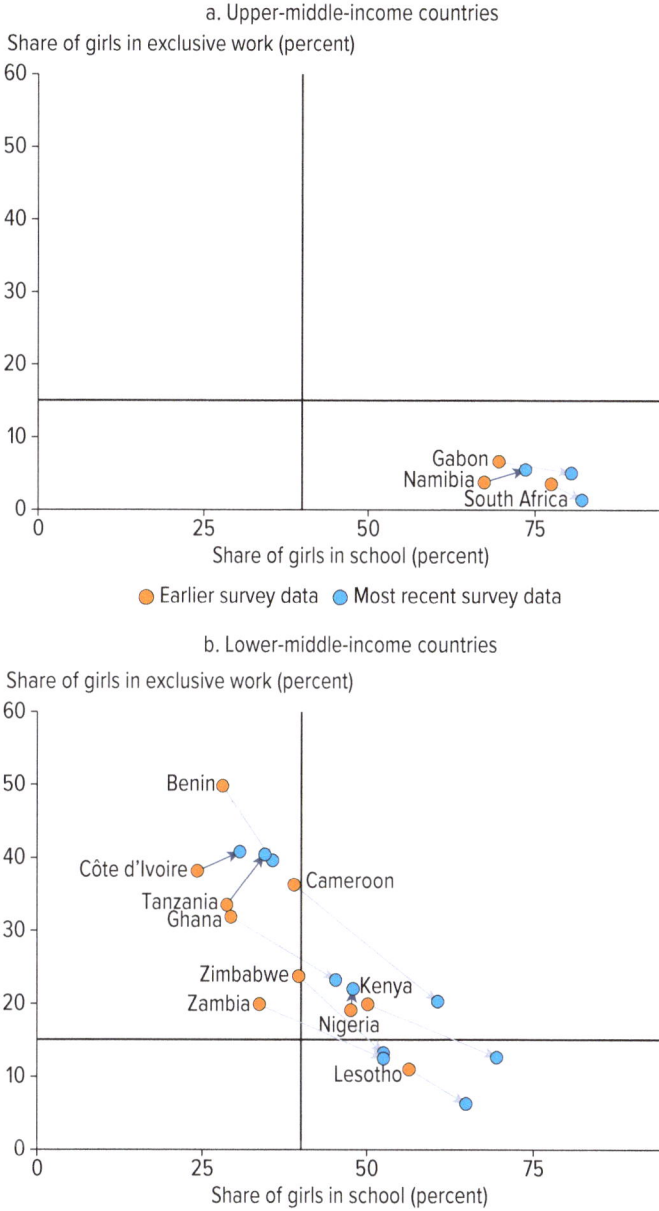

a. Upper-middle-income countries

Share of girls in exclusive work (percent)

Earlier survey data   Most recent survey data

b. Lower-middle-income countries

Share of girls in exclusive work (percent)

Share of girls in school (percent)

(continued)

FIGURE 2.4 School Enrollment Rates for 15- to 19-Year-Old Girls Have
Increased across the Region *(continued)*

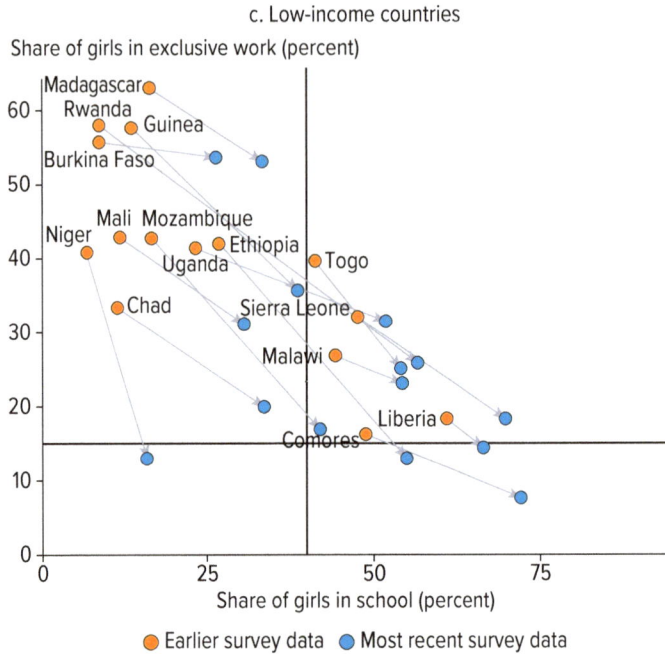

c. Low-income countries

Source: Original figure for this report, based on data from the US Agency for International Development's Demographic and Health Surveys, accessed March 17, 2024, https://www.dhsprogram.com.

Note: Orange dots show data from an earlier Demographic and Health Survey and blue dots data from the most recent one. Time between survey rounds varies; generally, for each country, the earlier round took place between 1990 and 2000 and the most recent one between 2010 and 2019, with an average difference between the two of 15 years (range = 10 to 23). Refer to table 2A.1 for the full list of countries and survey years. Black (rather than gray) arrows indicate four countries where the percentage of girls exclusively working has increased.

Although this progress in school enrollment gives much cause to celebrate, there is still work to be done. The primary school completion rate for girls in Africa is 69 percent, and the lower-secondary completion rate is 43 percent, compared with 89 percent and 75 percent, respectively, for all low- and middle-income countries,[2] indicating that grade progression is still a challenge. School-leaving exams present one potential barrier for adolescent girls' educational attainment (box 2.1). Additionally, there are still subgroups of girls who have not experienced increases in school enrollment, even within countries that have made substantial progress (Evans, Carvalho, and Mendez Acosta 2022).

BOX 2.1   School-Leaving Exams and Dropout Rates for Girls

Many African countries have primary-school-leaving exams, which determine access to secondary school (map B2.1.1). Girls often have a lower passing rate than boys do on these exams (figure B2.1.1). This gender gap in exam performance can exacerbate school dropout rates among girls and limit their transition to secondary school, even in cases in which girls are interested in continuing their schooling and have adequate academic ability, because factors such as gender bias in teachers' perceptions of student ability can undermine girls' performance on high-stakes exams (Carvalho and Cameron 2022). More than 80 percent of African countries have lower-secondary-school-leaving exams, which potentially reinforce this gender gap in schooling transition at tertiary education levels (Rossiter and Konate 2022).

MAP B2.1.1   Many African Countries Have a Primary-School-Leaving Exam That Determines Access to Secondary School, with Pass Rates That Vary Widely

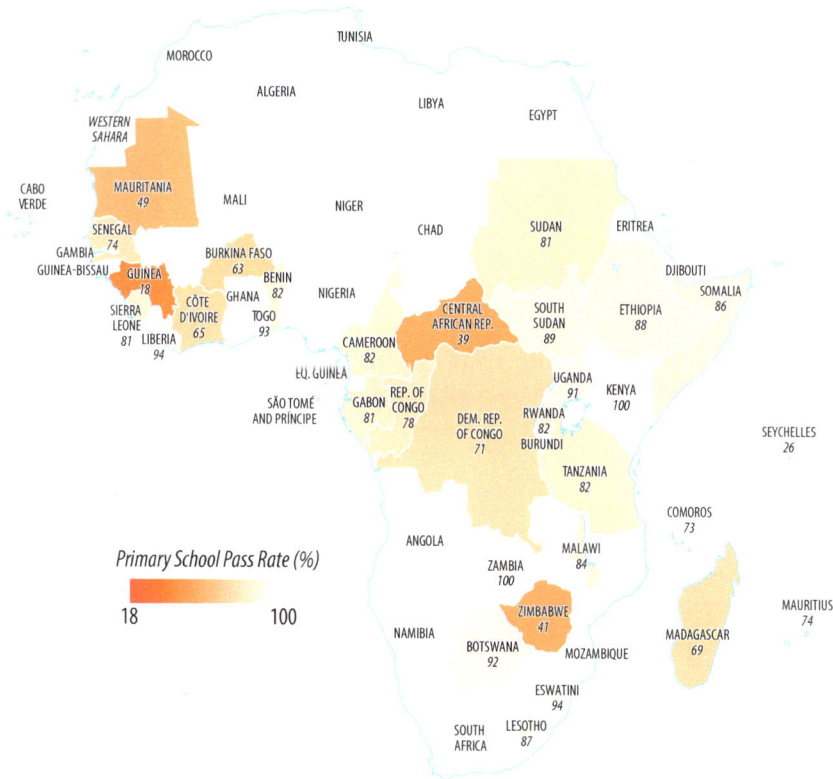

IBRD 48266 | AUGUST 2024

Source: Rossiter and Konate (2022).

(continued)

BOX 2.1 School-Leaving Exams and Dropout Rates for Girls *(continued)*

FIGURE B2.1.1 In Some Countries in Africa, Girls Are Less Likely Than Boys to Sit for Exams, and They Achieve Lower Pass Rates When They Do

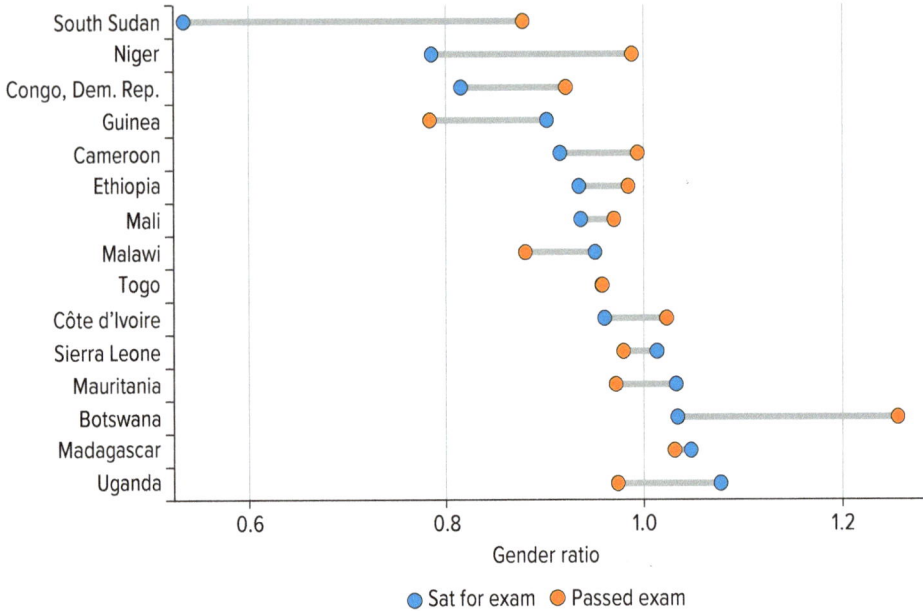

● Sat for exam   ● Passed exam

Source: Carvalho and Cameron (2022).
Note: The gender ratio is calculated by dividing the number of girls who sat for (or passed) an exam by the number of boys who did so. A ratio greater than 1 means more girls than boys sat for (or passed) the exam. Bars connecting orange and blue dots indicate the difference in gender ratios for exam sitting and exam passing.

Progress in reducing early marriage and childbearing in Africa has been more mixed than the robust positive trends in regard to schooling (figure 2.5). Adolescent girls' marriage rates have generally fallen across African countries over the past 10 to 20 years. However, some countries have seen increases, including Madagascar, Niger, Tanzania, and Zimbabwe. Additionally, the percentage of adolescent girls with children has largely declined, except in a few countries such as Burundi and Zambia. In the Comoros, Tanzania, and Zimbabwe, both the likelihood of adolescent girls' marriage and that of childbearing have increased over time.

FIGURE 2.5 Progress in Reducing Marriage and Childbearing among
15- to 19-Year-Old Girls Has Been Mixed

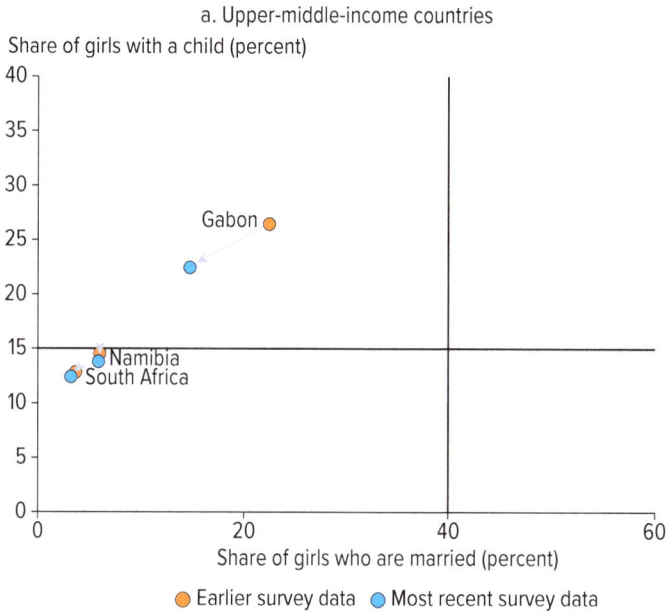

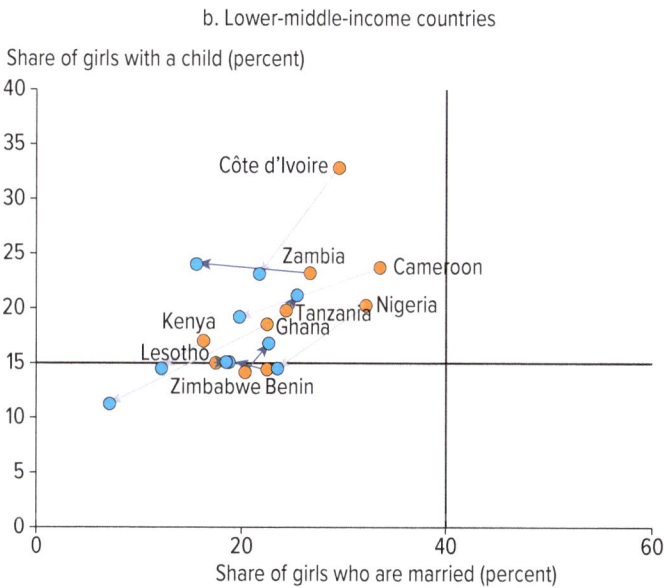

a. Upper-middle-income countries

Share of girls with a child (percent)

Gabon

Namibia
South Africa

Share of girls who are married (percent)

● Earlier survey data   ● Most recent survey data

b. Lower-middle-income countries

Share of girls with a child (percent)

Côte d'Ivoire

Zambia   Cameroon

Nigeria
Tanzania
Kenya   Ghana

Lesotho

Zimbabwe Benin

Share of girls who are married (percent)

(continued)

FIGURE 2.5 Progress in Reducing Marriage and Childbearing among 15- to 19-Year-Old Girls Has Been Mixed *(continued)*

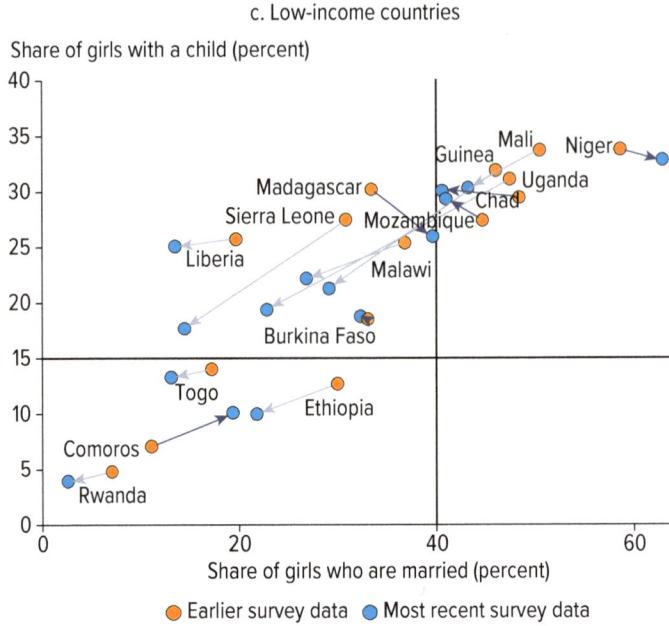

c. Low-income countries

Source: Original figure for this report, based on data from the US Agency for International Development's Demographic and Health Surveys, accessed March 17, 2024, https://www.dhsprogram.com.

Note: Orange dots show data from an earlier Demographic and Health Survey and blue dots data from the most recent one. Time between survey rounds varies; generally, for each country, the earlier round took place between 1990 and 2000 and the most recent one between 2010 and 2019, with an average difference between the two of 15 years (range = 10 to 23). Refer to table 2A.1 for the full list of countries and survey years. Black (rather than gray) arrows indicate countries where the percentage of girls who are married or have a child has increased.

Adolescent Girls' Experiences Vary across and within Countries, Partly Reflecting Girls' Cultural, Social, Legal, and Economic Contexts

Adolescent girls' experiences tend to vary across countries.

To further shed light on cross-country patterns, this report groups countries into five categories with common features that reflect the intersections among rates of schooling, work, marriage, and childbearing for older adolescent girls (figure 2.6).[3] These categories provide an instructive tool for understanding patterns in the experiences of adolescent girls and offer insight into approaches to support these girls' empowerment (table 2.1).

FIGURE 2.6 There Are Systematic Cross-Country Differences in Adolescent Girls' Experiences

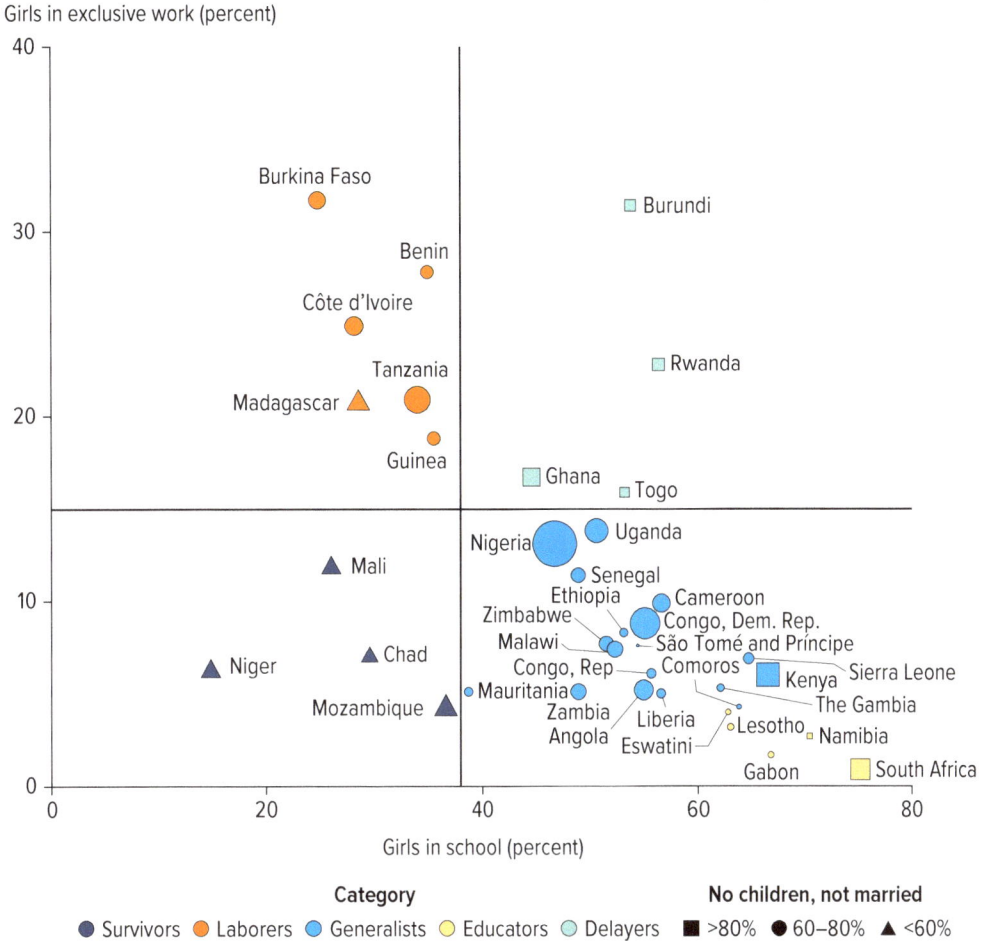

Source: Original figure for this report, based on data from the US Agency for International Development's Demographic and Health Surveys, accessed March 17, 2024, https://www.dhsprogram.com.
Note: Categorizations are based on the most recent Demographic and Health Surveys data for girls ages 15 to 19 years old. The size of the marker for each country reflects the country's population size. The shape of each marker indicates the share of adolescent girls who are not married and without children.

Marriage and childbearing delayers (the four countries in the upper-right quadrant in figure 2.6) have been most successful at delaying marriage and childbearing among adolescent girls. More than 80 percent of 15- to 19-year-old girls in these countries are still unmarried and have no children. These countries have a combination of high levels of school enrollment (above 40 percent) and high rates of work among girls who are out of school (that is, high rates of "exclusive work," at above 15 percent). This category includes both low- and lower-middle-income countries. A key policy question for these countries is how to further advance educational progress.

TABLE 2.1 Five Country Categories Provide a Data-Driven Tool to Guide Investments in Adolescent Girls

Marriage and Childbearing Delayers	Educators	Generalists	Laborers	Survivors
Burundi, Ghana, Rwanda, Togo	Eswatini, Gabon, Lesotho, Namibia, South Africa	Angola; Cameroon; Comoros; Congo, Dem. Rep.; Congo, Rep.; Ethiopia; Gambia, The; Kenya; Liberia; Malawi; Mauritania; Nigeria; São Tomé and Príncipe; Senegal; Sierra Leone; Uganda; Zambia; Zimbabwe	Benin, Burkina Faso, Côte d'Ivoire, Guinea, Madagascar, Tanzania	Chad, Mali, Mozambique, Niger
Low marriage and childbearing (>80% not married, no children)	Low marriage and childbearing (>70% not married, no children)	Moderate marriage and childbearing (65–85% not married, no children)	Moderate marriage and childbearing (55–80% not married, no children)	High marriage and childbearing (<60% not married, no children)
Moderate schooling (45–65% in school)	High schooling (60–75% in school)	Moderate schooling (45–65% in school)[a]	Low schooling (<40% in school)	Low schooling (<40% in school)
High work (>15% exclusively working)	Low work (<5% exclusively working)	Moderate work (5–15% exclusively working)	High work (>15% exclusively working)	High rates not in school and not working (>13%)
Low- and lower-middle-income countries	Lower-middle- and upper-middle-income countries	Low- and lower-middle-income countries	Low and lower-middle-income countries	Low-income countries

Source: Original table for this report, based on data from the US Agency for International Development's Demographic and Health Surveys, accessed March 17, 2024, https://www.dhsprogram.com.
Note: Categorizations are based on the most recent Demographic and Health Surveys data for 15- to 19-year-old girls.
[a]Mauritania is an exception, with a 39 percent school enrollment rate.

Educators (five countries in the lower-right quadrant of the figure) consist of a mix of lower-middle- and upper-middle-income countries. They have the highest levels of school enrollment among adolescent girls (universally above 60 percent). Yet they have extremely low levels of work participation in this group. Fewer than 5 percent of adolescent girls are out of school and working. A key policy question with respect to these countries is how to enhance the transition from schooling to safe and dignified work, which can be particularly challenging for young people in highly formalized labor markets that place a strong premium on credentials and work experience.

Generalists (the 18 remaining countries in the figure's lower-right quadrant) include a mix of low- and lower-middle-income countries. They achieve intermediate levels on indicators on all fronts, with 65 to 85 percent of 15- to 19-year-old girls who are unmarried or without children, 45 to 65 percent of them enrolled in school, and 5 to 10 percent exclusively working. Mauritania is a minor exception, with a school enrollment rate of 39 percent, but it is aligned along all the other dimensions. A key policy question for these countries is how to decide which of the available interventions to prioritize, given opportunities to improve adolescent girls' well-being on all fronts.

Laborers (the six countries in the figure's upper-left quadrant) have the highest levels of work participation, with more than 15 percent of 15- to 19-year-old girls exclusively working. Unlike the marriage and childbearing delayers, they have relatively low levels of schooling (below 40 percent enrollment rates) and moderate rates of marriage and childbearing. This category also includes a mix of low- and lower-middle-income countries. Key policy questions in regard to these countries are how to increase educational attainment and ensure access to safe and dignified work for the many adolescent girls who are already working.

Survivors (the four countries in the lower-left quadrant) exclusively consist of low-income countries classified as being in FCV contexts by the World Bank. Adolescent girls in these countries display the highest levels of vulnerability, with the highest rates of marriage and childbearing (fewer than 60 percent of 15- to 19-year-old girls are unmarried and without children), the lowest rates of school enrollment (below 40 percent), and a high share of adolescent girls who are not in work or schooling (fewer than 15 percent of girls are exclusively working). A key policy question with regard to these countries is how to address adolescent girls' vulnerabilities on all fronts.

Adolescent girls confront a range of experiences in countries across Africa (figure 2.7). Revisiting the five stylized profiles introduced in chapter 1, figure 2.7 illustrates the distribution of girls with these or similar profiles across countries grouped by category. The five stylized profiles capture the most commonly observed profiles of adolescent girls across countries. The marriage and childbearing delayers have the smallest share of adolescent girls with Aya's profile (married, with a child, not in school, and not working). By contrast, survivors have the largest share of adolescent girls with this profile. Educators have the largest share of girls with Grace's profile (not married, without children, in school, and not working). Both delayers and laborers have relatively large shares of adolescent girls with Chantal's profile (not married, without children, not in school, and working). In addition to the five stylized profiles, figure 2.7 includes a sixth group of girls who are married or have a child, but who differ from Aya's profile in some way (that is, by being enrolled in school, or working, or by being married with no child, or unmarried with a child). This sixth group of girls is most prevalent among survivors but least prevalent among marriage and childbearing delayers.

FIGURE 2.7 Countries Have Varying Profiles of Adolescent Girls

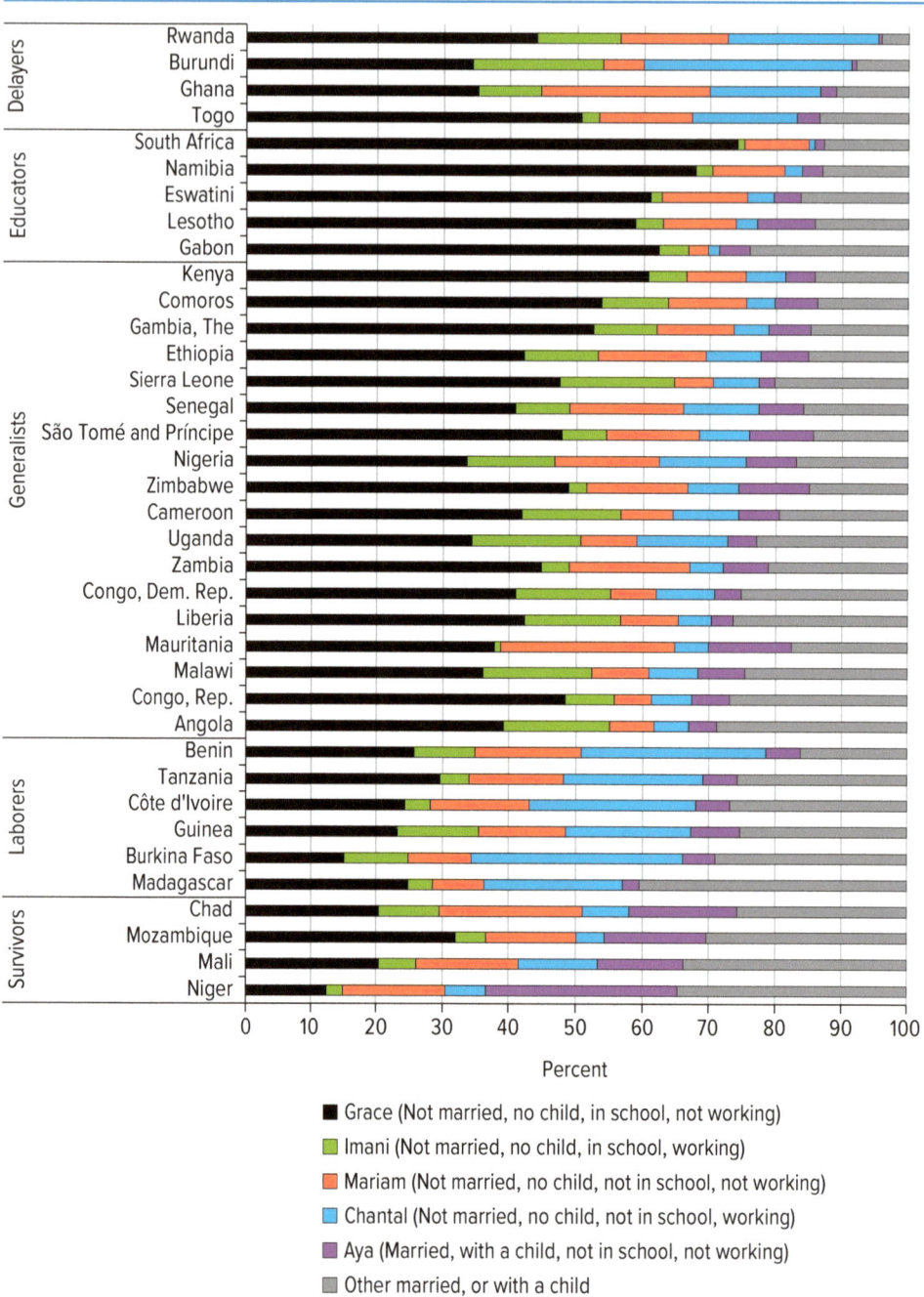

Source: Original figure for this report, based on data from the US Agency for International Development's Demographic and Health Surveys, accessed March 17, 2024, https://www.dhsprogram.com.

Note: Figure illustrates marriage, childbearing, school enrollment, and work statuses for 15- to 19-year-olds according to the five stylized profiles in chapter 1, which capture the majority of adolescent girls' experiences across countries. A sixth group—"Other married, or with a child"—represents girls who are married or have a child but who differ from Aya's profile in some way. Figure 2A.1 breaks out school enrollment and work statuses for adolescent girls in all groups.

Country categories correlate with the laws in each type of context (figure 2.8). Data from the World Bank's *Women, Business and the Law* study are employed here (World Bank 2020), along with information collected on ages for legal marriage and availability of free postprimary schooling, to examine the share of countries in each of the five categories that have adopted a given set of laws. This report uses data from 2020 to correspond to the most recent year of Demographic and Health Surveys data available (table 2A.2 presents the full set of indicators for each country).

- **Marriage and childbearing delayers** all have laws that a woman can get a job, open a bank account, and get identification documents in the same way as a man.

- **Educators** all have laws promoting education (free postprimary schooling) and an age of legal marriage above 18. They are also the most likely to have laws stating that sons and daughters have equal rights to inherit assets from their parents.

- **Generalists** do not stand out as leaders in any set of gender-related legal reforms.

FIGURE 2.8 Country Categories Correlate with Laws

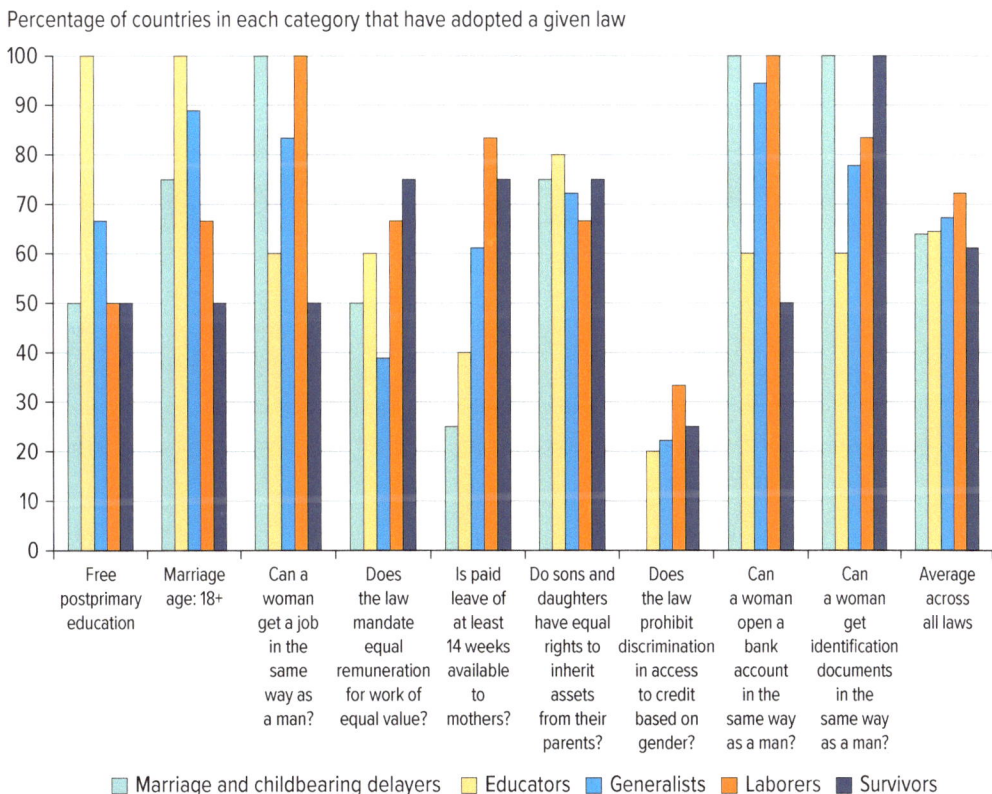

Percentage of countries in each category that have adopted a given law

Sources: Original figure for this report, based on World Bank (2020) and publicly available government sources.

- **Laborers** are more likely to have adopted gender-equitable labor laws (ensuring women can get a job in the same way as a man, equal work pay for equal work, and 14 weeks of paid leave for mothers), along with laws prohibiting gender discrimination in credit access and ensuring women can open a bank account in the same way as a man.
- **Survivors** have the lowest average level of gender-related legal reforms. All have laws that women and men can access national identification documents in the same way, presenting a foundation for access to social services.

These patterns suggest the potential importance of the legal context in shaping adolescent girls' experiences. However, the analysis presented here is purely descriptive and cannot be interpreted as demonstrating causal relationships (the causation could go in the opposite direction, to name just one other possibility). Chapter 4 discusses the implications of these patterns in more depth.

Country characteristics are not static, nor do they change uniformly. A number of countries have transitioned from one of the five categories to a different one over time (figure 2.9). Most of these changes have involved positive transitions into categories with lower rates of adolescent marriage and childbearing, along with higher rates of schooling. For example, out of the 12 countries that would have been categorized as laborers in the early 2000s, only 6 are currently in that same category. Two have transitioned into the category of marriage and childbearing delayers (Ghana and Togo). Another 4 have moved into the category of generalists (Cameroon, Ethiopia, Zambia, and Zimbabwe). Similarly, Uganda moved from being one of the survivors into being a generalist. However, there has also been some negative evolution. The Comoros started out as a marriage and childbearing delayer and switched to being a generalist, primarily because of increases in adolescent marriage and childbearing. Only the membership of the group of educators has remained unchanged over time. These multiple transitions indicate that country-level experiences of adolescent girls can dramatically transform (for better or worse) within a relatively short time span.

Altogether, multiple dimensions of vulnerability at a national level correlate with adolescent girls' experiences across countries (box 2.2). Country-level indicators are informative, but they are aggregate measures that mask subnational variation. There are often substantial differences in adolescent girls' experiences within countries (map 2.1 on page 83). In outcomes ranging from school enrollment to marriage, childbearing, and gender attitudes, variations within countries can be as large as variations across countries. For example, Nigeria is essentially a generalist country with subnational areas within its borders (for example, geographic zones and states) that would be categorized as survivors, laborers, and generalists. Understanding subnational differences is important for designing specialized interventions to improve outcomes for the most vulnerable adolescent girls within each country (box 2.3 on page 85).

FIGURE 2.9 A Number of Countries Have Transitioned from One Category to Another over Time

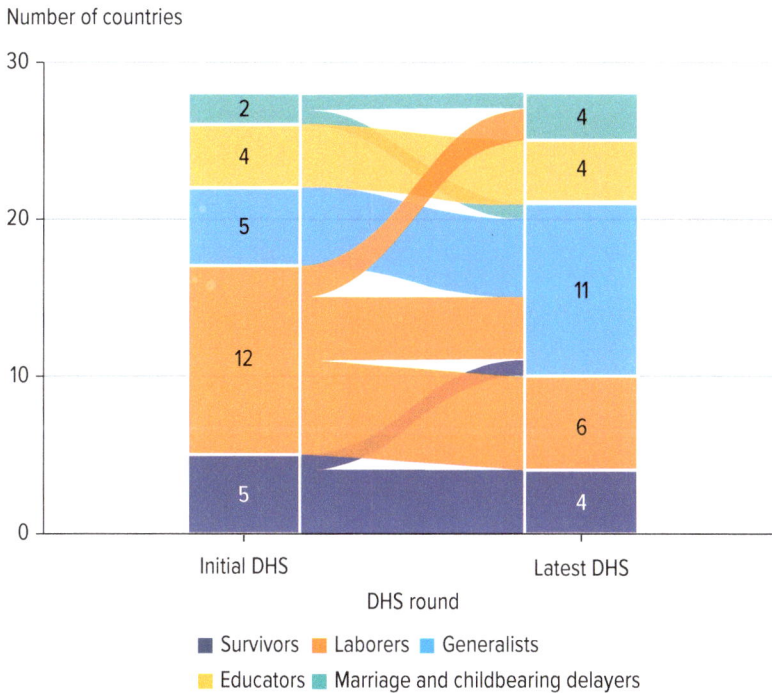

Number of countries

Survivors ■ Laborers ■ Generalists
Educators ■ Marriage and childbearing delayers

Source: Original figure for this report, based on data from the US Agency for International Development's Demographic and Health Surveys, accessed March 17, 2024, https://www .dhsprogram.com.
Note: Sample is restricted to countries for which rounds of Demographic and Health Survey (DHS) data within 20 years of one another are available (for additional details, refer to table 2A.1).

BOX 2.2 Dimensions of Vulnerability and Adolescent Girls' Trajectories across Countries

A country's status with regard to experience of fragility, conflict, and violence (FCV) and its national income classification are strongly correlated with adolescent girls' outcomes. In 2024, 20 African countries were classified as being in fragility and conflict-affected situations by the World Bank. Adolescent girls in countries experiencing FCV are more likely to be married and have children compared with those in countries not experiencing FCV; they also have lower rates of school enrollment (figure B2.2.1). In addition, there are gaps in indicators of financial inclusion, another dimension of empowerment (figure B2.2.2). Although they have rates of saving similar to those outside FCV contexts (at 40 percent), adolescent girls in FCV contexts are less likely to have a financial account. These differences in average experiences of adolescent girls in FCV contexts highlight the importance of considering fragility and conflict when thinking about the most effective ways to invest in adolescent girls' well-being, with certain dimensions being more crucial issues in some places than others. As outlined in chapter 1, status with respect to FCV is one of many contextual factors that shape adolescent girls' empowerment, so it is not the only determinant. Nonetheless, there are clear indications that adolescent girls living in contexts affected by fragility and violence often face greater barriers to realizing their full potential.

FIGURE B2.2.1 Adolescent Girls in Countries Experiencing FCV Are More Likely Than Other Girls to Be Married, Have Children, and Be Out of School

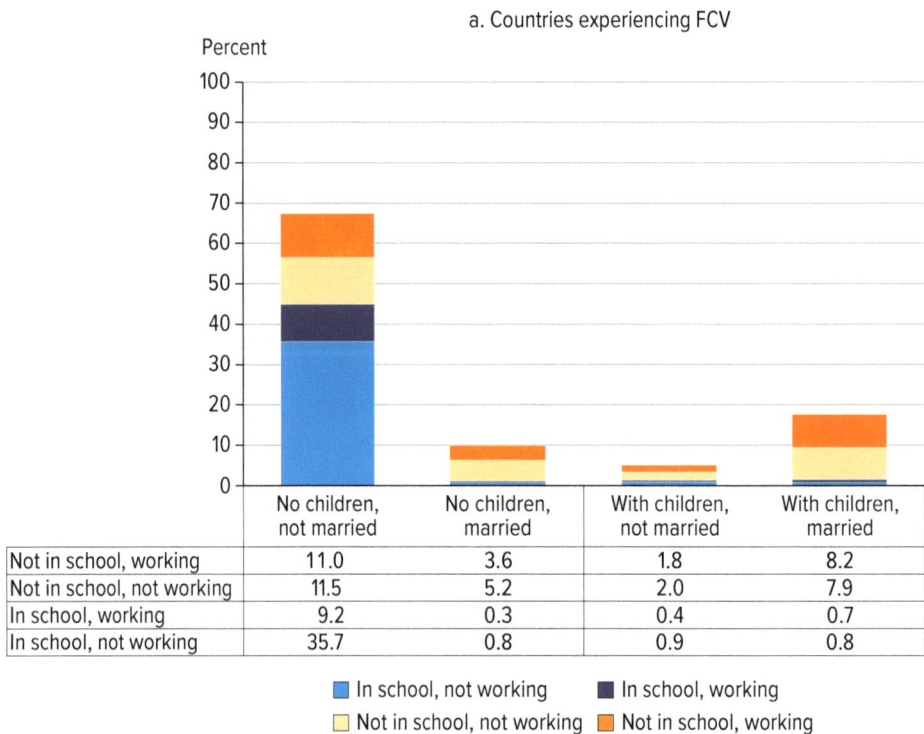

a. Countries experiencing FCV

Percent

	No children, not married	No children, married	With children, not married	With children, married
Not in school, working	11.0	3.6	1.8	8.2
Not in school, not working	11.5	5.2	2.0	7.9
In school, working	9.2	0.3	0.4	0.7
In school, not working	35.7	0.8	0.9	0.8

■ In school, not working   ■ In school, working
□ Not in school, not working   ■ Not in school, working

(continued)

BOX 2.2 Dimensions of Vulnerability and Adolescent Girls' Trajectories across Countries *(continued)*

FIGURE B2.2.1 Adolescent Girls in Countries Experiencing FCV Are More Likely Than Other Girls to Be Married, Have Children, and Be Out of School *(continued)*

b. Countries not experiencing FCV

Percent

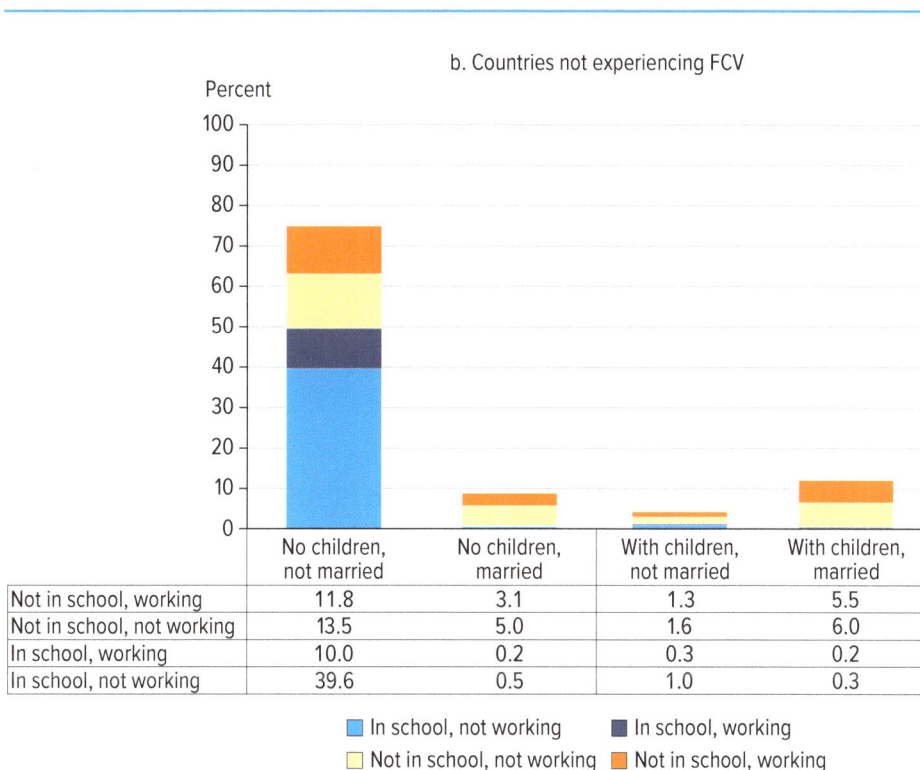

	No children, not married	No children, married	With children, not married	With children, married
Not in school, working	11.8	3.1	1.3	5.5
Not in school, not working	13.5	5.0	1.6	6.0
In school, working	10.0	0.2	0.3	0.2
In school, not working	39.6	0.5	1.0	0.3

■ In school, not working   ■ In school, working
■ Not in school, not working   ■ Not in school, working

Source: Original figure for this report, based on data from the US Agency for International Development's Demographic and Health Surveys, accessed March 17, 2024, https://www.dhsprogram.com.
Note: FCV = fragility, conflict, and violence.

(continued)

BOX 2.2 Dimensions of Vulnerability and Adolescent Girls' Trajectories
across Countries *(continued)*

FIGURE B2.2.2 Adolescent Girls in Countries Experiencing FCV Are Less Likely Than
Other Girls to Have a Financial Account

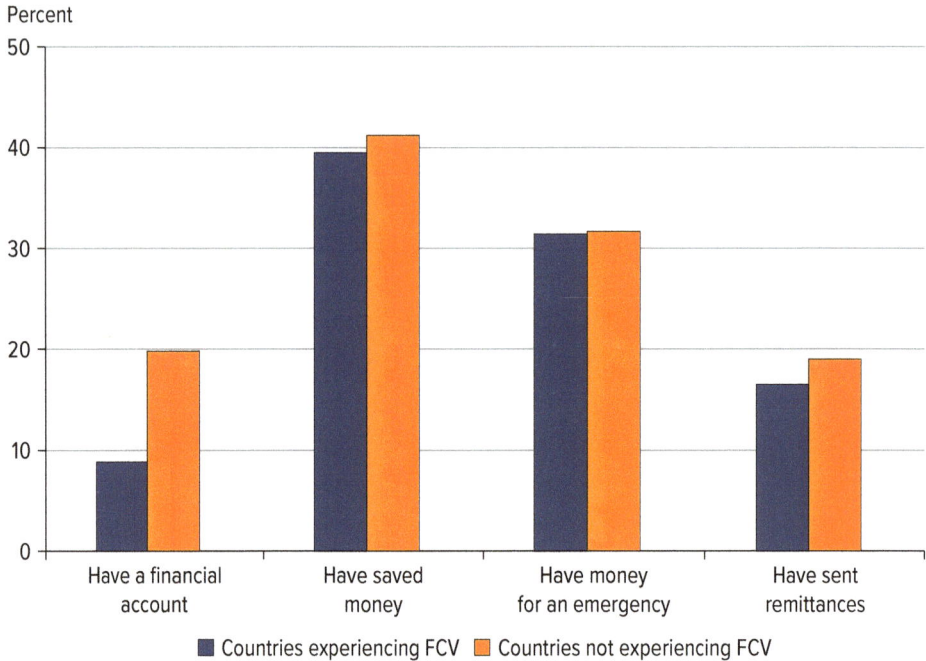

Source: Original figure for this report, based on data from the Global Financial Inclusion (Global Findex)
Database 2017 [data set], accessed August 22, 2023, https://doi.org/10.48529/FKZS-AT21.
Note: FCV = fragility, conflict, and violence.

Similarly, school enrollment rates increase and marriage and childbearing rates decline as
country income levels increase (figure B2.2.3). Among adolescent girls who have no children
and are not married, a much larger share in upper-middle-income countries are in school and
not working.

(continued)

BOX 2.2 Dimensions of Vulnerability and Adolescent Girls' Trajectories
across Countries *(continued)*

FIGURE B2.2.3 Country-Level Income Classifications Also Correlate with Adolescent
Girls' Experiences

a. Low-income countries

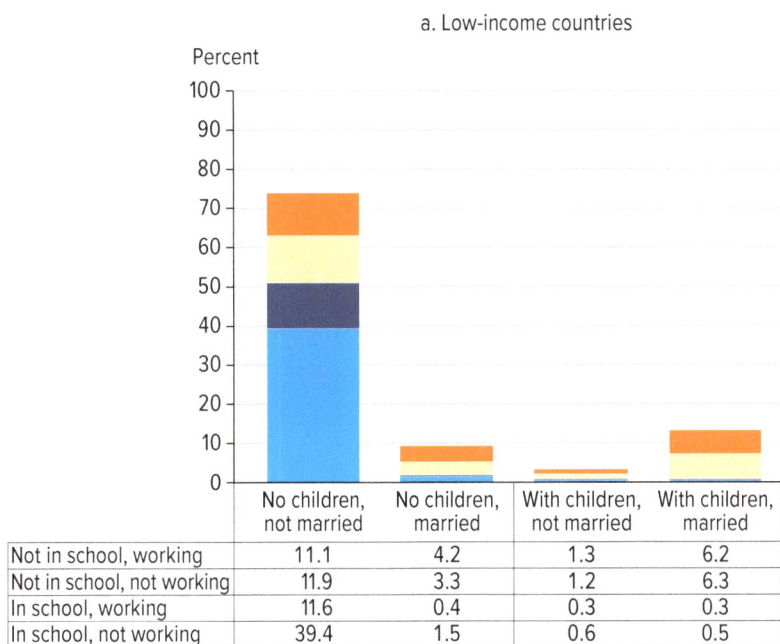

	No children, not married	No children, married	With children, not married	With children, married
Not in school, working	11.1	4.2	1.3	6.2
Not in school, not working	11.9	3.3	1.2	6.3
In school, working	11.6	0.4	0.3	0.3
In school, not working	39.4	1.5	0.6	0.5

b. Lower-middle-income countries

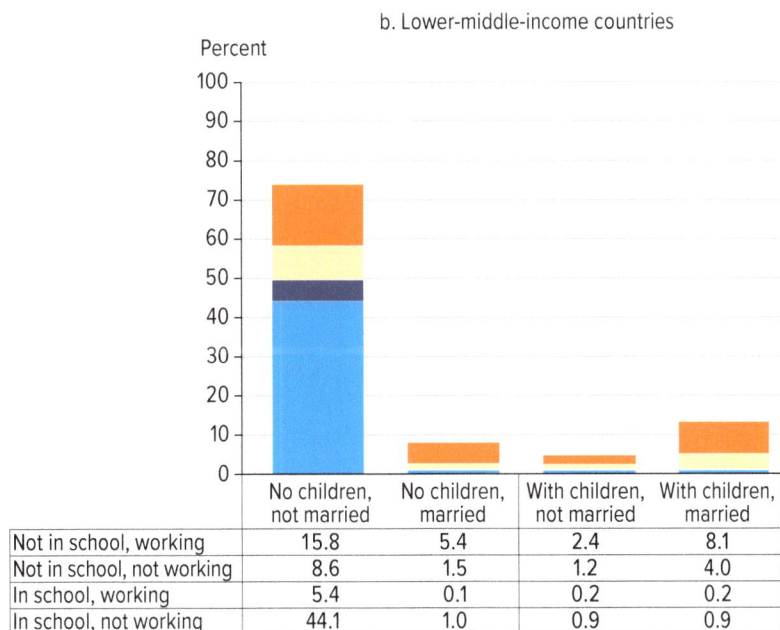

	No children, not married	No children, married	With children, not married	With children, married
Not in school, working	15.8	5.4	2.4	8.1
Not in school, not working	8.6	1.5	1.2	4.0
In school, working	5.4	0.1	0.2	0.2
In school, not working	44.1	1.0	0.9	0.9

■ In school, not working   ■ In school, working
□ Not in school, not working   ■ Not in school, working

(continued)

BOX 2.2 Dimensions of Vulnerability and Adolescent Girls' Trajectories
across Countries *(continued)*

FIGURE B2.2.3 Country-Level Income Classifications Also Correlate with Adolescent
Girls' Experiences *(continued)*

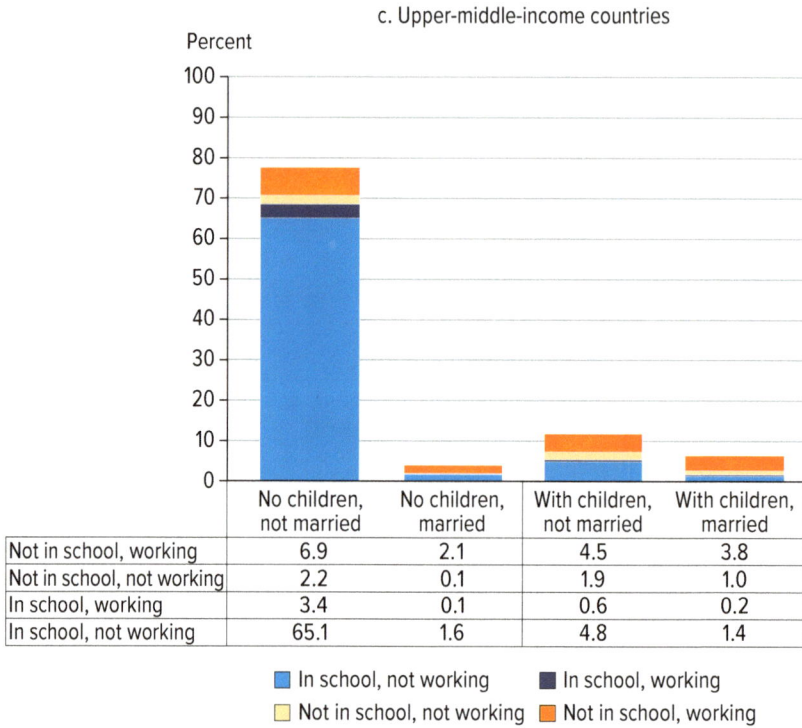

c. Upper-middle-income countries

	No children, not married	No children, married	With children, not married	With children, married
Not in school, working	6.9	2.1	4.5	3.8
Not in school, not working	2.2	0.1	1.9	1.0
In school, working	3.4	0.1	0.6	0.2
In school, not working	65.1	1.6	4.8	1.4

Legend: In school, not working; In school, working; Not in school, not working; Not in school, working

Source: Original figure for this report, based on data from the US Agency for International Development's Demographic and Health Surveys, accessed March 17, 2024, https://www.dhsprogram.com.

MAP 2.1 Some Subregions within Countries Have Worse Outcomes for
Adolescent Girls Than Others

a. Schooling for girls ages 10 to 14

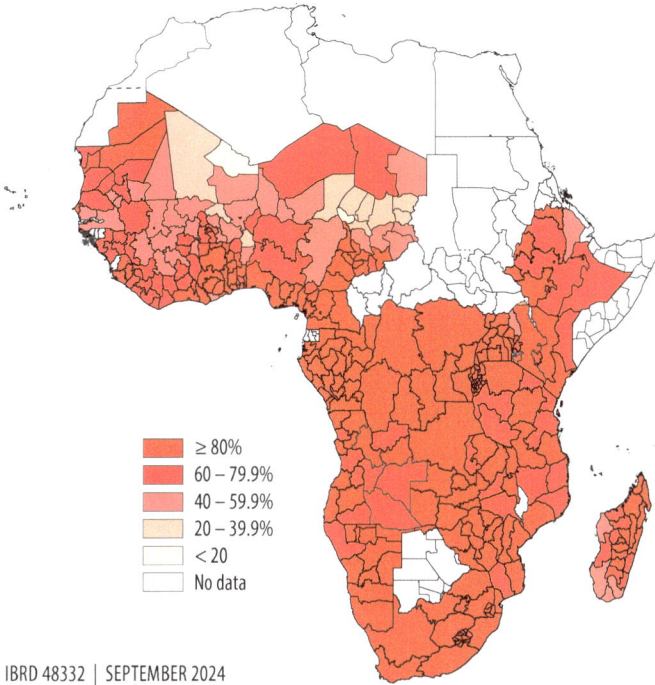

≥ 80%
60 – 79.9%
40 – 59.9%
20 – 39.9%
< 20
No data

IBRD 48332 | SEPTEMBER 2024

b. Girls ages 15 to 19 who are in school and not working

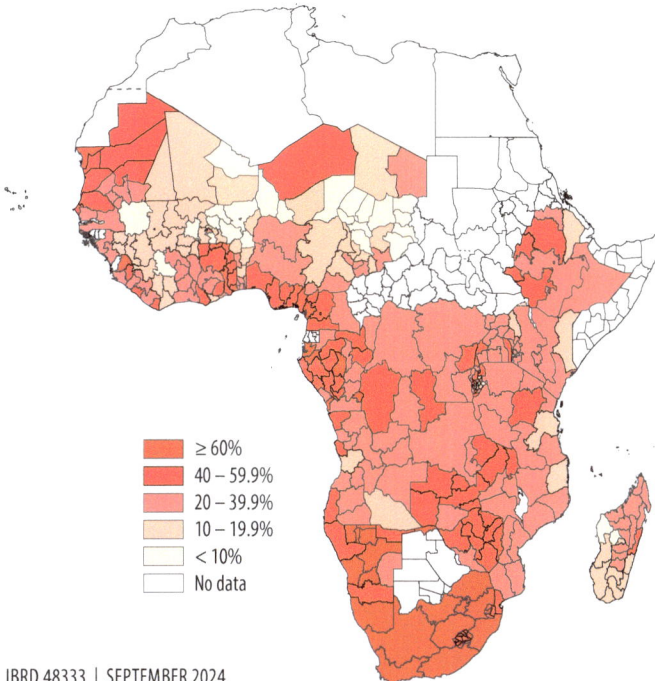

≥ 60%
40 – 59.9%
20 – 39.9%
10 – 19.9%
< 10%
No data

IBRD 48333 | SEPTEMBER 2024

(continued)

MAP 2.1 Some Subregions within Countries Have Worse Outcomes for
Adolescent Girls Than Others *(continued)*

c. Girls ages 15 to 19 who are not in school and not working

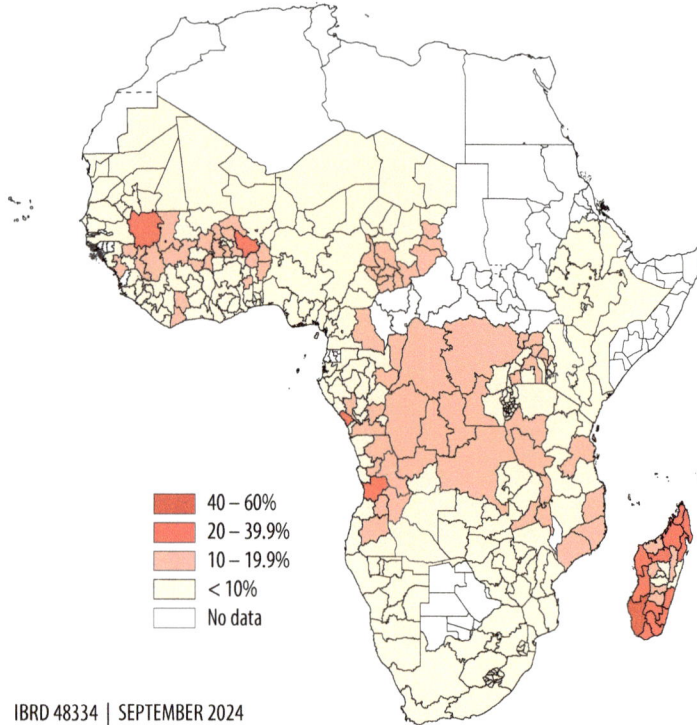

40 – 60%
20 – 39.9%
10 – 19.9%
< 10%
No data

IBRD 48334 | SEPTEMBER 2024

Source: Original map for this report, based on data from the US Agency for International
Development's Demographic and Health Surveys, accessed March 17, 2024, https://www
.dhsprogram.com.

Understanding Both Subnational and Regional Patterns Is Necessary to Optimize Policy Design

It is important to consider the inherent diversity in the experiences of
adolescent girls in Africa. Girls in the region continue to face gender-
specific challenges that have lasting implications even after girls make the
transition from adolescence to adulthood. Progress in school enrollment has
been significant, yet marriage and childbearing remain key constraints on
adolescent girls' empowerment. Notably, these two life transitions may have
different implications for adolescent girls' prospects for continuing their
education and participating in paid work.

Existing categorizations of vulnerabilities can get policy makers only so far in targeting interventions. It remains critical to identify both subnational and regional patterns to optimize policy design. Differences in individual-household wealth and country context strongly correlate with financial inclusion (one dimension of adolescent girls' empowerment), suggesting that there are strong correlations between adolescent girls' experiences and other dimensions of empowerment. Spotlight 2 highlights these correlations using more detailed data.

This chapter has focused on four aspects of adolescent girls' experiences that are reflected in data sets with wide coverage. However, there are several other important dimensions to consider, including, for example, experiences of gender-based violence. This report does not examine these dimensions, however, on account of data limitations.[4] Nonetheless, in a study using data from the 20 most populous African countries, 28.8 percent of girls ages 15 to 19 reported having ever experienced physical or sexual violence (Evans et al. 2023). This demonstrates the prevalence of this issue and establishes the importance of addressing it.

BOX 2.3 Dimensions of Vulnerability and Adolescent Girls' Trajectories within Countries

Within countries, factors such as household poverty and rurality correlate with adolescent girls' experiences. Adolescent girls from wealthier households are more likely to be enrolled in school, unmarried, and without children, while girls from less wealthy households are more likely to be on divergent paths. The share of adolescent girls who are exclusively schooling, are unmarried, and have no children is 30 percentage points higher among households in the top quintile of the wealth distribution compared with those in the bottom quintile (figure B2.3.1). Beyond its association with these differences in life transitions, household wealth is also strongly correlated with levels of financial inclusion. Adolescent girls from wealthier households are more likely to have a formal financial account, to have saved, to have money for an emergency, and to have sent remittances (figure B2.3.2).

(continued)

BOX 2.3 Dimensions of Vulnerability and Adolescent Girls' Trajectories within Countries *(continued)*

FIGURE B2.3.1 Adolescent Girls from Wealthier Households Are More Likely to Be Enrolled in School, Unmarried, and Without Children

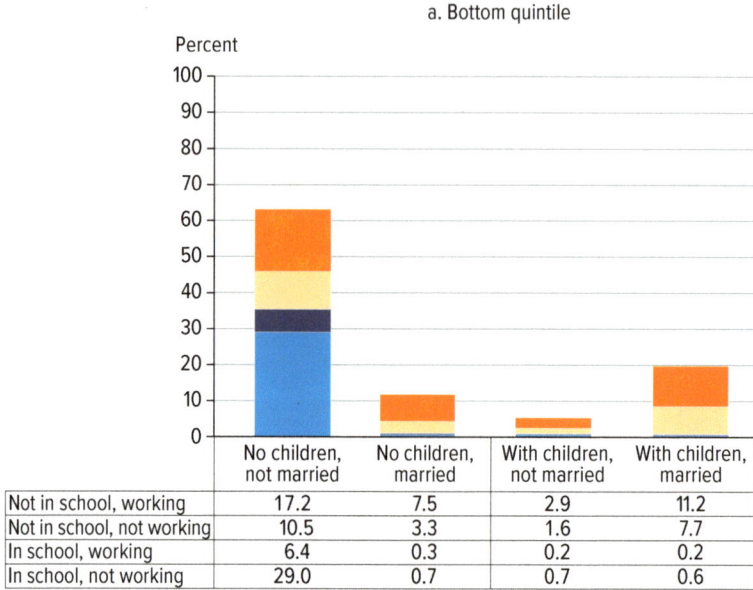

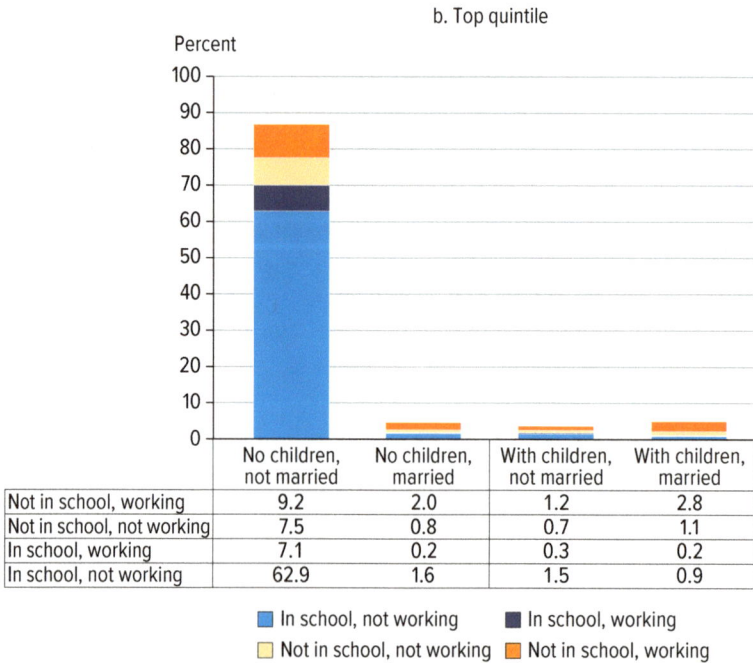

a. Bottom quintile

Percent

	No children, not married	No children, married	With children, not married	With children, married
Not in school, working	17.2	7.5	2.9	11.2
Not in school, not working	10.5	3.3	1.6	7.7
In school, working	6.4	0.3	0.2	0.2
In school, not working	29.0	0.7	0.7	0.6

b. Top quintile

Percent

	No children, not married	No children, married	With children, not married	With children, married
Not in school, working	9.2	2.0	1.2	2.8
Not in school, not working	7.5	0.8	0.7	1.1
In school, working	7.1	0.2	0.3	0.2
In school, not working	62.9	1.6	1.5	0.9

■ In school, not working   ■ In school, working
□ Not in school, not working   ■ Not in school, working

Source: Original figure for this report, based on data from the US Agency for International Development's Demographic and Health Surveys, accessed March 17, 2024, https://www.dhsprogram.com.

(continued)

BOX 2.3 Dimensions of Vulnerability and Adolescent Girls' Trajectories within Countries *(continued)*

FIGURE B2.3.2 Adolescent Girls from Wealthier Households Have Higher Levels of Financial Inclusion

Percent

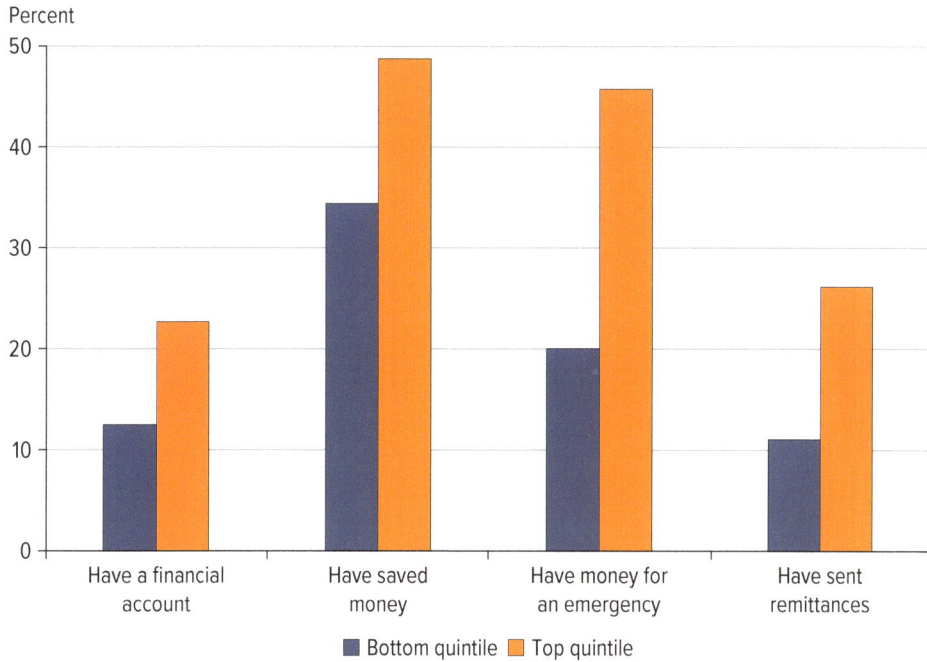

Source: Original figure for this report, based on data from the Global Financial Inclusion (Global Findex) Database 2017 [data set], accessed August 22, 2023, https://doi.org/10.48529/FKZS-AT21.

There are also striking differences between the experiences of adolescent girls in rural and urban areas (figure B2.3.3). Among 15- to 19-year-old girls in urban areas, 83 percent are not married and have no children, compared with less than 70 percent of their peers in rural areas. Adolescent girls in rural areas are also less likely to be enrolled in school and more likely to work, whether they attend school or not.

(continued)

BOX 2.3 Dimensions of Vulnerability and Adolescent Girls' Trajectories within Countries *(continued)*

FIGURE B2.3.3 Adolescent Girls in Urban Areas Are More Likely to Be Enrolled in School, Unmarried, and Without Children

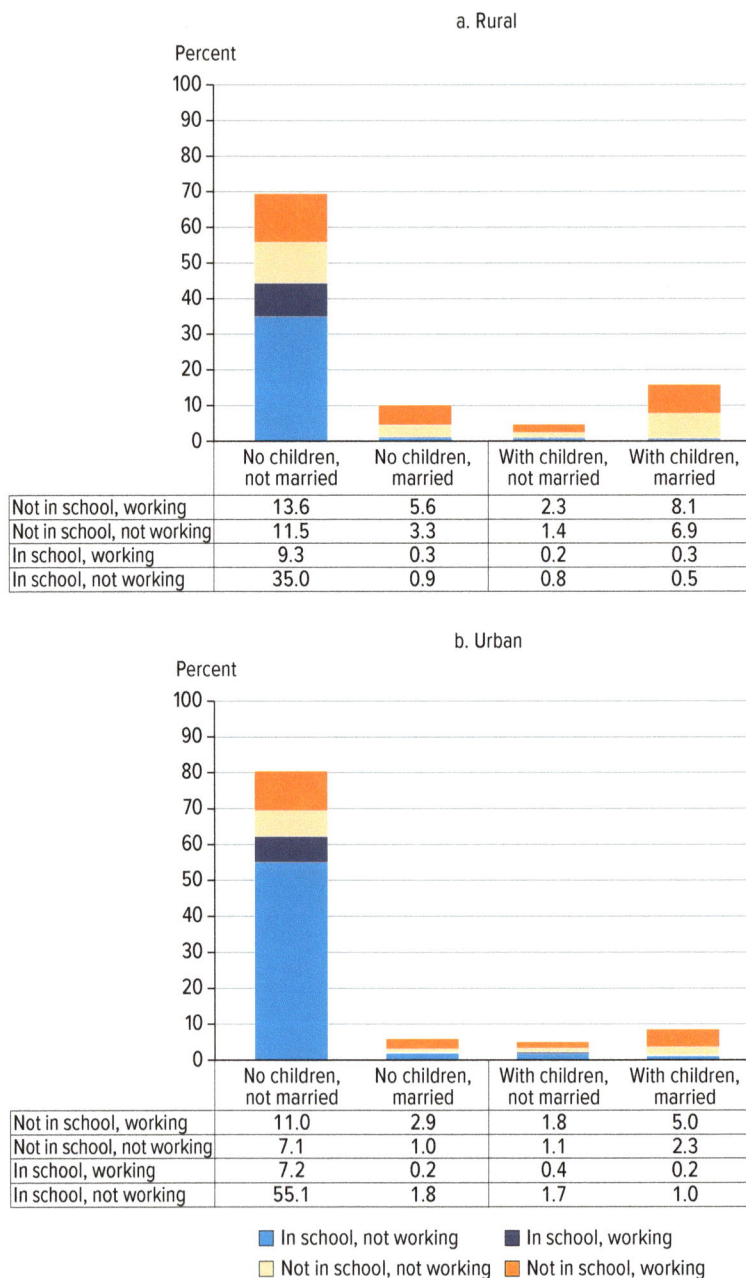

a. Rural

Percent

	No children, not married	No children, married	With children, not married	With children, married
Not in school, working	13.6	5.6	2.3	8.1
Not in school, not working	11.5	3.3	1.4	6.9
In school, working	9.3	0.3	0.2	0.3
In school, not working	35.0	0.9	0.8	0.5

b. Urban

Percent

	No children, not married	No children, married	With children, not married	With children, married
Not in school, working	11.0	2.9	1.8	5.0
Not in school, not working	7.1	1.0	1.1	2.3
In school, working	7.2	0.2	0.4	0.2
In school, not working	55.1	1.8	1.7	1.0

■ In school, not working   ■ In school, working
□ Not in school, not working   ■ Not in school, working

Source: Original figure for this report, based on data from the US Agency for International Development's Demographic and Health Surveys, accessed March 17, 2024, https://www.dhsprogram.com.

Annex 2A. Supplementary Data

TABLE 2A.1 The Demographic and Health Surveys, Multiple Indicator Cluster Survey, and Global Findex Database Provide Valuable but Incomplete Information about Adolescent Girls' Experiences in Africa

Country	Demographic and Health Surveys					Multiple Indicator Cluster Survey		2017 Global Findex Database
	Used for analysis	Most recent year	Earlier year	Used for trend analysis	Gap in years	Used for analysis	Year	Used for analysis
Angola	Yes	2015–16	n/a	No	n/a	No	n/a	No
Benin	Yes	2017–18	2001	Yes	16	Yes	2014	Yes
Botswana	No	n/a	n/a	n/a	n/a	No	n/a	Yes
Burkina Faso	Yes	2010	1998	Yes	12	Yes	2006	Yes
Burundi	Yes	2016–17	1987	No	n/a	Yes	2005	Yes
Cabo Verde	No	n/a	n/a	n/a	n/a	No	n/a	No
Cameroon	Yes	2018	1998	Yes	20	Yes	2014	Yes
Central African Republic	No	n/a	n/a	n/a	n/a	Yes	2018–19	Yes
Chad	Yes	2014–15	1996	Yes	19	Yes	2019	Yes
Comoros	Yes	2012	1996	Yes	16	No	n/a	No
Congo, Dem. Rep.	Yes	2013–14	2007	No	n/a	Yes	2017	Yes
Congo, Rep.	Yes	2011–12	2005	No	n/a	Yes	2014	Yes
Côte d'Ivoire	Yes	2011–12	1994	Yes	17	Yes	2016	Yes
Equatorial Guinea	No	n/a	n/a	n/a	n/a	No	n/a	No
Eritrea	No	n/a	n/a	n/a	n/a	No	n/a	No
Eswatini	Yes	2006–07	Not available	No	n/a	Yes	2014	No
Ethiopia	Yes	2016	2000	Yes	16	No	n/a	Yes

(continued)

TABLE 2A.1 The Demographic and Health Surveys, Multiple Indicator Cluster Survey, and Global Findex Database Provide Valuable but Incomplete Information about Adolescent Girls' Experiences in Africa *(continued)*

Country	Demographic and Health Surveys					Multiple Indicator Cluster Survey		2017 Global Findex Database
	Used for analysis	Most recent year	Earlier year	Used for trend analysis	Gap in years	Used for analysis	Year	Used for analysis
Gabon	Yes	2012	2000	Yes	12	No	n/a	Yes
Gambia, The	Yes	2019–20	2013	No	n/a	Yes	2018	Yes
Ghana	Yes	2014	1993	Yes	19	Yes	2017	Yes
Guinea	Yes	2018	1999	Yes	19	Yes	2016	Yes
Guinea-Bissau	No	n/a	n/a	n/a	n/a	Yes	2018	No
Kenya	Yes	2014	1998	Yes	16	No	n/a	Yes
Lesotho	Yes	2014	2004	Yes	10	Yes	2018	Yes
Liberia	Yes	2019–20	2007	Yes	12	No	n/a	Yes
Madagascar	Yes	2008–09	1997	Yes	11	Yes	2018	Yes
Malawi	Yes	2015–16	2000	Yes	15	Yes	2019–20	Yes
Mali	Yes	2018	1995	Yes	23	Yes	2015	Yes
Mauritania	Yes	2018–19	n/a	No	n/a	Yes	2015	Yes
Mauritius	No	n/a	n/a	n/a	n/a	No	n/a	Yes
Mozambique	Yes	2018	1997	Yes	19	Yes	2008	Yes
Namibia	Yes	2013	2000	Yes	13	No	n/a	Yes
Niger	Yes	2012	1998	Yes	14	No	n/a	Yes
Nigeria	Yes	2018	2003	Yes	15	Yes	2021	Yes
Rwanda	Yes	2019–20	2000	Yes	19	No	n/a	Yes
São Tomé and Príncipe	Yes	2008–09	n/a	No	n/a	Yes	2019	No

(continued)

TABLE 2A.1 The Demographic and Health Surveys, Multiple Indicator Cluster Survey, and Global Findex Database Provide Valuable but Incomplete Information about Adolescent Girls' Experiences in Africa (continued)

Country	Demographic and Health Surveys					Multiple Indicator Cluster Survey		2017 Global Findex Database
	Used for analysis	Most recent year	Earlier year	Used for trend analysis	Gap in years	Used for analysis	Year	Used for analysis
Senegal	Yes	2019	1999	No[a]	20	No	n/a	Yes
Seychelles	No	n/a	n/a	n/a	n/a	No	n/a	No
Sierra Leone	Yes	2019	2008	Yes	11	Yes	2017	Yes
Somalia	No	n/a	n/a	n/a	n/a	Yes	2006	No
South Africa	Yes	2016	1998	Yes	18	No	n/a	No
South Sudan	No	n/a	n/a	n/a	n/a	Yes	2010	Yes
Sudan	No	n/a	n/a	n/a	n/a	No	n/a	No
Tanzania	Yes	2015–16	1996	Yes	19	No	n/a	Yes
Togo	Yes	2013–14	1998	Yes	15	Yes	2017	Yes
Uganda	Yes	2016	1995	Yes	19	No	n/a	Yes
Zambia	Yes	2018	1996	Yes	22	No	n/a	Yes
Zimbabwe	Yes	2015	1994	Yes	21	Yes	2019	Yes

Source: Original table for this report, based on data from the US Agency for International Development's Demographic and Health Surveys, accessed March 17, 2024, https://www.dhsprogram.com; the United Nations Children's Fund's Multiple Indicator Cluster Surveys, accessed November 28, 2023, https://mics.unicef.org; and the Global Financial Inclusion (Global Findex) Database 2017 [data set], accessed August 22, 2023, https://doi.org/10.48529/FKZS-AT21.

Note: Year for all countries with data from the 2017 Global Findex Database is 2017. n/a = not applicable.

a. Although Senegal had two Demographic and Health Surveys available within the report's time range, definitions of variables were inconsistent between the two surveys. Six countries released newer Demographic and Health Surveys samples during the course of writing the report (Burkina Faso, Côte d'Ivoire, Ghana, Kenya, Madagascar, and Tanzania). The report's analysis retains the initial samples that were used; however, key results do not change when the newer samples are used.

TABLE 2A.2 Multiple Indicators Characterize a Country's Legal and Policy Context

Country	Income group	Report year	WBL Index	Free postprimary education	Marriage age: 18+	Do sons and daughters have equal rights to inherit assets from their parents?	Can a woman get a job in the same way as a man?	Does the law mandate equal remuneration for work of equal value?	Is paid leave of at least 14 weeks available to mothers?	Does the law prohibit discrimination in access to credit based on gender?	Can a woman open a bank account in the same way as a man?	Can a woman get identification documents in the same way as a man?
Angola	Lower middle income	2020	73.1	No	Yes	Yes	Yes	Yes	No	Yes	Yes	Yes
Benin	Lower middle income	2020	74.4	No	Yes	Yes	Yes	Yes	Yes	No	Yes	Yes
Botswana	Upper middle income	2020	63.8	Yes	Yes	No	Yes	No	No	No	Yes	No
Burkina Faso	Low income	2020	82.5	Yes	No	Yes	Yes	No	Yes	Yes	Yes	Yes
Burundi	Low income	2020	73.1	n/a	Yes	No	Yes	No	No	No	Yes	Yes
Cabo Verde	Lower middle income	2020	86.3	Yes	No	Yes	Yes	No	No	Yes	Yes	Yes

(continued)

TABLE 2A.2 Multiple Indicators Characterize a Country's Legal and Policy Context *(continued)*

Country	Income group	Report year	WBL Index	Free postprimary education	Marriage age: 18+	Do sons and daughters have equal rights to inherit assets from their parents?	Can a woman get a job in the same way as a man?	Does the law mandate equal remuneration for work of equal value?	Is paid leave of at least 14 weeks available to mothers?	Does the law prohibit discrimination in access to credit based on gender?	Can a woman open a bank account in the same way as a man?	Can a woman get identification documents in the same way as a man?
Cameroon	Lower middle income	2020	60.0	No	No	Yes	No	No	Yes	No	No	No
Central African Republic	Low income	2020	76.9	Yes	Yes	Yes	Yes	No	Yes	No	Yes	Yes
Chad	Low income	2020	66.3	Yes	Yes	Yes	No	Yes	Yes	No	No	Yes
Comoros	Lower middle income	2020	65.0	No	Yes	No	No	Yes	Yes	No	Yes	Yes
Congo, Dem. Rep.	Low income	2020	78.8	No	No	Yes	Yes	No	Yes	Yes	Yes	Yes
Congo, Rep.	Lower middle income	2020	49.4	Yes	Yes	Yes	Yes	No	Yes	No	Yes	No

(continued)

PATHWAYS TO PROSPERITY FOR ADOLESCENT GIRLS IN AFRICA

TABLE 2A.2 Multiple Indicators Characterize a Country's Legal and Policy Context *(continued)*

Country	Income group	Report year	WBL Index	Free postprimary education	Marriage age: 18+	Do sons and daughters have equal rights to inherit assets from their parents?	Can a woman get a job in the same way as a man?	Does the law mandate equal remuneration for work of equal value?	Is paid leave of at least 14 weeks available to mothers?	Does the law prohibit discrimination in access to credit based on gender?	Can a woman open a bank account in the same way as a man?	Can a woman get identification documents in the same way as a man?
Côte d'Ivoire	Lower middle income	2020	83.1	Yes	Yes	Yes	Yes	Yes	Yes	No	Yes	Yes
Equatorial Guinea	Upper middle income	2020	51.9	No	Yes	Yes	No	Yes	No	No	No	Yes
Eritrea	Low income	2020	69.4	Yes	Yes	Yes	Yes	No	No	No	Yes	Yes
Eswatini	Lower middle income	2020	46.3	Yes	Yes	No	No	No	No	No	No	Yes
Ethiopia	Low income	2020	71.9	Yes	Yes	Yes	Yes	No	No	No	Yes	Yes
Gabon	Upper middle income	2020	57.5	Yes	Yes	Yes	No	No	Yes	No	No	Yes

(continued)

TABLE 2A.2 Multiple Indicators Characterize a Country's Legal and Policy Context *(continued)*

Country	Income group	Report year	WBL Index	Free postprimary education	Marriage age: 18+	Do sons and daughters have equal rights to inherit assets from their parents?	Can a woman get a job in the same way as a man?	Does the law mandate equal remuneration for work of equal value?	Is paid leave of at least 14 weeks available to mothers?	Does the law prohibit discrimination in access to credit based on gender?	Can a woman open a bank account in the same way as a man?	Can a woman get identification documents in the same way as a man?
Gambia, The	Low income	2020	69.4	Yes	Yes	No	Yes	No	Yes	No	Yes	Yes
Ghana	Lower middle income	2020	75.0	Yes	Yes	Yes	Yes	No	No	No	Yes	Yes
Guinea	Low income	2020	73.8	No	No	Yes	Yes	Yes	Yes	Yes	Yes	Yes
Guinea-Bissau	Low income	2020	42.5	Yes	Yes	Yes	No	No	No	No	No	Yes
Kenya	Lower middle income	2020	80.6	Yes	Yes	Yes	Yes	Yes	No	No	Yes	Yes
Lesotho	Lower middle income	2020	78.1	Yes	Yes	Yes	Yes	Yes	No	No	Yes	Yes
Liberia	Low income	2020	81.3	No	Yes	Yes	Yes	Yes	Yes	No	Yes	Yes

(continued)

TABLE 2A.2 Multiple Indicators Characterize a Country's Legal and Policy Context *(continued)*

Country	Income group	Report year	WBL Index	Free postprimary education	Marriage age: 18+	Do sons and daughters have equal rights to inherit assets from their parents?	Can a woman get a job in the same way as a man?	Does the law mandate equal remuneration for work of equal value?	Is paid leave of at least 14 weeks available to mothers?	Does the law prohibit discrimination in access to credit based on gender?	Can a woman open a bank account in the same way as a man?	Can a woman get identification documents in the same way as a man?
Madagascar	Low income	2020	66.9	No	Yes	No	Yes	No	Yes	No	Yes	No
Malawi	Low income	2020	77.5	Yes	Yes	Yes	Yes	Yes	No	No	Yes	No
Mali	Low income	2020	63.8	Yes	No	Yes	Yes	Yes	Yes	No	Yes	Yes
Mauritania	Lower middle income	2020	48.1	Yes	Yes	No	No	No	Yes	No	Yes	Yes
Mauritius	Upper middle income	2020	89.4	Yes	Yes	Yes	Yes	Yes	Yes	Yes	Yes	Yes
Mozambique	Low income	2020	82.5	n/a	Yes	Yes	Yes	No	No	Yes	Yes	Yes
Namibia	Upper middle income	2020	86.3	Yes	Yes	Yes	Yes	Yes	No	No	Yes	No

(continued)

TABLE 2A.2 Multiple Indicators Characterize a Country's Legal and Policy Context (continued)

Country	Income group	Report year	WBL Index	Free postprimary education	Marriage age: 18+	Do sons and daughters have equal rights to inherit assets from their parents?	Can a woman get a job in the same way as a man?	Does the law mandate equal remuneration for work of equal value?	Is paid leave of at least 14 weeks available to mothers?	Does the law prohibit discrimination in access to credit based on gender?	Can a woman open a bank account in the same way as a man?	Can a woman get identification documents in the same way as a man?
Niger	Low income	2020	56.9	n/a	No	No	No	Yes	Yes	No	No	Yes
Nigeria	Lower middle income	2020	63.1	Yes	Yes	Yes	Yes	No	No	No	Yes	Yes
Rwanda	Low income	2020	81.3	No	Yes	Yes	Yes	Yes	No	No	Yes	Yes
São Tomé and Príncipe	Lower middle income	2020	83.1	No	Yes	Yes	Yes	No	Yes	No	Yes	Yes
Senegal	Lower middle income	2020	63.8	Yes	Yes	No	Yes	No	Yes	No	Yes	Yes
Seychelles	High income	2020	76.3	Yes	Yes	Yes	Yes	No	Yes	No	Yes	No

(continued)

TABLE 2A.2 Multiple Indicators Characterize a Country's Legal and Policy Context *(continued)*

Country	Income group	Report year	WBL Index	Free postprimary education	Marriage age: 18+	Do sons and daughters have equal rights to inherit assets from their parents?	Can a woman get a job in the same way as a man?	Does the law mandate equal remuneration for work of equal value?	Is paid leave of at least 14 weeks available to mothers?	Does the law prohibit discrimination in access to credit based on gender?	Can a woman open a bank account in the same way as a man?	Can a woman get identification documents in the same way as a man?
Sierra Leone	Low income	2020	63.1	Yes	Yes	Yes	Yes	No	No	No	Yes	Yes
Somalia	Low income	2020	46.9	n/a	Yes	No	Yes	Yes	Yes	No	Yes	Yes
South Africa	Upper middle income	2020	88.1	Yes	Yes	Yes	Yes	Yes	Yes	Yes	Yes	Yes
South Sudan	Low income	2020	67.5	Yes	Yes	Yes	Yes	Yes	No	No	Yes	Yes
Sudan	Low income	2020	29.4	Yes	Yes	No	No	No	No	No	Yes	No
Tanzania	Lower middle income	2020	81.3	Yes	Yes	No	Yes	Yes	No	No	Yes	Yes

(continued)

TABLE 2A.2 Multiple Indicators Characterize a Country's Legal and Policy Context (*continued*)

Country	Income group	Report year	WBL Index	Free postprimary education	Marriage age: 18+	Do sons and daughters have equal rights to inherit assets from their parents?	Can a woman get a job in the same way as a man?	Does the law mandate equal remuneration for work of equal value?	Is paid leave of at least 14 weeks available to mothers?	Does the law prohibit discrimination in access to credit based on gender?	Can a woman open a bank account in the same way as a man?	Can a woman get identification documents in the same way as a man?
Togo	Low income	2020	84.4	Yes	No	Yes	Yes	Yes	Yes	No	Yes	Yes
Uganda	Low income	2020	73.1	Yes	Yes	No	Yes	Yes	No	No	Yes	Yes
Zambia	Low income	2020	81.3	Yes	Yes	Yes	Yes	Yes	Yes	Yes	Yes	No
Zimbabwe	Lower middle income	2020	86.9	Yes	Yes	Yes	Yes	No	Yes	Yes	Yes	Yes

Source: Original table for this report, based on data from World Bank (2020) and publicly available government sources.

Note: n/a = not applicable; WBL = *Women, Business and the Law* (World Bank 2020).

FIGURE 2A.1 The Distribution of Adolescent Girls' Experiences Varies across Country Categories

a. 15- to 19-year-olds who are not married and have no children

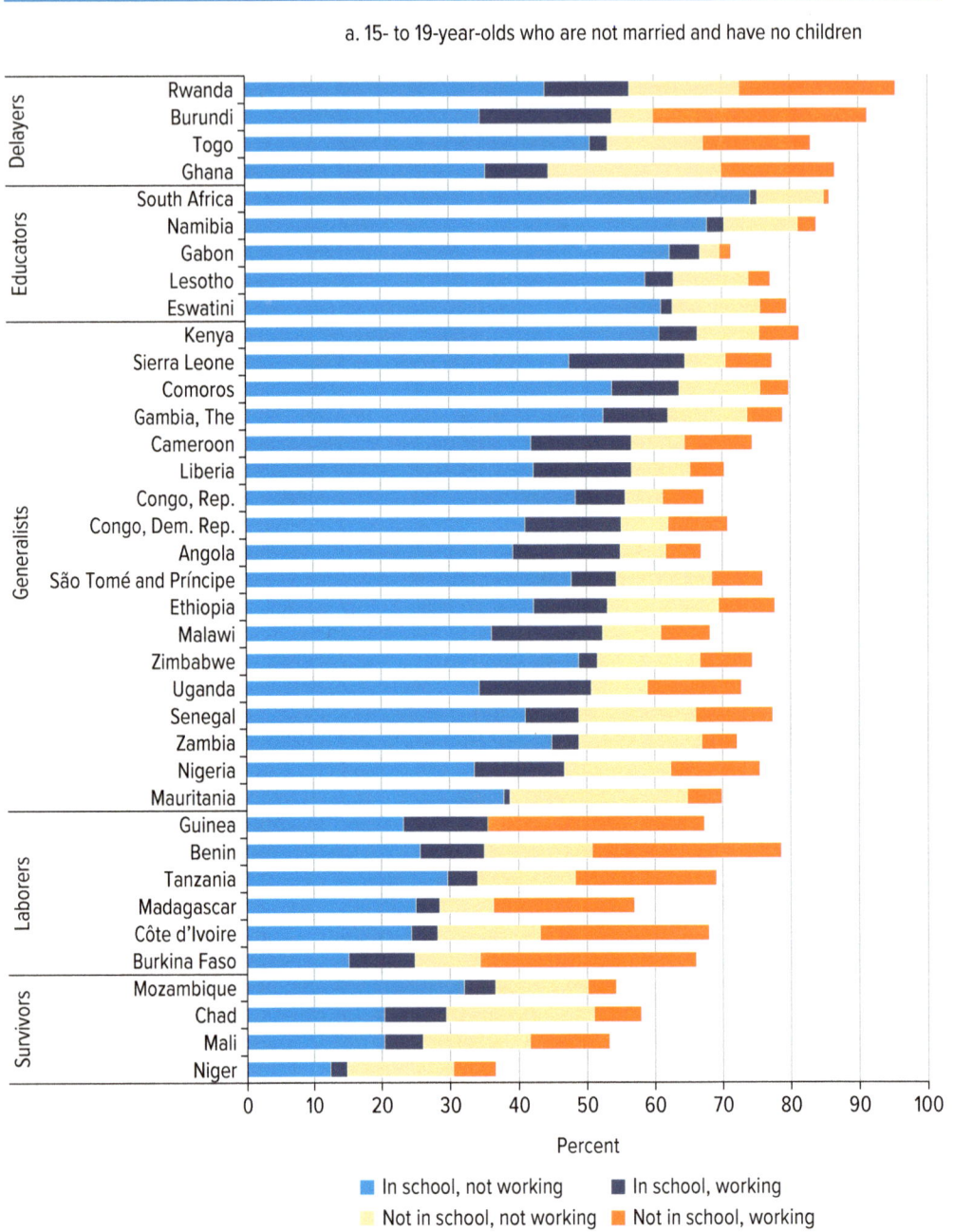

■ In school, not working   ■ In school, working
■ Not in school, not working   ■ Not in school, working

b. 15- to 19-year-olds who are married and have children

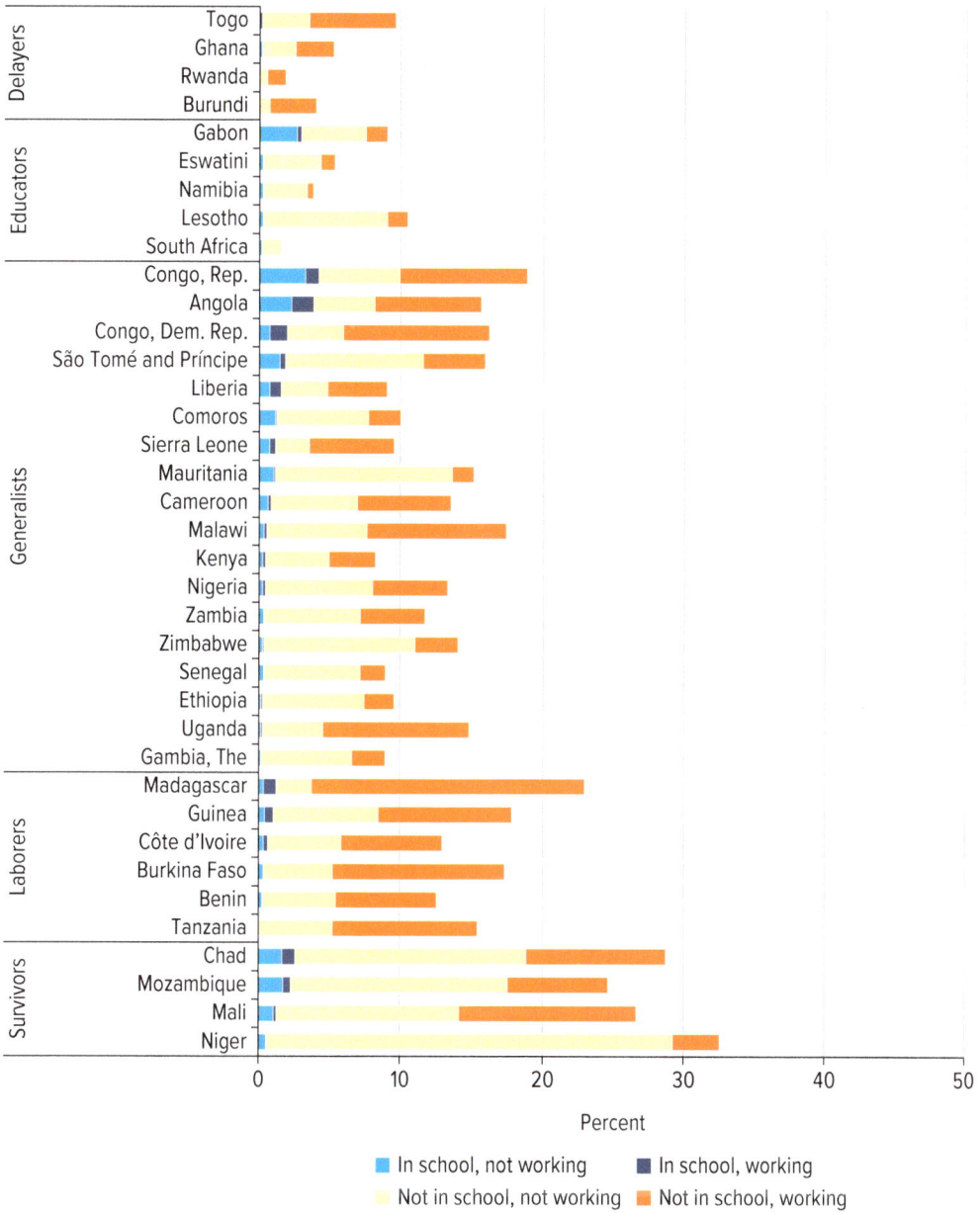

In school, not working   In school, working
Not in school, not working   Not in school, working

c. 15- to 19-year-olds who are not married and have children

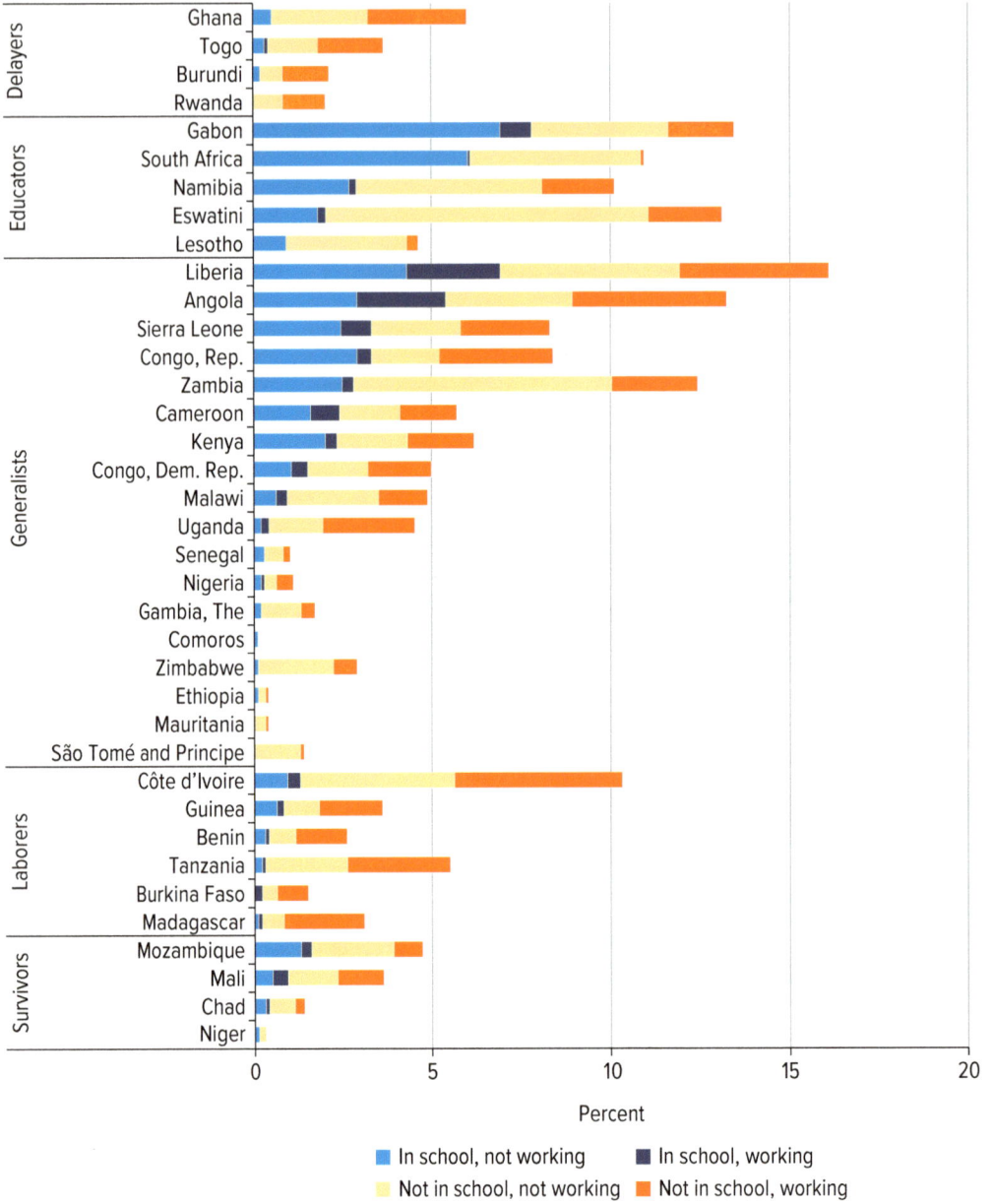

Percent

- In school, not working
- In school, working
- Not in school, not working
- Not in school, working

d. 15- to 19-year-olds who are married and do not have children

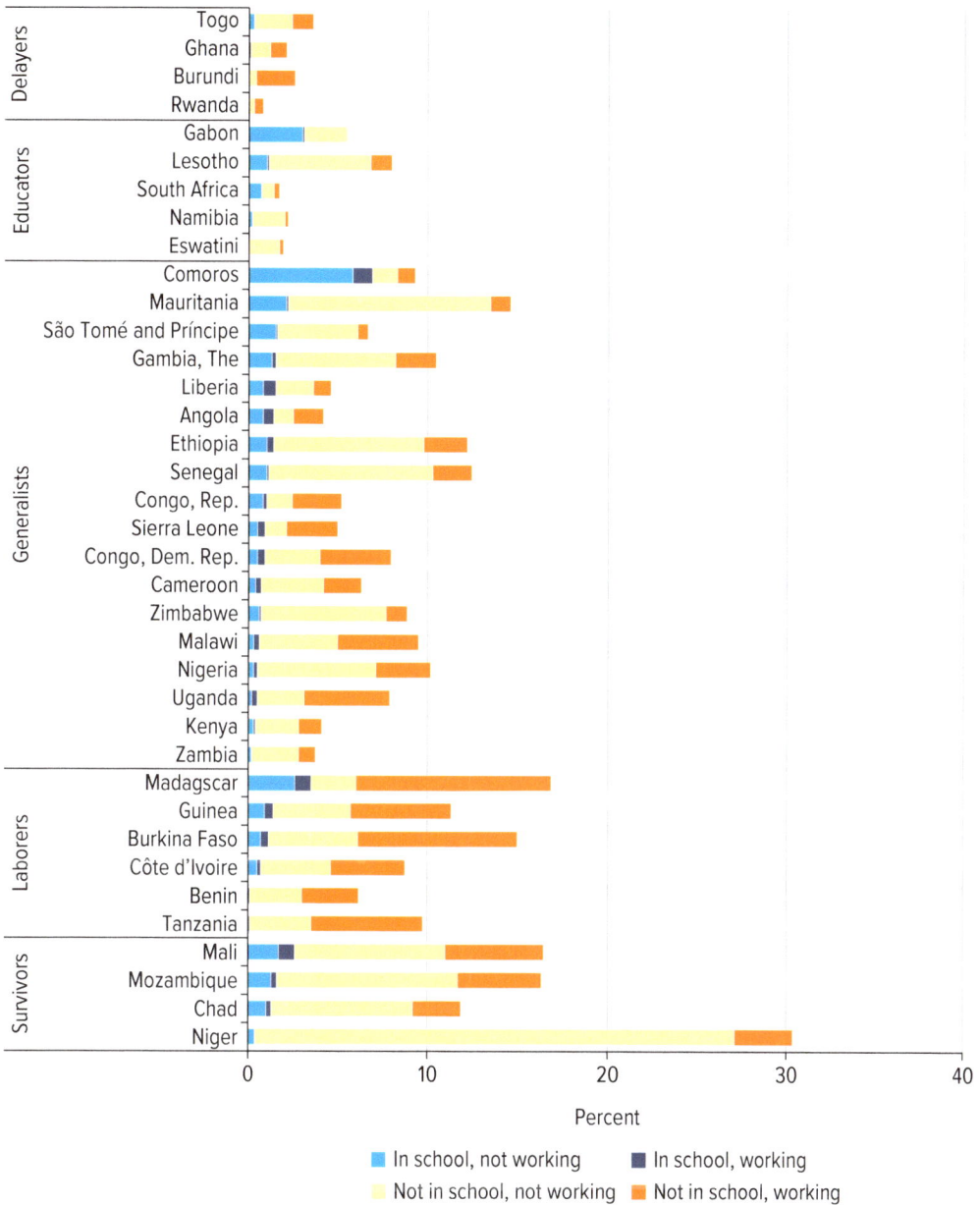

Source: Original figure for this report, based on data from the US Agency for International Development's Demographic and Health Surveys, accessed March 17, 2024, https://www.dhsprogram.com.

Notes

1. Bergstrom and Özler (2023) discuss the rationale for focusing on these three outcomes.
2. According to data from the World Bank's World Development Indicators (accessed January 30, 2024, https://databank.worldbank.org/source/world -development-indicators).
3. The Global Financing Facility uses a similar categorization approach to provide guidance on investments to improve adolescent girls' sexual and reproductive health and rights, based on four typologies of early pregnancy.
4. Demographic and Health Surveys questionnaires administer modules on gender-based violence only to married and cohabiting adults.

References

Bergstrom, Katy, and Berk Özler. 2023. "Improving the Well-Being of Adolescent Girls in Developing Countries." *World Bank Research Observer* 38 (2): 179–212. https://doi.org/10.1093/wbro/lkac007.

Carvalho, Shelby, and Emma Cameron. 2022. "How Can Education Systems Contribute More Effectively to Equality?" In *Girls' Education and Women's Equality: How to Get More out of the World's Most Promising Investment*, edited by Shelby Carvalho and David K. Evans, 80–92. Washington, DC: Center for Global Development.

Evans, David K., Shelby Carvalho, and Amina Mendez Acosta. 2022. "Which Girls Are Still Being Left Behind?" In *Girls' Education and Women's Equality: How to Get More out of the World's Most Promising Investment*, edited by Shelby Carvalho and David K. Evans, 43–52. Washington, DC: Center for Global Development.

Evans, David K., Susannah Hares, Peter A. Holland, and Amina Mendez Acosta. 2023. "Adolescent Girls' Safety In and Out of School: Evidence on Physical and Sexual Violence from across Sub-Saharan Africa." *Journal of Development Studies* 59 (5): 739–57. https://doi.org/10.1080/00220388.2023.2172333.

ILO (International Labour Organization). 2020. *Global Employment Trends for Youth 2020: Technology and the Future of Jobs*. Geneva: ILO Publishing.

Rossiter, Jack, and Maimouna Konate. 2022. "Studying School Exams: A New Database." Center for Global Development, Washington, DC.

World Bank. 2020. *Women, Business and the Law*. Washington, DC: World Bank.

Exploring the Complexity of Adolescent Girls' Empowerment: Insights from Impact Evaluation Surveys in Africa

Wei Chang, Riddhi Kalsi, Estelle Koussoubé and Léa Rouanet

Key Messages

- Empowerment is multidimensional. Adolescent girls can exhibit empowerment in one domain while lacking it in another.
- Weak associations between human capital fundamentals and other empowerment dimensions underscore the need for holistic intervention strategies.
- Life transitions like marriage and childbearing can hinder girls' acquisition of human capital and agency, yet certain resources and achievements persist across these changes.

Understanding the Multidimensional Nature of Adolescent Girls' Empowerment in Africa

The empowerment of adolescent girls is a complex and multidimensional concept, encompassing various aspects essential for these girls' development and success. Chapter 1 highlights that empowerment extends beyond just education and health; it also encompasses dimensions such as resources, agency, and economic achievement. While interventions focusing on education and health are crucial for laying the foundation of success in adulthood, they may not be sufficient to increase girls' empowerment in all its dimensions, potentially constraining sustainable economic success for girls in Africa.

A comprehensive understanding of adolescent girls' empowerment is hindered by data gaps and insufficient consideration of the interrelationships among various dimensions of empowerment. Closing the data gaps is essential for developing effective strategies that can empower adolescent girls in Africa. Furthermore, the multidimensionality of empowerment can vary for adolescent girls at different stages of life based on girls' demographic profiles and circumstances. As illustrated in chapter 1, adolescent girls in Africa may follow various pathways to empowerment, whether a

A reproducibility package is available for this book in the Reproducible Research Repository at https://reproducibility.worldbank.org.

path of building solid human capital fundamentals or facing challenging circumstances such as early marriage and motherhood. Understanding these differences with respect to demographic profiles and adapting interventions accordingly is crucial if policy makers and practitioners are to support adolescent girls at different life stages in realizing their full potential.

This spotlight delves into the multidimensionality of empowerment among adolescent girls in Africa, building upon the framework for adolescent girls' empowerment presented in chapter 1. It explores the interrelationships among various dimensions of empowerment, with particular emphasis on whether enhancements in human capital fundamentals can translate into improvements in other dimensions. Additionally, it investigates how empowerment manifests itself at different life stages experienced by adolescent girls, offering insights into the design of targeted interventions. To explore these issues, this spotlight analyzes data from impact evaluation surveys across Africa (refer to box S2.1.1 for details on the research methodology).

BOX S2.1.1 Insights from Impact Evaluation Surveys in Africa: Research Methodology

The analysis in this spotlight combines baseline survey data from 12 evaluations of the impact of empowerment programs targeting vulnerable adolescent girls and young women in 10 African countries (see table S2A.1 in annex S2A). These impact evaluations are being led by the World Bank's Africa Gender Innovation Lab and the Population Council. It is important to note that these surveys are not nationally representative and vary in sample compositions (for example, some surveys have solely rural participants, whereas others include both rural and urban samples, and respondents' age ranges vary from survey to survey). These variations are based on each program's definition of vulnerability and the corresponding targeting criteria. Despite these differences, these surveys offer a more comprehensive view of the various dimensions of adolescent girls' empowerment as described in the framework for adolescent girls' empowerment presented in chapter 1.

The spotlight first uses baseline survey data from these impact evaluations, focusing on the subsample of adolescents ages 10 to 19, to provide a descriptive overview of the empowerment levels of adolescent girls targeted by empowerment programs in Africa. Subsequently, it examines the relationships among various dimensions of empowerment by presenting Pearson correlations among all empowerment outcomes captured in the surveys. It then uses regression analysis to explore the extent to which human capital fundamentals are associated with other dimensions of empowerment, controlling for age, marital status, childbearing status, urban versus rural status, and survey fixed effects. Specifically, it evaluates the correlations among human capital fundamentals and other empowerment outcomes and assesses improvement in explaining each outcome's variance by comparing the adjusted R^2 statistics in two sets of models: one with education and health indicators as predictors, along with demographic and context predictors, and the other omitting education and health indicators as predictors. Additionally, the spotlight uses regression analysis to explore how levels of empowerment may differ based on various profiles of adolescent girls, controlling for urban versus rural status, age, and survey fixed effects. Individual weights are computed at the survey level and then applied to the models to ensure that each survey is given equal importance.

How Does Empowerment Manifest Itself among Adolescent Girls?

Empowerment among adolescent girls encompasses various dimensions, including human capital fundamentals, resources, and agency, all of which interact to influence girls' long-term economic achievements. Human capital fundamentals, namely, education and health, are vital not only in their own right, but also for realizing the potential of adolescent girls in adulthood. However, access to education remains a challenge for many girls, as on average 30 percent of girls in the aggregated impact evaluation sample reported having never attended school, and this challenge is especially pronounced in rural areas of the Sahel region (table S2.1). For instance, 55 percent of girls surveyed in rural Mali, 62 percent in rural Niger, and 77 percent in rural Burkina Faso reported they had never attended school. Health knowledge also varies significantly across contexts, with fewer than half of the girls surveyed in the impact evaluations reporting awareness of modern contraceptives in Mali (46 percent) and Chad (48 percent), whereas about three-quarters indicated having this knowledge in Côte d'Ivoire (77 percent), Benin (78 percent and 72 percent in two separate impact evaluation samples), and Mauritania (81 percent).

Beyond education and health, resources and agency are crucial dimensions of girls' empowerment. Whereas only 16 percent of girls in the sample said they had managed to accumulate financial resources through savings (table S2.1), a larger proportion, 62 percent, reported living in households that own cell phones.

"Agency" in respect to adolescent girls refers to their ability to define goals, act on those goals, and exert control over their lives. On average, 59 percent of girls surveyed reported aspiring to attain at least a high school education, whereas only 47 percent said they aspired to pursue skilled work that necessitates professional training, such as health work, engineering, and civil service. In addition, there is a discrepancy between girls' aspirations regarding marriage and education and the realities they face. Although 59 percent of girls surveyed indicated they aspired to attain a high school education, only 54 percent were in school. Likewise, the desired age of marriage among unmarried survey participants was 21.7 years across age groups, yet the average age of marriage among those already wedded stood at less than 16 years. Furthermore, gender attitudes reveal persistent inequalities. While 52 percent of girls acknowledged the importance of girls completing secondary education at par with boys, only 32 percent endorsed equal sharing of housework between genders. Moreover, attitudes toward gender-based violence are concerning. On average, 44 percent of girls surveyed across the sample justified wife beating in certain circumstances. This percentage varied significantly across countries, ranging from 80 percent in Mali to 13 percent in the sample from Benin.

TABLE S2.1 Empowerment Indicators Highlight Significant Challenges among Adolescent Girls across Different Impact Evaluation Surveys

Component	Demographics Variable	Number of observations	Weighted pooled average	AGEP Zambia (2016)	AGI Kenya (2015)	AGILE Nigeria (2023)	PASS Tanzania (2016)	SWEDD Cash Transfers Benin (2022)	SWEDD Safe Spaces Benin (2022)	SWEDD Burkina Faso (2017)	SWEDD Chad (2017)	SWEDD Côte d'Ivoire (2017)	SWEDD Mali (2017)	SWEDD Mauritania (2017)	SWEDD Niger (2017)
	Ages 15 to 19	51,241	63%	72%	4%	100%	54%	50%	51%	66%	57%	59%	77%	100%	60%
	Rural	51,215	64%	35%	41%	37%	100%	59%	72%	100%	36%	48%	100%	44%	100%
	Married	47,420	20%	8%	0%	1%	2%	1%	10%	49%	25%	23%	32%	22%	68%
	Age of marriage among married girls	7,152	15.5	17	–	–	–	15	16	16	15	15	16	15	15
	Has children	42,941	14%	14%	0%	–	4%	0%	7%	25%	20%	22%	22%	15%	24%
	Variable														
Human capital fundamentals	Never enrolled in school	51,172	30%	1%	10%	0%	1%	0%	47%	77%	56%	50%	55%	12%	62%
	Presently in school	50,888	54%	93%	88%	100%	95%	100%	0%	12%	33%	38%	26%	66%	0%
	Knowledge of family planning	28,316	65%	71%	–	–	–	78%	72%	55%	48%	77%	46%	81%	55%
Enabling resources	Saves	42,849	16%	36%	16%	–	14%	8%	11%	12%	2%	25%	27%	15%	11%
	Average savings amount for girls who save[a]	37,191	$38.38	$16.91	$10.88	–	$47.14	$23.20	$95.66	$54.98	$90.04	$61.01	$37.82	$44.73	$11.02
	Household owns a mobile phone	39,616	62%	28%	2%	–	–	67%	39%	73%	75%	98%	84%	93%	67%

(continued)

TABLE S2.1 Empowerment Indicators Highlight Significant Challenges among Adolescent Girls across Different Impact Evaluation Surveys *(continued)*

Component	Demographics / Variable	Number of observations	Weighted pooled average	AGEP Zambia (2016)	AGI Kenya (2015)	AGILE Nigeria (2023)	PASS Tanzania (2016)	SWEDD Cash Transfers Benin (2022)	SWEDD Safe Spaces Benin (2022)	SWEDD Burkina Faso (2017)	SWEDD Chad (2017)	SWEDD Côte d'Ivoire (2017)	SWEDD Mali (2017)	SWEDD Mauritania (2017)	SWEDD Niger (2017)
Agency	Aspirations for high school education and above	44,807	59%	—	98%	100%	99%	65%	100%	28%	30%	24%	—	30%	17%
	Aspirations for high-status work	41,075	47%	—	—	92%	—	51%	2%	46%	40%	52%	34%	69%	36%
	Marriage age aspiration (if not married)	29,591	21.7	25	26	22	—	25	21	20	19	22	19	22	17
	Self-efficacy (0–1)	47,717	0.71	0.72	0.51	0.88	—	0.73	0.76	0.81	0.55	0.67	0.73	0.76	0.67
	Locus of control (0–1)	34,806	0.62	0.39	0.46	—	—	0.61	0.60	0.72	0.69	0.71	—	0.72	0.70
	Gender attitudes: education	47,440	52%	96%	17%	99%	—	45%	22%	51%	29%	43%	50%	72%	42%

(continued)

TABLE S2.1 Empowerment Indicators Highlight Significant Challenges among Adolescent Girls across Different Impact Evaluation Surveys (*continued*)

Component	Variable	Number of observations (Pooled sample size)	Weighted pooled average	AGEP Zambia (2016)	AGI Kenya (2015)	AGILE Nigeria (2023)	PASS Tanzania (2016)	SWEDD Cash Transfers Benin (2022)	SWEDD Safe Spaces Benin (2022)	SWEDD Burkina Faso (2017)	SWEDD Chad (2017)	SWEDD Côte d'Ivoire (2017)	SWEDD Mali (2017)	SWEDD Mauritania (2017)	SWEDD Niger (2017)
AG (Demographics)	Gender attitudes: housework	41,417	32%	—	—	74%	—	12%	13%	32%	32%	30%	31%	32%	33%
Agency	Gender-based violence attitudes: justifying wife beating	39,686	44%	65%	51%	62%	—	13%	14%	28%	48%	64%	80%	18%	—
	Employed for pay in the past year	50,484	29%	17%	1%	36%	18%	60%	97%	11%	13%	56%	25%	9%	12%
Economic achievement (EA)	Number of observations per survey			1,120	5,145	8,197	3,402	6,044	4,344	4,328	1,064	3,225	4,749	2,683	6,940

Source: Original table for this report, based on data from impact evaluation surveys.
Note: Dashes indicate data that are not available. AGEP = Adolescent Girls' Empowerment Program; AGI = Adolescent Girls Initiative; AGILE = Adolescent Girls Initiative for Learning and Empowerment; PASS = Promoting Safe Sex Among Adolescents; SWEDD = Sahel Women's Empowerment and Demographic Dividend.
a. In dollars at purchasing-power parity.

In terms of economic achievement, although only girls' contemporaneous achievement is measured here, this information remains important, especially considering the large proportion of out-of-school girls in the sample. Only 29 percent of adolescent girls in the sample were engaged in paid employment, with the range spanning from 1 percent of girls surveyed in Kenya to 97 percent of girls surveyed in Benin, as part of the Sahel Women's Empowerment and Demographic Dividend Benin safe spaces impact evaluation (table S2.1). Most of these girls were employed as domestic workers, nonagricultural laborers, beauticians, cooks, and vendors. However, working for pay, especially at a younger age while attending school, may not always equate to meaningful economic achievements later in life, owing to factors such as job quality and the appropriateness of the work for one's age. While transitioning into professional careers may be achievable through continued skill development in specific occupations, it poses considerable challenges for the most vulnerable girls, who often lack adequate resources, agency, and support networks to enable them to make such a transition.

What Is the Connection between Human Capital Fundamentals and Other Dimensions of Empowerment?

While exploring the relationship between various dimensions of girls' empowerment, the research reported in this spotlight finds generally weak correlations among indicators measuring different dimensions of empowerment, with most correlation coefficients falling below 0.3 (table S2.2). However, education, as measured by self-reported school enrollment status, exhibits moderate positive correlations with several indicators of agency, including educational and career aspirations, and aspirational age of marriage. In contrast, knowledge of modern contraceptive methods, a health indicator, appears to be either not correlated or only weakly correlated with most other empowerment outcomes.

Despite the associations between human capital fundamentals and other empowerment dimensions, the explanatory power of human capital fundamentals is relatively small, especially in comparison with that of other demographic and contextual factors (figure S2.1). These findings suggest that the effect of human capital fundamentals—represented by school attendance and knowledge of sexual and reproductive health—on other aspects of girls' empowerment is, at most, only minimal. Although the possibility cannot be ruled out that using alternative measures of empowerment could affect these results, additional analysis using other measures on a subset of girls largely confirms these findings.

TABLE S2.2 Analysis of Correlations among Dimensions of Adolescent Girls' Empowerment Reveals Generally Weak Correlations

Component	Variable	Human capital fundamentals		Enabling resources			Agency						Economic achievement
		Attends school	Knows of modern contraception	Saves	Savings amount	Mobile phone at home	Aspires for high school education and above	Aspires for high-status job	Aspirational age of marriage	Gender attitudes: education	Gender attitudes: household chores	Attitudes toward normalizing GBV	Employed in the past year
Human capital fundamentals	Attends school	1	0.140***	0.012**	−0.051***	−0.122***	0.455***	0.458***	0.424***	0.235***	0.262***	0.032***	−0.063***
	Knows of modern contraception	0.140***	1	0.109***	0.077***	0.035***	0.094***	0.107***	0.259***	0.078***	−0.085***	0.011*	0.106***
Enabling resources	Saves	0.012**	0.109***	1	0.487***	0.054***	0.000	0.025***	0.040***	0.023***	0.012**	0.128***	0.106***
	Savings amount	−0.051***	0.077***	0.487***	1	0.035***	0.012**	−0.015***	−0.025***	−0.009	0.006	0.081***	0.117***
	Mobile phone at home	−0.122***	0.035***	0.054***	0.035***	1	−0.306***	0.138***	−0.193***	0.108***	0.066***	0.017***	0.017***
Agency	Aspires for high school education and above	0.455***	0.094***	0.000	0.012**	−0.306***	1	0.263***	0.205***	0.129***	0.187***	0.055***	0.131***
	Aspires for high-status job	0.458***	0.107***	0.025***	−0.015***	0.138***	0.263***	1	0.166***	0.294***	0.308***	0.114***	−0.121***
	Aspirational age of marriage	0.424***	0.259***	0.040***	−0.025***	−0.193***	0.205***	0.166***	1	−0.004	−0.035***	−0.072***	−0.031***
	Gender attitudes: education	0.235***	0.078***	0.023***	−0.009	0.108***	0.129***	0.294***	−0.004	1	0.408***	0.082***	−0.038***
	Gender attitudes: household chores	0.262***	−0.085***	0.012**	0.006	0.066***	0.187***	0.308***	−0.035***	0.408***	1	0.234***	−0.143***
	Gender attitudes: normalizing GBV	0.032***	0.011*	0.128***	0.081***	0.017***	0.055***	0.114***	−0.072***	0.082***	0.234***	1	−0.077***
Economic achievement	Employed for pay in the past year	−0.063***	0.106***	0.106***	0.117***	0.017***	0.131***	−0.121***	−0.031***	−0.038***	−0.143***	−0.077***	1

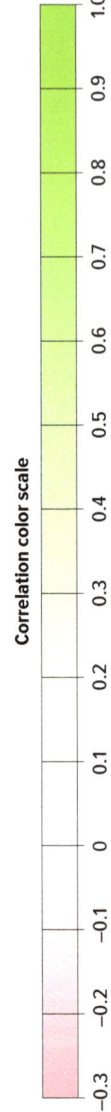

Correlation color scale

−0.3 −0.2 −0.1 0 0.1 0.2 0.3 0.4 0.5 0.6 0.7 0.8 0.9 1.0

Source: Original table for this report, based on data from impact evaluation surveys.

Note: GBV = gender-based violence.

*** $p<0.01$, ** $p<0.05$, * $p<0.1$

FIGURE S2.1 Human Capital Fundamentals Have Minimal Explanatory Power with Regard to Other Empowerment Dimensions

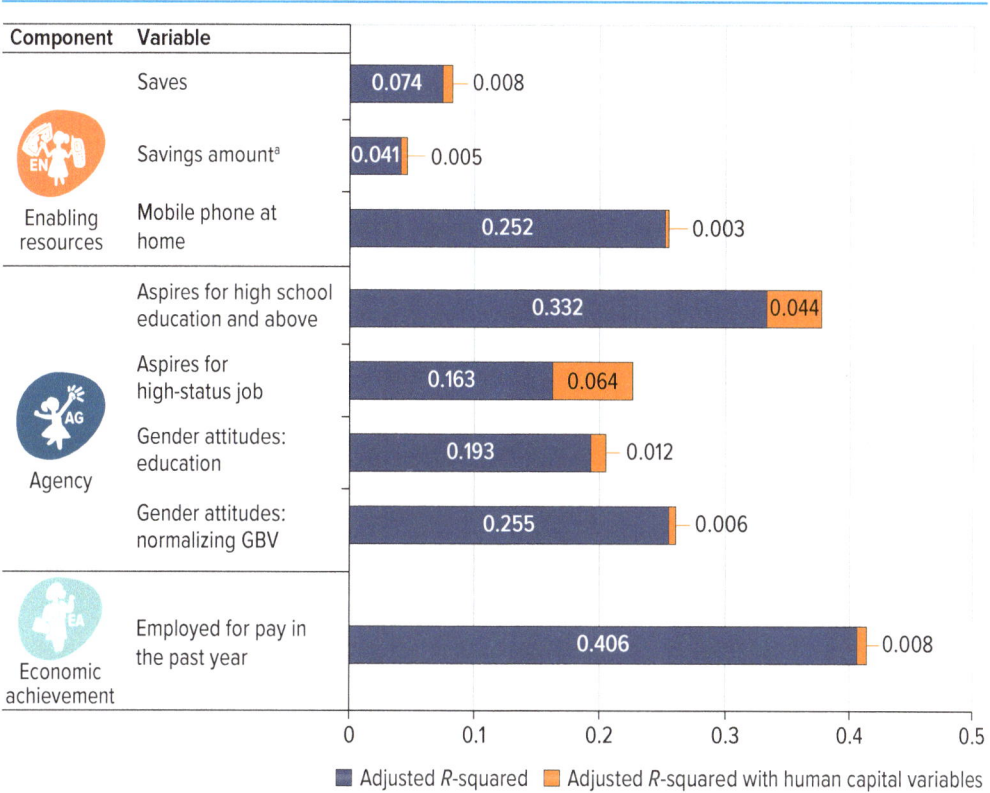

Component	Variable	Adjusted R-squared	Adjusted R-squared with human capital variables
Enabling resources	Saves	0.074	0.008
	Savings amount[a]	0.041	0.005
	Mobile phone at home	0.252	0.003
Agency	Aspires for high school education and above	0.332	0.044
	Aspires for high-status job	0.163	0.064
	Gender attitudes: education	0.193	0.012
	Gender attitudes: normalizing GBV	0.255	0.006
Economic achievement	Employed for pay in the past year	0.406	0.008

■ Adjusted *R*-squared ■ Adjusted *R*-squared with human capital variables

Source: Original figure for this report, based on data from impact evaluation surveys.
Note: GBV = gender-based violence
a. In dollars at purchasing-power parity.

How Do Life Transitions, Such as Marriage and Childbearing, Influence Girls' Empowerment?

Life transitions, specifically marriage and childbearing, influence girls' ability to acquire resources and gain agency. Such life transitions can often lead to girls' discontinuing their education, giving up education or career aspirations, and other negative consequences. Among the adolescent girls in the sample examined here,[1] approximately 10 percent reported being married without children, 3 percent said they were unmarried single mothers, and about 12 percent indicated they both were married and had children.

Compared with unmarried girls without children, married girls with or without children and single mothers are less likely to be attending school and more likely never to have received any formal education (figure S2.2). Similarly, it is unsurprising that married girls and single mothers have lower aspirations for professional careers. Adolescent mothers are also more inclined to tolerate instances of spousal abuse. However, even after going through life transitions such as marriage and childbearing, some girls still manage to retain or even gain certain resources. For instance, married girls without children are 17% more likely to have savings, unmarried mothers are 38% more likely, and married mothers are 28% more likely to have savings compared to unmarried girls without children.

FIGURE S2.2 Marriage and Childbearing Significantly Influence Adolescent Girls' Education, Aspirations, and Acceptance of Violence

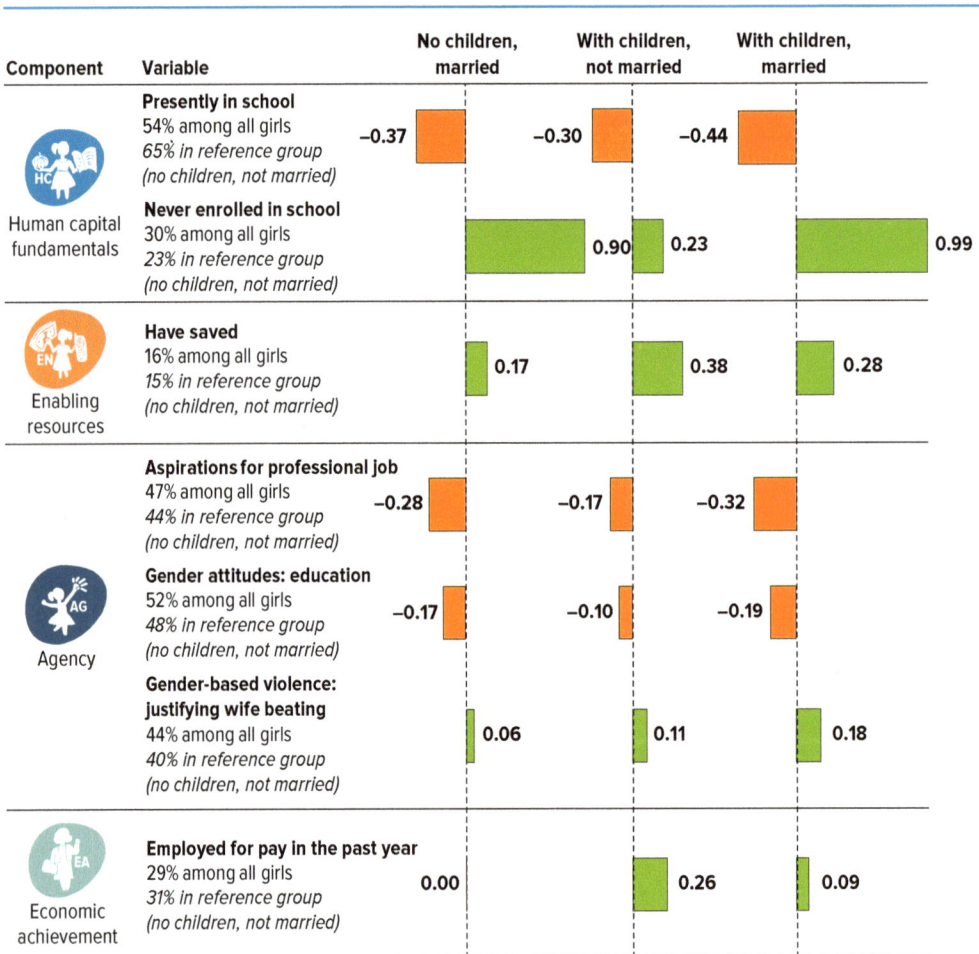

Component	Variable	No children, married	With children, not married	With children, married
Human capital fundamentals	**Presently in school** 54% among all girls 65% in reference group (no children, not married)	−0.37	−0.30	−0.44
	Never enrolled in school 30% among all girls 23% in reference group (no children, not married)	0.90	0.23	0.99
Enabling resources	**Have saved** 16% among all girls 15% in reference group (no children, not married)	0.17	0.38	0.28
Agency	**Aspirations for professional job** 47% among all girls 44% in reference group (no children, not married)	−0.28	−0.17	−0.32
	Gender attitudes: education 52% among all girls 48% in reference group (no children, not married)	−0.17	−0.10	−0.19
	Gender-based violence: justifying wife beating 44% among all girls 40% in reference group (no children, not married)	0.06	0.11	0.18
Economic achievement	**Employed for pay in the past year** 29% among all girls 31% in reference group (no children, not married)	0.00	0.26	0.09

Source: Original figure for this report, based on data from impact evaluation surveys.

Note: Figure uses linear regressions to examine whether selected empowerment indicators vary by demographic profile, with the "no children, not married" group as the reference group. Regressions control for urban versus rural status, age, and survey fixed effects and are weighted such that each survey has equal representation. Values represent the difference between each group and the reference group ('no children, not married'), expressed as a percentage of the reference group's mean. For example, a value of -0.37 indicates that the group is 37% lower than the reference group on the given indicator, while a value of 0.90 indicates it is 90% higher. Darker shading indicates a statistical significance of at least 10 percent.

Empowering Adolescent Girls Will Require Expanding Strategies to Address Their Multidimensional Needs across Life Stages

This spotlight argues that human capital alone falls short in capturing the multidimensionality of adolescent girls' empowerment. Moreover, adolescent girls face unique challenges associated with contextual factors, demographic characteristics, and life stages. Based on these findings, policies and programs should expand their focus beyond education and health interventions, incorporate a wider spectrum of empowerment strategies, and respond to the evolving needs of adolescent girls across life stages.

In various contexts, many girls, including those attending school while also caring for children, are involved in paid employment, highlighting the need for skills development and social-protection measures to support working girls, especially young working mothers. Young mothers who are working while going to school often face significant challenges in keeping up with their education. Policies should be designed to assist them in assigning schooling a higher priority than work, enabling them to acquire the necessary educational qualifications for better job opportunities. For young working mothers who are not enrolled in school and may no longer consider returning to the traditional education system, alternative paths like technical and vocational training are essential to equip them with practical skills and knowledge aligned with market demands. To enable these girls to participate effectively in both work and educational pursuits, policies that provide accessible childcare options are crucial. Moreover, policies that facilitate the reentry of out-of-school married girls or girls with children into the education system, should they desire it, are essential. Although information regarding the quality of work and working conditions for girls is lacking, it is crucial to consider these factors when designing programs and policies to empower girls. In addition to considering differences in contexts, the design of programs and policies should also take into account girls' age. For young girls in school, it is particularly important to assess whether work is hindering their educational attainment.

High aspirations can yield positive development outcomes, such as increased educational attainment, savings, and investments. However, when aspirations are set unrealistically high, especially given the existing context, it can also lead to frustration, resulting in negative outcomes (Genicot and Ray 2017; Lybbert and Wydick 2018). The analysis shows that, on average, most adolescent girls in Africa aspire to complete at least high school. However, married girls and those with children tend to have lower aspirations for educational attainment. This pattern is consistent with job aspirations, and these girls' aspirations also vary across countries in the analysis. These results highlight the potential for targeted interventions aimed at raising girls' aspirations and interventions designed to create an enabling environment for their economic success. Indeed, aspirations are influenced by the context, highlighting the importance of creating conditions that allow aspirations to flourish and high aspirations to be achieved.

Restrictive gender attitudes and norms can lower adolescent access to resources as well as their health and education outcomes (Cislaghi and Heise 2020; Levy et al. 2020). In the sample used here, many adolescent girls reported they believed that household chores should not be equally divided between men and women and that wife beating is acceptable. This finding highlights the need for interventions to promote equitable gender attitudes and transform norms that perpetuate inequitable attitudes and those that condone or encourage gender-based violence. Such interventions should be tailored to accommodate the evolving life stages of adolescent girls.

When it comes to promising opportunities, many adolescent girls across demographic categories have access to cell phones in their households. However, girls may not always own a mobile phone themselves, especially considering the large gender gap in digital access and usage (Tyers-Chowdhury and Binder 2021). In an era in which digital tools and platforms hold the potential to transform lives and job opportunities across Africa (Choi, Dutz, and Usman 2020), it is essential for programs and policies not only to leverage the potential of mobile technologies, but also to increase girls' access to devices, data, and networks. Additionally, designing digital products and services for girls and providing them with digital literacy training is also important to enhance girls' awareness, skills, and confidence in using digital tools and services. Such an approach is essential for effectively reaching, engaging, and supporting adolescent girls, especially those who are most disadvantaged.

Annex S2A. Overview of Impact Evaluation Surveys

Table S2A.1 provides an overview of the impact evaluation surveys analyzed in this spotlight.

TABLE S2A.1 Summary of Impact Evaluation Surveys

Impact evaluation survey	Survey year	Number of observations	Intervention	Age range	Out of school (%)	Rural (%)
AGEP Zambia	2016	1,120	• Safe spaces • Health services vouchers • Savings accounts	10–19	6.7	35
AGI Kenya	2015	5,145	• Community dialogue • Cash transfers • Health education • Savings and financial education	11–14	12.0	41
AGILE Nigeria	2023	8,197	• In-school safe spaces • Soft skills training • Digital skills training	15–21	0	37
PASS Tanzania	2016	3,402	• Health education • Free contraceptives	12–23	5.1	100
SWEDD Cash Transfers Benin	2022	6,044	• Safe spaces for life skills and health knowledge • Financial support (grants/loans) • Technical or business training • School course support, cash transfers, school supplies	10–19	0	59
SWEDD Safe Spaces Benin	2021	4,344	• Safe spaces for life skills and health knowledge • Financial support (grants/loans) • Technical or business training • School course support, cash transfers, school supplies	10–19	100	72
SWEDD Burkina Faso	2017	4,328	• Safe spaces for life skills and health knowledge • Financial support (grants/loans) • Technical or business training • School course support, cash transfers, school supplies	10–24	87.6	100

(continued)

TABLE S2A.1 Summary of Impact Evaluation Surveys *(continued)*

Impact evaluation survey	Survey year	Number of observations	Intervention	Age range	Out of school (%)	Rural (%)
SWEDD Chad	2017	1,064	• Safe spaces for life skills and health knowledge • Financial support (grants/loans) • Technical or business training • School course support, cash transfers, school supplies	12–24	66.7	36
SWEDD Côte d'Ivoire	2017	3,225	• Safe spaces for life skills and health knowledge • Financial support (grants/loans) • Technical or business training • School course support, cash transfers, school supplies	12–24	61.8	48
SWEDD Mali	2017	4,749	• Safe spaces for life skills and health knowledge • Financial support (grants/loans) • Technical or business training • School course support, cash transfers, school supplies	12–24	73.9	100
SWEDD Mauritania	2017	2,683	• Safe spaces for life skills and health knowledge • Financial support (grants/loans) • Technical or business training • School course support, cash transfers, school supplies	15–29	33.9	44
SWEDD Niger	2017	6,940	• Safe spaces for life skills and health knowledge • Financial support (grants/loans) • Technical or business training • School course support, cash transfers, school supplies	10–19	99.5	100

Source: Original table for this report, based on data from impact evaluation surveys.

Note: AGEP = Adolescent Girls Empowerment Program; AGI = Adolescent Girls Initiative; AGILE = Adolescent Girls Initiative for Learning and Empowerment; PASS= Promoting Safe Sex Among Adolescents; SWEDD = Sahel Women's Empowerment and Demographic Dividend.

Note

1. The analysis sample consists of the subsample of adolescent girls in the pooled sample with available information on their childbearing and marital status.

References

Choi, Jieun, Mark A. Dutz, and Zainab Usman. 2020. *The Future of Work in Africa: Harnessing the Potential of Digital Technologies for All*. Africa Development Forum. Washington, DC: World Bank. https://documents1.worldbank.org/curated/en /511511592867036615/pdf/The-Future-of-Work-in-Africa-Harnessing-the -Potential-of-Digital-Technologies-for-All.pdf.

Cislaghi, Beniamino, and Lori Heise. 2020. "Gender Norms and Social Norms: Differences, Similarities and Why They Matter in Prevention Science." *Sociology of Health & Illness* 42 (2): 407–22. https://doi.org/10.1111/1467-9566.13008.

Genicot, Garance, and Debraj Ray. 2017. "Aspirations and Inequality." *Econometrica* 85 (2): 489–519. https://doi.org/10.3982/ECTA13865.

Levy, Jessica K., Gary L. Darmstadt, Caitlin Ashby, Mary Quandt, Erika Halsey, Aishwarya Nagar, and Margaret E. Greene. 2020. "Characteristics of Successful Programmes Targeting Gender Inequality and Restrictive Gender Norms for the Health and Wellbeing of Children, Adolescents, and Young Adults: A Systematic Review." *Lancet: Global Health* 8 (2): e225–36. https://doi.org/10.1016/S2214 -109X(19)30495-4.

Lybbert, Travis J., and Bruce Wydick. 2018. "Poverty, Aspirations, and the Economics of Hope." *Economic Development and Cultural Change* 66 (4): 709–53. https://doi.org /10.1086/696968.

Tyers-Chowdhury, Alexandra, and Gerda Binder. 2021. "Innovation and Technology for Gender Equality: What We Know about the Gender Digital Divide for Girls; A Literature Review." United Nations Children's Fund, New York. https://www.unicef .org/eap/reports/innovation-and-technology-gender-equality-0.

CHAPTER 3

What Do We Know about Improving Human Capital Fundamentals among Adolescent Girls in Africa?

Ioana Botea and Kehinde Ajayi, with contributions from Karen Austrian, Chiara Pasquini and Sara Troiano

Key Messages

- Evidence definitively shows that reducing direct and indirect costs of schooling through fee elimination, scholarships, school meals, and cash transfers is the most effective way to improve education outcomes—especially for girls—in Africa. Improving quality of school instruction is also crucial.

- Compared with what we know about improving education outcomes, adolescent health remains relatively understudied in Africa. Multicomponent interventions combining education in sexual and reproductive health with the provision of youth-friendly services emerge as the most promising approaches.

- There is a mutually reinforcing connection between building a robust human capital foundation and delaying marriage and childbearing. Interventions that support girls' schooling through (conditional) cash transfers show the clearest pattern of success in delaying marriage and childbearing.

Providing Girls with a Solid Foundation in Human Capital Promotes Their Successful Transition to Adulthood

A robust foundation in human capital is essential for a successful transition to adulthood and the achievement of empowerment. Adolescence is a period in which girls experience rapid physical, emotional, social, and cognitive changes. Prioritizing investment in developing human capital fundamentals during these years can profoundly influence girls' adulthood and even shape the trajectory of the next generation. This includes building core education and health resources and largely corresponds to a life path in which girls

A reproducibility package is available for this book in the Reproducible Research Repository at https://reproducibility.worldbank.org.

can attend school, adopt healthy lifestyles, and delay family formation and employment. For girls who are already out of school or married or have children, core resources are instrumental for skills development and broader capital accumulation (additional details are provided in chapter 4).

Based on the conceptual framework introduced in chapter 1, this chapter synthesizes what is known about how to improve the education and health outcomes of adolescent girls in Africa (table 3.1). It draws on recent literature reviews of interventions aimed at improving education and health outcomes for adolescent girls (Bergstrom and Özler 2023; Evans, Mendez Acosta, and Yuan 2024; Evans and Yuan 2022; Malhotra and Elnakib 2021; Meherali et al. 2021; Psaki et al. 2022). Annex 4A details the criteria for rating evidence strength and maps the evidence across intervention categories and empowerment components and indicators from the conceptual framework.

TABLE 3.1 Evidence Reveals the Varying Effectiveness of Interventions Aimed at Improving Adolescent Girls' Human Capital Fundamentals

Intervention category	Degree of effectiveness in improving adolescent girls' human capital fundamentals
School fee reduction or elimination	Effective
Improving quality of instruction	Effective
In-kind transfers for schooling	Effective
Cash transfers	Effective
School feeding	Effective
Sexual and reproductive health education	Effective
Health services	Effective
Employment opportunities for women	Promising
Engaging boys, parents, and community	Promising
Information on return to education or training	Promising
Child marriage ban	Promising
Educational entertainment programs	Promising
Inheritance law reform	Promising
School construction	Promising
Girls' group empowerment programs	Mixed
Other life skills training, mentoring, and empowerment programs	Mixed
Comprehensive economic empowerment programs	Unknown
Financial inclusion programs	Unknown
Traditional vocational and business skills training	Unknown

Source: Original table for this report.

The chapter is structured into three sections. First, it highlights interventions for which there is robust evidence in regard to Africa, focusing on enhancing adolescent girls' education and health. Second, it examines interventions that either demonstrate promise within the African context or show potential based on evidence from other contexts, albeit with limited evidence in regard to Africa. Third, it addresses interventions for which the evidence is mixed but that are deemed worthy of consideration, potentially requiring refinement or adaptation. The chapter concludes with a discussion of future areas of research and experimentation. Altogether, a great deal is known about how to get adolescent girls in school, keep them in school, and improve their education outcomes. Much less is known about how to improve their health outcomes and how to sustain impacts over long horizons. Interventions aimed at improving girls' human capital fundamentals also have significant interactions with efforts to reduce their exposure to violence and to delay marriage and childbearing (boxes 3.1 and 3.2).

BOX 3.1 Interventions to Reduce Girls' Exposure to Violence

Although exposure to violence is an issue of substantial relevance to the lives of adolescent girls in Africa, there is limited evidence on effective interventions to reduce it. The growing evidence on effective interventions to eliminate violence includes relatively little research from Africa. Out of 33 studies included in a recent review of evidence on school-based interventions to reduce violence in schools, only three were from programs implemented in Africa (Smarrelli et al. 2024). Only one of those three studies found a significant reduction in violence, primarily through a reduction in teacher-perpetrated violence. School-based interventions to reduce violence typically include focusing on students to build their life skills, knowledge, and awareness or to provide psychosocial support; enhancing skills training for school staff members; or adopting a whole-school approach to create sustained structural change by holistically engaging the school community: students, parents, teachers, head teachers, and sometimes members or leaders of the broader community. However, all three types of interventions have been found to lead to improvements in student learning and mental health. These three studies demonstrate that although lessons on what works to address girls' exposure to violence are still emerging, efforts to improve school climate can have positive impacts on education and mental health outcomes.

Beyond school-based interventions, another emerging approach to reduce violence is through girls' empowerment clubs and other empowerment programs. A low-cost, behaviorally informed action plan intervention for young women in Tanzania significantly reduced reports of intimate-partner violence (Shah et al. 2023). Similarly, a girls' club empowerment intervention in Uganda increased girls' knowledge in the area of sexual and reproductive health and reduced the incidence of sex against girls' will (Bandiera et al. 2020). Although the studies that yielded

(continued)

BOX 3.1 Interventions to Reduce Girls' Exposure to Violence *(continued)*

these findings did not directly measure impacts on school enrollment as a potential pathway to improvements in long-term outcomes, the interventions studied may have large impacts in adulthood.

Edwards et al. (2024, 593) review evidence on interventions to reduce gender-based violence among adolescent girls in Africa and find that

> programs that focus on (1) economic strengthening, (2) teachers [or] schools, (3) entire families, (4) caregivers only, and (5) children only are generally effective in reducing violence against children by promoting focused action on the mechanisms of change (e.g., parenting skills, enhanced parent–child relationships, resistance skills for children). To date, no research in SSA [Sub-Saharan Africa] has examined the impact of policy interventions on childhood victimization or community-level interventions to change norms and values that support violence against children. Future research is needed to examine the impacts of comprehensive efforts to prevent violence against children in SSA as well as factors that predict uptake and sustainability of such prevention efforts in SSA.

A global review of research from low- and middle-income countries concludes that the most favorable impacts emerge from bundled individual-level interventions and multilevel interventions (Yount, Krause, and Miedema 2017). Moreover, promising interventions also include those that involve community engagement, skill building to enhance girls' voice and agency, and social-network expansion. Yount, Krause, and Miedema (2017) recommend an increased focus on polyvictimization to understand how impacts vary over the course of adolescence and to provide more evidence on excluded populations such as urban, out-of-school, married, and displaced or conflict-affected populations with higher potential risk.

BOX 3.2 Interventions to Delay Marriage and Childbearing

Building foundational human capital is closely linked to preventing early marriage and childbearing, adverse outcomes that endanger the life trajectories of girls in multiple ways, including through lower educational attainment (Delprato et al. 2015; Nguyen and Wodon 2014) and health outcomes (Delprato and Akyeampong 2017; Nour 2006), which, in turn, lead to reduced economic participation (Chaaban and Cunningham 2011). The evidence base on what works to prevent child marriage, particularly in Africa, has substantially expanded over the past 20 years (Malhotra and Elnakib 2021).[a]

Provide incentives for education through cash and in-kind transfers

In Africa, cash and in-kind transfers supporting education emerge as the strategy with the strongest evidence base for preventing child marriage and early childbearing. In Zimbabwe, a five-year program providing financial and material aid for educating orphan adolescent girls reduced child marriage rates by 53 percent (Hallfors et al. 2015). In Ghana, a scholarship to attend senior high school decreased pregnancy among female scholarship recipients by 7 percentage

(continued)

BOX 3.2 Interventions to Delay Marriage and Childbearing *(continued)*

points (Duflo, Dupas, and Kremer 2021). Similarly, a program in Kenya that provided free school uniforms led to a 19 percent decrease in the teenage pregnancy rate within marriages (Duflo, Dupas, and Kremer 2015). In Malawi, conditional cash transfers reduced marriage and pregnancy for girls not in school before the start of the program by 40 and 30 percent, respectively—but showed no effects for girls already in school (Baird et al. 2010).

Interestingly, cash transfers appear to have an impact on marriage and childbearing only when linked to education outcomes. In the Malawi study mentioned previously, although an unconditional version of the cash transfers led to similar results in the short run, nonbeneficiaries caught up with beneficiaries shortly after the end of the intervention. Baird, McIntosh, and Özler (2019) posit that when the cash payments stop, unconditional cash transfers provide no value added for girls. In the case of conditional cash transfers, on the other hand, staying in school is forging a different life trajectory for girls. Moreover, neither of two studies of government-run unconditional cash transfer programs in Africa showed any effects on rates of child marriage (Dake et al. 2018; Handa et al. 2015). Handa et al. (2015) did, however, find reduced pregnancy rates among young women in Kenya through increased school enrollment and delayed age at first sex. Taken together, these findings suggest that it may be the human capital investment in girls and provision of an alternative option, rather than the money itself, that matters the most in early marriage and childbearing prevention.

Improve knowledge regarding sexual and reproductive health

School-based interventions targeting HIV/AIDS transmission among students have been proven to have a positive impact on adolescent girls' pregnancy and childbearing rates. A recent review of evidence from Africa identifies three studies supporting this conclusion (Costa et al. 2023). First, in Kenya, an intervention informing students about HIV infection risks associated with partner age (including an education video on "sugar daddies") led to a substantial reduction in teenage pregnancy rates, indicating a shift away from older partners (Dupas 2011). Second, in rural Cameroon, four interventions[b] that provided HIV/AIDS information to adolescent schoolgirls reduced the incidence of teenage pregnancy by up to 48 percent (Dupas, Huillery, and Seban 2018). Finally, also in Cameroon, a teacher-training program led to a significant reduction in early childbearing among girls ages 15 to 17, likely as a result of a significant increase in condom use (Arcand and Wouabe 2010). For younger girls (ages 12 to 13), the program resulted in an increase in self-reported abstinence and condom use and a decrease in the likelihood of having multiple partners.

Consider offering girls' group empowerment programs

There is mixed evidence on the effect of girls' group empowerment programs on marriage and childbearing. In Uganda, an adolescent girls' group empowerment program led to a 34 percent drop in adolescent fertility and a 62 percent drop in marriage four years after the intervention (Bandiera et al. 2020). In Ethiopia, a program that combined girls' groups with financial support to stay in school and community awareness was associated with an increase in age at marriage, through reduced marriage among 10- to 14-year-old girls and increased marriage among 15- to 19-year-olds (Erulkar

(continued)

BOX 3.2 Interventions to Delay Marriage and Childbearing *(continued)*

and Muthengi 2009). However, studies of girls' group interventions in other countries, including Tanzania, have found null effects, likely on account of differences in implementation quality. This variation in effects of girls' clubs highlights the importance of building evidence on ways to ensure effective implementation of programs and interventions (for additional details, refer to spotlight 3).

Reform policy

Banning child marriage can meaningfully increase adolescent girls' empowerment. Wilson (2022) exploits data from policy changes in 17 low- and middle-income countries to measure the effects of child marriage bans on female schooling and labor market outcomes. He finds that banning child marriage (by raising the minimum legal age of marriage to 18) increases age at marriage, age at birth of first child, and likelihood of employment. Additionally, such bans reduce child marriage rates and increase educational attainment in urban areas. Although the effects appear to be generally less pronounced in rural areas, the bans appear to have led to a greater effect on employment than in urban areas, without increasing the years of schooling. And although positive effects are observed even in places where enforcement is not strict, the continued prevalence of child marriage in countries with legal bans underscores the necessity of supplementing legal reforms with complementary measures (for example, communication campaigns and engagement with community leaders) to enhance the likelihood of their success in achieving the desired results (Collin and Talbot 2023). Indeed, evidence from Ethiopia shows that, for some groups, cultural norms prevail over the law (McGavock 2021). Therefore, legal reforms will have limited impacts in the absence of supportive frameworks (the World Bank [2024] indicates that African countries have the weakest mechanisms for implementing laws supporting gender equality, highlighting the importance of strengthening these mechanisms in the region).

Eliminating tuition fees is another policy reform with the potential to reduce child marriage significantly at the national level. Koski et al. (2018) use data on women born between 1970 and 2000 in 16 African countries to estimate the impact of removing primary school fees on the prevalence of child marriage. Their study reveals that the removal of tuition fees resulted in a modest average decline in child marriage rates across the pooled sample of countries studied. However, there was substantial heterogeneity among countries in the estimated impacts. The prevalence of child marriage declined by 10 to 15 percentage points in Ethiopia and Rwanda following tuition elimination but did not change in Cameroon or Malawi. The authors conclude that enhancing the quality of available education could amplify the impacts of fee removal and further advance progress toward various other objectives.

a. There has been a surge in the number of studies on child marriage: from 193 publications between 2000 and 2016 to another 193 publications between 2016 and 2019. The evidence base for Africa expanded from 20 studies between 2000 and 2011 to 34 more studies between 2012 and 2015 and 79 more studies between 2016 and 2019.

b. The four interventions—one an in-class quiz, two providing general information on prevention of HIV infection, and one providing additional information on HIV risk by partner age and gender—all presented the use of condoms as a strategy to avoid HIV infection instead of promoting abstinence only.

Some Approaches Have Proven Their Effectiveness

Educational expenses are the largest barrier to schooling in many contexts. Therefore, lowering schooling costs has positive impacts for adolescent girls' educational and other outcomes. A key policy question, however, is how to choose among alternative approaches for reducing schooling costs. In contrast to the substantial evidence on approaches to boost education outcomes, there is less evidence on effective interventions to improve health outcomes.

Reduction or Elimination of School Fees Increases Girls' Educational Attainment

Policies lowering school fees have consistently led to significant increases in enrollment and attainment for girls. Most African countries mandated free primary school education in the 1980s or 1990s, dramatically increasing enrollment in subsequent years. Studies reporting sex-disaggregated results demonstrate that free primary education had positive impacts on girls' education outcomes in Ethiopia (Chicoine 2016), Tanzania (Hoogeveen and Rossi 2013), and Uganda (Grogan 2009).

Given that most countries in Africa have already eliminated fees for education at the primary level, reducing or eliminating fees for secondary education is the next frontier (Mastercard Foundation 2020). Universally providing free secondary education tends to be more politically favorable than providing subsidies or financial support exclusively for vulnerable individuals or households. However, this approach can be costly, because it subsidizes secondary education for many households that could otherwise afford to pay for it. Partial approaches of eliminating fees in certain high-poverty geographic regions, exclusively for girls, or only for other vulnerable groups can offer a more cost-effective approach for delivering free secondary education (Sandefur 2022).

Complementing fee elimination with increased resources to expand schools' capacity has greater effects than simply eliminating school fees without explicitly increasing resources to accommodate more students. Moreover, accompanying enrollment gains with complementary policies to reduce unintended consequences such as overcrowding and greater competition for limited formal employment is crucial (Duflo, Dupas, and Kremer 2021). Finally, entrance exams often ration access to secondary schools even when families can afford to pay and are eager for their children to attend, because of high failure rates on the exams. Therefore, addressing entrance exam bottlenecks by revising or removing entrance exam requirements may also be necessary to expand secondary school access after fees are eliminated.

In-Kind Transfers for Schooling Remove Financial Barriers

Five studies from African countries unambiguously show that removing the financial barrier of schooling costs through scholarships improves a range of girls' education outcomes. In Ghana, a four-year full scholarship for low-income, academically qualified students increased educational enrollment, attainment, and knowledge (Duflo, Dupas, and Kremer 2021). Similarly, the provision of full scholarships to attend low-cost private schools in Uganda substantially increased total enrollment for early secondary grades among both male and female students (Barrera-Osorio et al. 2020). Another scholarship program—for more than 100,000 girls in upper-primary and lower-secondary grades in the Democratic Republic of Congo—boosted both reading and mathematics scores (Randall and Garcia 2020). A program that paid school fees in Tanzania and covered other informal costs for tens of thousands of secondary school girls who had been identified by their communities as highly vulnerable resulted in lower dropout rates and much higher test scores (Sabates et al. 2021). Finally, a five-year program providing financial and material aid for educating orphan adolescent girls in Zimbabwe increased school enrollment and school attendance and improved the girls' sexual and reproductive health (Hallfors et al. 2015).

Distance to school is a major constraint on girls' education, undermining punctuality, attendance, and learning and exposing girls to risks of harassment and assault. Evidence from Zambia points to the provision of bicycles as another potential avenue for improving girls' access to school. Fiala et al. (2022) find that providing bicycles to girls living more than three kilometers from the school they attend significantly reduces commuting time and late arrival, decreases absenteeism, and increases math test scores. The study also finds improvements in girls' attendance and retention that are sustained up to four years after the intervention. The results are consistent with similar research conducted in India, where giving bicycles to secondary school girls reduced travel time and led to a substantial increase in girls' enrollment (Muralidharan and Prakash 2017).

School Feeding Programs Provide Incentives for Enrollment and Can Improve Academic Achievement and Health

School feeding programs, typically offered in primary schools, have been proven to offer incentives for enrollment and improve academic performance for both girls and boys. In northern Burkina Faso, providing girls with either lunch at school or take-home rations of 10 kilograms of cereal flour each month is found to increase enrollment by 3 to 5 percentage points (Kazianga, de Walque, and Alderman 2012) and to improve girls' math scores as well.

Similarly, another study finds that both school meals and take-home rations have a positive impact on school participation in camps for internally displaced people in northern Uganda, including increasing enrollment among girls not enrolled before the school feeding program began (Alderman, Gilligan, and Lehrer 2012). In Ghana, a large-scale school feeding program increased enrollment and led to moderate increases in both math and literacy test scores (Aurino et al. 2023). The impacts were more pronounced for girls, children from households living below the poverty line, and children from the northern region of the country, emphasizing the role of underlying conditions in mediating the impact of an intervention.

Although most nutrition literature focuses on a child's first thousand days, there is increased recognition of the need for nutritional interventions during adolescence. Malnutrition during formative years has long-term implications for adult morbidity (Lassi, Moin, and Bhutta 2017) and economic outcomes, including a wage penalty due to obesity (Cawley 2015). A recent systematic review of school feeding programs in low- and middle-income countries finds significant increases in height and weight for children (Wang et al. 2021). There is not enough evidence specifically about adolescent girls in Africa to draw any definitive conclusions about the anthropometric effects of these programs in that group. However, a randomized evaluation in Uganda finds that a school feeding program providing meals fortified with multiple micronutrients reduced anemia among adolescent girls ages 10 to 13 (Alderman, Gilligan, and Lehrer 2012).

In addition, a growing body of research points to micronutrient supplementation as an intervention to improve nutrition outcomes for girls. A 2017 review of reviews found that iron, iron–folic acid, zinc, and multiple micronutrient supplementation in adolescents can significantly improve serum hemoglobin concentrations (Lassi, Moin, and Bhutta 2017). Evidence from African countries is still evolving. Whereas an early study in Tanzania found that weekly iron supplementation increased iron levels and weight gain but had no impact on hemoglobin concentrations among adolescent girls (Beasley et al. 2000), a similar study in Mali subsequently found increased hemoglobin concentrations and reduced anemia among a population of adolescent girls with higher initial rates of anemia (Hall et al. 2002). Studies from Kenya and Mozambique measure the impact of administering iron and either folic acid or vitamin A, respectively, and determine that the positive effects on hemoglobin concentration materialize only among girls who are iron deficient (Horjus et al. 2005; Leenstra et al. 2009). Taken together, this evidence indicates that micronutrient supplementation is an especially effective intervention for adolescent girls at risk of nutrient deficiency.

Improving the Quality of Instruction Leads to Better Outcomes

There is promising evidence on the effectiveness of interventions designed to improve the quality of instruction in Africa, especially in regard to school attainment. First, evidence from a multifaceted program[1] in Kenya and performance pay in Tanzania suggests that teacher incentives can lead to literacy and learning gains, particularly for girls (Freudenberger and Davis 2017; Mbiti et al. 2019; Piper and Mugenda 2014; Piper et al. 2018). Second, Psaki et al. (2022) find evidence that remedial support programs can also be effective at improving learning outcomes for girls (in Kenya, Malawi, Zambia, and Zimbabwe, among other countries). More recent research in Ghana similarly finds that different models of a remedial reading program lead to significant gains in student learning that are again higher for girls than for boys (Duflo, Kiessel, and Lucas 2020). Based on a global review of the evidence, however, improving the quality of education has mixed impacts on school participation (JPAL 2017). This is likely because of the difficulty parents have in accurately perceiving the quality of education their children are receiving and, consequently, in changing their behavior in response to improvements.

Cash Transfers Consistently Increase School Enrollment and Attendance

Direct cash transfers to households have consistently led to increased child school enrollment and attendance, particularly when they have been targeted toward the most disadvantaged groups. Global evidence shows that cash transfers can improve access to school in the short term by removing direct and indirect financial barriers to education (Bastagli et al. 2016; Bergstrom and Özler 2023). This finding holds as well in Africa, where cash transfers have shown notable success in enhancing school participation, especially among girls (Akresh, de Walque, and Kazianga 2013; Evans et al. 2014). The provision of cash to families tends to primarily benefit children on the margin of school attendance, who may otherwise have a lower likelihood of attending school (Akresh, de Walque, and Kazianga 2013). This effect predominantly favors girls, although exceptions have been documented in Lesotho and South Africa, where boys are more disadvantaged than girls with respect to school attendance because of their herding and farming responsibilities (Edmonds 2006; Pellerano et al. 2014).[2]

In contrast to their robust impacts on school participation, the effects of cash transfers on learning outcomes have been more muted. In both Burkina Faso and Malawi, gains in test scores were attained only when cash transfers were conditional on school attendance (Akresh, de Walque, and Kazianga 2013; Baird, McIntosh, and Özler 2011). A conditional cash transfer was also successful in increasing literacy rates among children from beneficiary households in Tanzania (Evans et al. 2014). Even so, results either dissipated (Evans et al. 2014) or failed to translate into improved competencies (Baird, McIntosh, and Özler 2019) after a couple of years. The evidence base for impacts on adolescent girls' health and nutrition in Africa is limited. While there is robust evidence on the impacts of cash transfers on girls' nutritional status in early childhood, relatively little empirical evidence exists on the effects of cash transfers on nutrition outcomes during adolescence. Preliminary research from South Africa finds that adolescents from households receiving the country's Child Support Grant have higher body mass index z-scores and are less likely to be either underweight or obese (Chakroborty and Villa 2022).

Increasing Demand for Health Services through Education and Improving the Quality of Youth-Friendly Services Available Enhances Girls' Health

The most definitive evidence regarding interventions to promote adolescent girls' health in Africa supports multicomponent interventions that combine education to increase demand for health services with efforts to enhance the quality of delivery of these services. In Tanzania, providing in-school education with youth-friendly health services was associated with long-term improvements in sexual and reproductive health knowledge among females and an increase in reported condom use during their most recent sexual activity with a partner other than a regular partner (Doyle et al. 2010). In Kenya, a culturally consistent package of activities, including community-based education for youth and parents, advocacy, and subsidized clinical services, led to considerable changes in young people's knowledge and behavior related to sexual and reproductive health (Erulkar et al. 2004). Adolescent girls were also significantly more likely to either abstain from sex or have fewer than three sex partners. A quasi-experimental evaluation of the multicomponent African Youth Alliance program in Ghana, Tanzania, and Uganda finds positive results in terms of sexual and reproductive health knowledge and—especially among young women—an increase in contraceptive use and a decrease in the number of sexual partners (Williams et al. 2007). Additionally, a quasi-experimental evaluation of South Africa's National Adolescent Friendly Clinic Initiative finds that access to youth-friendly clinics delayed pregnancy and increased education (Branson and Byker 2018). In Cameroon, an intervention that provided adolescent girls and young women with personal digital counseling on modern contraceptive methods increased adoption of long-acting reversible contraceptives without compromising the girls' and women's use of short-acting methods, indicating that technology and individualized advice can be effective at improving sexual and reproductive health outcomes (Athey et al. 2023).

Altogether, integrating youth-friendly adaptations into the delivery of health services is important for ensuring that adolescent girls have adequate access to health services (especially those relating to their sexual and reproductive health). Increases in access to skilled birth attendants and in institutional births in Africa (UNICEF 2024) have likely had a positive impact on the well-being of adolescent mothers. However, adolescent girls risk falling through the cracks of health care systems in the absence of an intentional focus on addressing their unique circumstances. Factors such as regulations regarding consent to use health services and attitudes of health care providers toward adolescent girls seeking care are critical to consider (Bergstrom and Özler 2023). Sexual and reproductive health education can increase girls' level of knowledge in this area.

An emerging body of evidence[3] suggests that sex and HIV education programs can increase sexual and reproductive health knowledge, but that effectiveness is highly sensitive to intervention design and implementation. For instance, a review of school-based HIV education programs for African youth suggests that the introduction of condoms as a preventive measure is most effective among older youth, especially when teachers are not the primary program implementers and when there is clear community support (Gallant and Maticka-Tyndale 2004). Moreover, Dupas (2011) finds that providing information on the relative risk of HIV infection based on partner age is more effective at reducing risky sexual behavior among adolescent girls than the official abstinence-only HIV curriculum in Kenya. The HIV risk information leads not just to better sexual and reproductive health knowledge, but also to a decrease in teen pregnancy.

There is also evidence regarding the potential of peer-led interventions at the school and community level. A recent global review finds that school-based peer-led interventions can improve sexual and reproductive health knowledge and attitudes (Mason-Jones et al. 2023). However, peers need to be meaningfully engaged and recognized as experts with real-life experience for these interventions to work effectively. In contrast with school-based interventions, community-focused peer-based[4] interventions are premised on the role of community support and shared affinity and have the added benefit of reaching out-of-school adolescents. Impact evidence from Africa is scarce, except for that obtained from quasi-experimental evaluations in Ghana and Nigeria showing that peer education can measurably enhance reproductive health knowledge among youth in secondary schools (Brieger et al. 2001). Although evidence from Africa is still nascent, there is a sufficient global knowledge base to enable those responsible for implementing education interventions to determine what factors are essential to ensure they are effective.

Other Promising Approaches Are Emerging as Possible Solutions

School Construction May Boost Both Enrollment and Attendance

In areas where few schools exist, creating new schools can increase enrollment and attendance. Although the evidence base for Africa remains thin, research on girl-friendly schools in Burkina Faso and Niger is encouraging. In both countries, the construction of primary schools with latrines in rural areas, when combined with other complementary measures (for example, hiring of more female teachers and provision of school supplies) improved enrollment, attendance, and learning outcomes (Bagby et al. 2016; Kazianga et al. 2013). In the Burkina Faso study, the impacts were consistently greater among girls than among boys, eliminating gender gaps in test scores and grade progression (Kazianga et al. 2013). Moreover, earlier quasi-experimental evidence from Nigeria shows that primary school construction in the 1970s significantly boosted female educational achievement and lowered early fertility rates (Osili and Long 2008).

Edutainment May Help Girls Achieve Educational and Developmental Objectives

"Edutainment," also known as educational entertainment, uses content from various forms of media such as video, music, or games to achieve educational and developmental objectives. There is limited, yet promising, evidence regarding the effects of edutainment on girls' health and fertility outcomes. For instance, Banerjee, La Ferrara, and Orozco-Olvera (2019) find that MTV Shuga, a popular serial aiming to provide information on HIV and change attitudes and behaviors related to HIV and risky behaviors, led to significant improvements in young people's knowledge and attitudes toward HIV and risky sexual behavior—measured by the acceptability and reported incidence of concurrent sexual partnerships, as well as the likelihood of testing positive for sexually transmitted diseases—in urban Nigeria. Although the evidence is still limited for the African context, a growing body of research from both high-income and middle- to low-income countries suggests that edutainment may be a cost-effective tool for reducing risky sexual behaviors among young people (Orozco-Olvera, Shen, and Cluver 2019).

Allowing Pregnant Girls to Remain in School May Reduce Dropout Rates and Improve Outcomes

Instituting policies that allow adolescent girls to return to school after giving birth enhances their education outcomes without the negative consequences sometimes feared. Policies that prevent young mothers from returning to school, often as a result of the belief that allowing them to return could encourage more adolescent pregnancies, contribute to high dropout rates among adolescent girls. However, Evans, Mendez Acosta, and Yuan (2024) examine data from nine African countries that lifted bans on pregnant girls returning to school between 1993 and 2015 and find no evidence that allowing young mothers to attend school increases fertility rates. Instead, their findings suggest that such policies improve the human capital of these girls. The policy reform also leads to an increase in the proportion of girls who have been pregnant and are attending school. Although introduction of school reentry policies requires creation of adequate awareness among girls and families about the policy change, the recent introduction of such policies in these African countries signals a promising shift in the right direction.

Eliminating Child Marriage May Improve Education Outcomes for Girls

As discussed in box 3.2, banning child marriage can reduce child marriage and generate positive effects on school enrollment in some contexts (Wilson 2022). However, the effects of child marriage bans depend on the extent of enforcement and on the adoption of complementary interventions to address countervailing social norms. Establishing supportive frameworks to strengthen the implementation of legal reforms is therefore crucial to the success of child marriage.

Other Policies Promoting Girls' Education Also Show Promise

Additional policies that show promise include the introduction of instruction conducted in girls' mother tongue, which led to a significant increase in primary and secondary attainment for girls in Ethiopia (Argaw 2016). In Uganda, an automatic promotion policy, allowing students to progress from one class to the next irrespective of their academic performance, that included remedial classes for academically weak students was also effective at improving literacy and numeracy for both girls and boys (Okurut 2015). Single-sex education has also been demonstrated to have positive impacts on adolescent girls' education outcomes in Trinidad and Tobago, improving exam performance and increasing the likelihood that female students took advanced courses (Jackson 2021). Evidence obtained by using random variation in peer composition in Ethiopian schools indicates that having a greater share of female classmates reduces school absenteeism and increases math test scores among girls (Borbely, Norris, and Romiti 2023). Finally, a policy reform in Kenya that gave daughters inheritance rights equal to those of sons led to increases in girls' schooling along with delays in marriage and childbearing (Harari 2019).

Increasing Employment Opportunities for Women Can Boost Girls' Human Capital Fundamentals

Despite a lack of evidence from Africa, studies of the effects of garment factories in Bangladesh (Heath and Mobarak 2015) and of business centers in India (Jensen 2012; Oster and Steinberg 2013) suggest that increased labor market opportunities for women can spark improvements in human capital fundamentals for adolescent girls, particularly when girls and their families are well informed about these employment opportunities.

Information on Returns to Education or Training May Increase Girls' Enrollment and Improve Their Academic Performance

Providing adolescent girls and their families with information on returns to schooling can boost girls' school enrollment and performance. Although there is limited evidence from Africa—with positive effects on school enrollment documented only in one study in Madagascar (Nguyen 2008)—additional evidence from other regions points to providing this information as a potentially low-cost approach to improve education outcomes. Notably, the range of effects estimated in global studies suggests that impacts may be context specific, with one study in Mexico finding larger effects for girls than boys (Avitabile and de Hoyos 2018) and two other studies documenting effects on boys in the Dominican Republic (Jensen 2010) and Peru (Neilson, Gallego, and Molina 2015).

Engaging Boys, Parents, and Communities in the Quest May Lead to Better Health Outcomes for Girls

Beyond working with girls directly, engaging boys, parents, and communities can have positive impacts on adolescent girls' health outcomes. In Tanzania, a soccer-based curriculum that offered sexual and reproductive health education to male partners of adolescent girls improved male attitudes regarding sexual and reproductive health and violence and improved adolescent girls' sexual and reproductive health outcomes (Shah et al. 2023). In Côte d'Ivoire, combining a girls' group intervention with an intervention focused on equipping boys and men with life skills, sexual and reproductive health knowledge, and information on girls' and women's rights improved girls' sexual and reproductive health behavior and knowledge (Boulhane et al. 2024). Additional evidence from India demonstrates the positive effects of engaging male and female peers in discussions about gender equality (Dhar, Jain, and Jayachandran 2022).

Insights from Interventions with Mixed Impacts Point to Potential Areas for Further Exploration

Girls' Group Empowerment Programs Offer a Promising Way to Reach Adolescent Girls, but Results Have Been Mixed

Girls' empowerment clubs, or "safe spaces," are increasingly being adopted as platforms to reach adolescent girls, especially those out of school. The evidence on their impact on human capital outcomes such as education and health is, however, mixed (Psaki et al. 2022).

Training in Life Skills and Mentoring and Empowerment Programs Show Mixed Results

Beyond group-based empowerment programs, interventions designed to provide adolescent girls with life skills have mixed effects on education outcomes. In Zambia, a program focused on equipping adolescent girls with negotiation skills increased school enrollment (Ashraf et al. 2020). However, Melnikas et al. (2021) find that the Marriage: No Child's Play project implemented by the More than Brides Alliance had positive effects on school enrollment and learning outcomes in Malawi, no effects on either in Mali, and negative effects on both in Niger. Additionally, Brar et al. (2023) find that the Choices program (designed to promote equitable gender attitudes and behaviors among adolescents through interactive activities) had limited effects on school enrollment in Somalia.

Additional Interventions Should Be Considered for Future Directions

The evidence review presented here has highlighted a number of interventions to develop adolescent girls' human capital fundamentals. Although these interventions have been identified as either effective or promising based on evidence from multiple studies and countries, their applicability remains highly context specific. Choices of strategies to be pursued should be based on local constraints and challenges. For example, school construction should be accorded priority in areas where schools are scarce. In the same vein, school feeding programs should be given priority where child malnutrition is identified as a binding constraint. Evidence-based interventions adapted to local contexts are most likely to achieve the intended impacts.

Beyond overall evidence on effectiveness, it is critical also to consider cost-effectiveness, as well as cost-effectiveness at scale (Crawfurd, Hares, and Sandefur 2022; Evans, Mendez Acosta, and Yuan 2024). Although there is a growing set of cost-effectiveness estimates for interventions to improve education, these estimates typically focus on a single outcome, without accounting for the fact that some interventions are effective at improving multiple outcomes and thus might be more cost-effective overall, even if they are less cost-effective when a single outcome is considered. One example is school feeding, which affects both education and nutrition outcomes (Bedasso 2022). A recent evidence review concludes that the most cost-effective way to improve learning outcomes is through remedial education (Banerjee et al. 2023). Limited cost-effectiveness estimates exist regarding interventions to improve adolescent girls' health.

Restricting the analysis of available evidence to African countries reflects key takeaway findings on intervention effectiveness, while also revealing areas in which further experimentation is needed. More research is needed to determine the effectiveness of interventions that either have been proven to work in other parts of the world or have had limited or mixed results in Africa. This is particularly salient in regard to adolescent health outcomes, especially those related to nutrition and mental health, which have garnered increased focus globally but remain understudied in African countries.

Notes

1. The program included detailed teachers' guides, training for teachers and head teachers, teacher coaching, and literacy and math books for every student.
2. In Lesotho, girls benefited significantly more than boys, maintaining their relatively higher rates of school enrollment and attendance (Pellerano et al. 2014). A potential explanation is that the current opportunity cost of boys' time is perceived as being higher than the future benefit of human capital accumulation and that this difference for boys exceeds that for girls. In South Africa, the girls' relative advantage in terms of school outcomes is used to explain the more muted impact of cash transfers. Whereas access to social pensions leads to an 18 percentage point increase in schooling attendance for boys, it is associated with a small, non-statistically-significant increase for girls (Edmonds 2006).
3. Quality evidence from Africa remains limited, however (Lopez, Bernholc, et al. 2016; Lopez, Grey, et al. 2016).
4. Also referred to as peer education, peer counseling, and peer-led, peer-driven, peer-facilitated, or peer-assisted interventions.

References

Akresh, Richard, Damien de Walque, and Harounan Kazianga. 2013. "Cash Transfers and Child Schooling: Evidence from a Randomized Evaluation of the Role of Conditionality." World Bank Policy Research Working Paper 6340, World Bank, Washington, DC.

Alderman, Harold, Daniel O. Gilligan, and Kim Lehrer. 2012. "The Impact of Food for Education Programs on School Participation in Northern Uganda." *Economic Development and Cultural Change* 61 (1): 187–218. https://doi.org/10.1086/666949.

Arcand, Jean-Louis, and Eric Djimeu Wouabe. 2010. "Teacher Training and HIV/ AIDS Prevention in West Africa: Regression Discontinuity Design Evidence from the Cameroon." *Health Economics* 19 (S1): 36–54. https://doi.org/10.1002/hec.1643.

Argaw, Bethlehem Asres. 2016. "Quasi-Experimental Evidence on the Effects of Mother Tongue-Based Education on Reading Skills and Early Labour Market Outcomes." Discussion Paper 16-016, ZEW—Centre for European Economic Research, Mannheim, Germany. http://dx.doi.org/10.2139/ssrn.2760337.

Ashraf, Nava, Natalie Bau, Corinne Low, and Kathleen McGinn. 2020. "Negotiating a Better Future: How Interpersonal Skills Facilitate Intergenerational Investment." *Quarterly Journal of Economics* 135 (2): 1095–151. https://doi.org/10.1093/qje/qjz039.

Athey, Susan, Katy Bergstrom, Vitor Hadad, Julian C. Jamison, Berk Özler, Luca Parisotto, and Julius Dohbit Sama. 2023. "Can Personalized Digital Counseling Improve Consumer Search for Modern Contraceptive Methods?" *Science Advances* 9 (40): eadg4420. https://doi.org/10.1126/sciadv.adg4420.

Aurino, Elisabetta, Aulo Gelli, Clement Adamba, Isaac Osei-Akoto, and Harold Alderman. 2023. "Food for Thought?: Experimental Evidence on the Learning Impacts of a Large-Scale School Feeding Program." *Journal of Human Resources* 58 (1): 74–111. https://doi.org/10.3368/jhr.58.3.1019-10515R1.

Avitabile, Ciro, and Rafael de Hoyos. 2018. "The Heterogeneous Effect of Information on Student Performance: Evidence from a Randomized Control Trial in Mexico." *Journal of Development Economics* 135: 318–48. https://doi.org/10.1016/j .jdeveco.2018.07.008.

Bagby, Emilie, Anca Dumitrescu, Cara Orfield, and Matt Sloan. 2016. "Long-Term Evaluation of the IMAGINE Project in Niger." Mathematica Policy Research, Washington, DC. https://ideas.repec.org//p/mpr/mprres/f8404bbfd4eb4276a 7925d3004a16bf7.html.

Baird, Sarah, Ephraim Chirwa, Craig McIntosh, and Berk Özler. 2010. "The Short-Term Impacts of a Schooling Conditional Cash Transfer Program on the Sexual Behavior of Young Women." *Health Economics* 19 (S): 55–68. https://doi.org /10.1002/hec.1569.

Baird, Sarah, Craig McIntosh, and Berk Özler. 2011. "Cash or Condition? Evidence from a Cash Transfer Experiment." *Quarterly Journal of Economics* 126 (4): 1709–53. https://doi.org/10.1093/qje/qjr032.

Baird, Sarah, Craig McIntosh, and Berk Özler. 2019. "When the Money Runs Out: Do Cash Transfers Have Sustained Effects on Human Capital Accumulation?" *Journal of Development Economics* 140: 169–85. https://doi.org/10.1016/j.jdeveco.2019.04.004.

Bandiera, Oriana, Niklas Buehren, Robin Burgess, Markus Goldstein, Selim Gulesci, Imran Rasul, and Munshi Sulaiman. 2020. "Women's Empowerment in Action: Evidence from a Randomized Control Trial in Africa." *American Economic Journal: Applied Economics* 12 (1): 210–59. https://doi.org/10.1257/app.20170416.

Banerjee, Abhijit, Tahir Andrab, Rukmini Banerji, Susan Dynarski, Rachel Glennerster, Sally Grantham-Mcgregor, Karthik Muralidharan, et al. 2023. *2023 Cost-Effective Approaches to Improve Global Learning—What Does Recent Evidence Tell Us Are "Smart Buys" for Improving Learning in Low- and Middle-Income Countries?* Washington, DC: World Bank. https://policycommons.net/artifacts/4310772/2023-cost-effective-approaches-to-improve-global-learning/5121024/.

Banerjee, Abhijit, Eliana La Ferrara, and Victor H. Orozco-Olvera. 2019. "The Entertaining Way to Behavioral Change: Fighting HIV with MTV." Working Paper 26096, National Bureau of Economic Research, Cambridge, MA. https://doi.org/10.3386/w26096.

Barrera-Osorio, Felipe, Pierre de Galbert, James Habyarimana, and Shwetlena Sabarwal. 2020. "The Impact of Public-Private Partnerships on Private School Performance: Evidence from a Randomized Controlled Trial in Uganda." *Economic Development and Cultural Change* 68 (2): 429–69. https://doi.org/10.1086/701229.

Bastagli, Francesca, Jessica Hagen-Zanker, Luke Harman, Valentina Barca, Georgina Sturge, and Tanja Schmidt. 2016. "Cash Transfers: What Does the Evidence Say?" Overseas Development Institute, London.

Beasley, N. M. R., A. M. Tomkins, A. Hall, W. Lorri, C. M. Kihamia, and D. A. P. Bundy. 2000. "The Impact of Weekly Iron Supplementation on the Iron Status and Growth of Adolescent Girls in Tanzania." *Tropical Medicine and International Health* 5 (11): 794–99. https://doi.org/10.1046/j.1365-3156.2000.00641.x.

Bedasso, Biniam. 2022. "Feeding Kids May Look Expensive by Standard Value-for-Money Metrics, but It Promotes Equity in Outcomes beyond Just Test Scores." In *Schooling for All Feasible Strategies to Achieve Universal Education*, edited by Justin Sandefur, 36–48. Washington, DC: Center for Global Development.

Bergstrom, Katy, and Berk Özler. 2023. "Improving the Well-Being of Adolescent Girls in Developing Countries." *World Bank Research Observer* 38 (2): 179–212. https://doi.org/10.1093/wbro/lkac007.

Borbely, Daniel, Jonathan Norris, and Agnese Romiti. 2023. "Peer Gender and Schooling: Evidence from Ethiopia." *Journal of Human Capital* 17 (2): 207–49. https://doi.org/10.1086/723111.

Boulhane, Othmane, Claire Boxho, Désiré Kanga, Estelle Koussoubé, and Léa Rouanet. 2024. "Empowering Adolescent Girls through Safe Spaces and Accompanying Measures in Côte d'Ivoire." Policy Research Working Paper 10721, World Bank, Washington, DC.

Branson, Nicola, and Tanya Byker. 2018. "Causes and Consequences of Teen Childbearing: Evidence from a Reproductive Health Intervention in South Africa." *Journal of Health Economics* 57: 221–35. https://doi.org/10.1016/j.jhealeco.2017.11.006.

Brar, Rajdev, Niklas Buehren, Sreelakshmi Papineni, and Munshi Sulaiman. 2023. "Rebel with a Cause: Effects of a Gender Norms Intervention for Adolescents in

Somalia." Policy Research Working Paper 10567, World Bank, Washington, DC. https://doi.org/10.1596/1813-9450-10567.

Brieger, William R, Grace E. Delano, Catherine G. Lane, Oladimeji Oladepo, and Kola A. Oyediran. 2001. "West African Youth Initiative: Outcome of a Reproductive Health Education Program." *Journal of Adolescent Health* 29 (6): 436–46. https://doi .org/10.1016/S1054-139X(01)00264-6.

Cawley, John. 2015. "An Economy of Scales: A Selective Review of Obesity's Economic Causes, Consequences, and Solutions." *Journal of Health Economics* 43 (September): 244–68. https://doi.org/10.1016/j.jhealeco.2015.03.001.

Chaaban, Jad, and Wendy Cunningham. 2011. "Measuring the Economic Gain of Investing in Girls: The Girl Effect Dividend." Policy Research Working Paper 5753, World Bank, Washington, DC. https://doi.org/10.1596/1813-9450-5753.

Chakroborty, Kritika Sen, and Kira M. Villa. 2022. "Cash Transfers and Adolescent Nutrition Outcomes: Evidence from the Child Support Grant in South Africa." Unpublished manuscript.

Chicoine, Luke. 2016. "Free Primary Education, Schooling, and Fertility: Evidence from Ethiopia." IZA Discussion Paper 10387, IZA Institute of Labor Economics, Bonn, Germany. https://papers.ssrn.com/abstract=2879794.

Collin, Matthew, and Theodore Talbot. 2023. "Are Age-of-Marriage Laws Enforced? Evidence from Developing Countries." *Journal of Development Economics* 160 (January): 102950. https://doi.org/10.1016/j.jdeveco.2022.102950.

Costa, R., A. Kalle, D. Lopez Avila, M. Magalhaes, M. Muller, and E. Salazar. 2023. "What Works to Narrow Gender Gaps and Empower Women in Sub-Saharan Africa? An Evidence-Review of Selected Impact Evaluation Studies." World Bank, Washington, DC.

Crawfurd, Lee, Susannah Hares, and Justin Sandefur. 2022. "What Has Worked at Scale?" In *Schooling for All Feasible Strategies to Achieve Universal Education*, edited by Justin Sandefur, 11–31. Washington, DC: Center for Global Development.

Dake, Fidelia, Luisa Natali, Gustavo Angeles, Jacobus de Hoop, Sudhanshu Handa, and Amber Peterman. 2018. "Cash Transfers, Early Marriage, and Fertility in Malawi and Zambia." *Studies in Family Planning* 49 (4): 295–317. https://doi.org/10.1111/sifp .12073.

Delprato, Marcos, and Kwame Akyeampong. 2017. "The Effect of Early Marriage Timing on Women's and Children's Health in Sub-Saharan Africa and Southwest Asia." *Annals of Global Health* 83 (3): 557–67. https://doi.org/10.1016/j .aogh.2017.10.005.

Delprato, Marcos, Kwame Akyeampong, Ricardo Sabates, and Jimena Hernandez-Fernandez. 2015. "On the Impact of Early Marriage on Schooling Outcomes in Sub-Saharan Africa and South West Asia." *International Journal of Educational Development* 44 (September): 42–55. https://doi.org/10.1016/j.ijedudev.2015.06.001.

Dhar, Diva, Tarun Jain, and Seema Jayachandran. 2022. "Reshaping Adolescents' Gender Attitudes: Evidence from a School-Based Experiment in India." *American Economic Review* 112 (3): 899–927. https://doi.org/10.1257/aer.20201112.

Doyle, Aoife M., David A. Ross, Kaballa Maganja, Kathy Baisley, Clemens Masesa, Aura Andreasen, Mary L. Plummer, et al. 2010. "Long-Term Biological and Behavioural Impact of an Adolescent Sexual Health Intervention in Tanzania:

Follow-Up Survey of the Community-Based MEMA Kwa Vijana Trial." *PLOS Medicine* 7 (6): e1000287. https://doi.org/10.1371/journal.pmed.1000287.

Duflo, Annie, Jessica Kiessel, and Adrienne Lucas. 2020. "External Validity: Four Models of Improving Student Achievement." Working Paper 27298, National Bureau of Economic Research, Cambridge, MA.

Duflo, Esther, Pascaline Dupas, and Michael Kremer. 2015. "Education, HIV, and Early Fertility: Experimental Evidence from Kenya." *American Economic Review* 105 (9): 2757–97. https://doi.org/10.1257/aer.20121607.

Duflo, Esther, Pascaline Dupas, and Michael Kremer. 2021. "The Impact of Free Secondary Education: Experimental Evidence from Ghana." Working Paper 28937, National Bureau of Economic Research, Cambridge, MA. https://doi.org/10.3386/w28937.

Dupas, Pascaline. 2011. "Do Teenagers Respond to HIV Risk Information? Evidence from a Field Experiment in Kenya." *American Economic Journal: Applied Economics* 3 (1): 1–34. https://doi.org/10.1257/app.3.1.1.

Dupas, Pascaline, Elise Huillery, and Juliette Seban. 2018. "Risk Information, Risk Salience, and Adolescent Sexual Behavior: Experimental Evidence from Cameroon." *Journal of Economic Behavior and Organization* 145 (January): 151–75. https://doi.org/10.1016/j.jebo.2017.10.007.

Edmonds, Eric V. 2006. "Child Labor and Schooling Responses to Anticipated Income in South Africa." *Journal of Development Economics* 81 (2): 386–414. https://doi.org/10.1016/j.jdeveco.2005.05.001.

Edwards, Katie M., Manasi Kumar, Emily A. Waterman, Natira Mullet, Beatrice Madeghe, and Otsetswe Musindo. 2024. "Programs to Prevent Violence against Children in Sub-Saharan Africa: A Systematic Review." *Trauma, Violence, and Abuse* 25 (1): 593–612. https://doi.org/10.1177/15248380231160742.

Erulkar, Annabel S., Linus I. A. Ettyang, Charles Onoka, Fredrick K. Nyagah, and Alex Muyonga. 2004. "Behavior Change Evaluation of a Culturally Consistent Reproductive Health Program for Young Kenyans." *International Family Planning Perspectives* 30 (2): 58–67.

Erulkar, Annabel S., and Eunice Muthengi. 2009. "Evaluation of Berhane Hewan: A Program to Delay Child Marriage in Rural Ethiopia." *International Perspectives on Sexual and Reproductive Health* 35 (1): 6–14. https://www.guttmacher.org/journals/ipsrh/2009/03/evaluation-berhane-hewan-program-delay-child-marriage-rural-ethiopia.

Evans, David, Stephanie Hausladen, Katrina Kosec, and Natasha Reese. 2014. *Community-Based Conditional Cash Transfers in Tanzania: Results from a Randomized Trial*. Washington, DC: World Bank.

Evans, David, Amina Mendez Acosta, and Fei Yuan. 2024. "Girls' Education at Scale." *World Bank Research Observer* 39 (1): 47–74. https://doi.org/10.1093/wbro/lkad002.

Evans, David, and Fei Yuan. 2022. "What We Learn about Girls' Education from Interventions That Do Not Focus on Girls." *World Bank Economic Review* 36 (1): 244–67.

Fiala, Nathan, Ana Garcia-Hernandez, Kritika Narula, and Nishith Prakash. 2022. "Wheels of Change: Transforming Girls' Lives with Bicycles." CESifo Working Paper 9865, Munich.

Freudenberger, Elizabeth, and Jeff Davis. 2017. "Tusome External Evaluation Midline Report." U.S. Agency for International Development, Washington, DC. https://ierc-publicfiles.s3.amazonaws.com/public/resources/Tusome%20Midline%20evaluation%202017%20final%20report%20from%20DEC.pdf.

Gallant, Melanie, and Eleanor Maticka-Tyndale. 2004. "School-Based HIV Prevention Programmes for African Youth." *Social Science and Medicine* 58 (7): 1337–51. https://doi.org/10.1016/S0277-9536(03)00331-9.

Grogan, Louise. 2009. "Universal Primary Education and School Entry in Uganda." *Journal of African Economies* 18 (2): 183–211. https://doi.org/10.1093/jae/ejn015.

Hall, Andrew, Natalie Roschnik, Fatimata Ouattara, Idrissa Touré, Fadima Maiga, Moussa Sacko, Helen Moestue, and Mohamed Ag Bendech. 2002. "A Randomised Trial in Mali of the Effectiveness of Weekly Iron Supplements Given by Teachers on the Haemoglobin Concentrations of Schoolchildren." *Public Health Nutrition* 5 (3): 413–18. https://doi.org/10.1079/PHN2001327.

Hallfors, Denise Dion, Hyunsan Cho, Simbarashe Rusakaniko, John Mapfumo, Bonita Iritani, Lei Zhang, Winnie Luseno, and Ted Miller. 2015. "The Impact of School Subsidies on HIV-Related Outcomes among Adolescent Female Orphans." *Journal of Adolescent Health* 56 (1): 79–84. https://doi.org/10.1016/j.jadohealth.2014.09.004.

Handa, Sudhanshu, Amber Peterman, Carolyn Huang, Carolyn Halpern, Audrey Pettifor, and Harsha Thirumurthy. 2015. "Impact of the Kenya Cash Transfer for Orphans and Vulnerable Children on Early Pregnancy and Marriage of Adolescent Girls." *Social Science and Medicine* 141 (September): 36–45. https://doi.org/10.1016/j.socscimed.2015.07.024.

Harari, Mariaflavia. 2019. "Women's Inheritance Rights and Bargaining Power: Evidence from Kenya." *Economic Development and Cultural Change* 68 (1): 189–238. https://doi.org/10.1086/700630.

Heath, Rachel, and A. Mushfiq Mobarak. 2015. "Manufacturing Growth and the Lives of Bangladeshi Women." *Journal of Development Economics* 115 (July): 1–15. https://doi.org/10.1016/j.jdeveco.2015.01.006.

Hoogeveen, Johannes, and Mariacristina Rossi. 2013. "Enrolment and Grade Attainment Following the Introduction of Free Primary Education in Tanzania." *Journal of African Economies* 22 (3): 375–93. https://doi.org/10.1093/jae/ejt003.

Horjus, Peter, Victor M. Aguayo, Julie A. Roley, Maurício C. Pene, and Stephan P. Meershoek. 2005. "School-Based Iron and Folic Acid Supplementation for Adolescent Girls: Findings from Manica Province, Mozambique." *Food and Nutrition Bulletin* 26 (3): 281–86. https://doi.org/10.1177/156482650502600305.

Jackson, C. Kirabo. 2021. "Can Introducing Single-Sex Education into Low-Performing Schools Improve Academics, Arrests, and Teen Motherhood?" *Journal of Human Resources* 56 (1): 1–39. https://doi.org/10.3368/jhr.56.1.0618-9558R2.

Jensen, Robert. 2010. "The (Perceived) Returns to Education and the Demand for Schooling." *Quarterly Journal of Economics* 125 (2): 515–48. https://doi.org/10.1162/qjec.2010.125.2.515.

Jensen, Robert. 2012. "Do Labor Market Opportunities Affect Young Women's Work and Family Decisions? Experimental Evidence from India." *Quarterly Journal of Economics* 127 (2): 753–92. https://doi.org/10.1093/qje/qjs002.

JPAL (Abdul Latif Jameel Poverty Action Lab). 2017. "Roll Call: Getting Children into School." JPAL, Cambridge, MA.

Kazianga, Harounan, Damien de Walque, and Harold Alderman. 2012. "Educational and Child Labour Impacts of Two Food-for-Education Schemes: Evidence from a Randomised Trial in Rural Burkina Faso." *Journal of African Economies* 21 (5): 723–60. https://doi.org/10.1093/jae/ejs010.

Kazianga, Harounan, Dan Levy, Leigh L. Linden, and Matt Sloan. 2013. "The Effects of 'Girl-Friendly' Schools: Evidence from the BRIGHT School Construction Program in Burkina Faso." *American Economic Journal: Applied Economics* 5 (3): 41–62. https://doi.org/10.1257/app.5.3.41.

Koski, Alissa, Erin C. Strumpf, Jay S. Kaufman, John Frank, Jody Heymann, and Arijit Nandi. 2018. "The Impact of Eliminating Primary School Tuition Fees on Child Marriage in Sub-Saharan Africa: A Quasi-Experimental Evaluation of Policy Changes in 8 Countries." *PLOS ONE* 13 (5): e0197928. https://doi.org/10.1371PLOS/journal.pone.0197928.

Lassi, Zohra, Anoosh Moin, and Zulfiqar Bhutta. 2017. "Nutrition in Middle Childhood and Adolescence." In *Child and Adolescent Health and Development*, edited by Donald A. P. Bundy, Nilanthi de Silva, Susan Horton, Dean T. Jamison, and George C. Patton, 133–46. Vol. 8 of *Disease Control Priorities*. Washington, DC: World Bank. https://doi.org/10.1596/978-1-4648-0423-6.

Leenstra, T., S. K. Kariuki, J. D. Kurtis, A. J. Oloo, P. A. Kager, and F. O. ter Kuile. 2009. "The Effect of Weekly Iron and Vitamin A Supplementation on Hemoglobin Levels and Iron Status in Adolescent Schoolgirls in Western Kenya." *European Journal of Clinical Nutrition* 63 (2): 173–82. https://doi.org/10.1038/sj.ejcn.1602919.

Lopez, Laureen M., Alissa Bernholc, Mario Chen, and Elizabeth E. Tolley. 2016. "School-Based Interventions for Improving Contraceptive Use in Adolescents." *Cochrane Database of Systematic Reviews* 2016 (6): CD012249. https://doi.org/10.1002/14651858.CD012249.

Lopez, Laureen M., Thomas W. Grey, Elizabeth E. Tolley, and Mario Chen. 2016. "Brief Educational Strategies for Improving Contraception Use in Young People." *Cochrane Database of Systematic Reviews* 2016 (3): CD012025. https://doi.org/10.1002/14651858.CD012025.pub2.

Malhotra, Anju, and Shatha Elnakib. 2021. "20 Years of the Evidence Base on What Works to Prevent Child Marriage: A Systematic Review." *Journal of Adolescent Health* 68 (5): 847–62. https://doi.org/10.1016/j.jadohealth.2020.11.017.

Mason-Jones, Amanda J., Marlon Freeman, Theo Lorenc, Tina Rawal, Shalini Bassi, and Monika Arora. 2023. "Can Peer-Based Interventions Improve Adolescent Sexual and Reproductive Health Outcomes? An Overview of Reviews." *Journal of Adolescent Health* 73 (6): 975–82. https://doi.org/10.1016/j.jadohealth.2023.05.035.

Mastercard Foundation. 2020. *Secondary Education in Africa: Preparing Youth for the Future of Work.* Toronto: Mastercard Foundation. https://doi.org/10.15868/socialsector.35972.

Mbiti, Isaac, Karthik Muralidharan, Mauricio Romero, Youdi Schipper, Constantine Manda, and Rakesh Rajani. 2019. "Inputs, Incentives, and Complementarities in

Education: Experimental Evidence from Tanzania." *Quarterly Journal of Economics* 134 (3): 1627–73. https://doi.org/10.1093/qje/qjz010.

McGavock, Tamara. 2021. "Here Waits the Bride? The Effect of Ethiopia's Child Marriage Law." *Journal of Development Economics* 149 (March): 102580. https://doi .org/10.1016/j.jdeveco.2020.102580.

Meherali, Salima, Komal Abdul Rahim, Sandra Campbell, and Zohra S. Lassi. 2021. "Does Digital Literacy Empower Adolescent Girls in Low- and Middle-Income Countries: A Systematic Review." Frontiers in Public Health 9. https://doi .org/10.3389/fpubh.2021.761394.

Melnikas, Andrea J., Grace Saul, Michelle Chau, Neelanjana Pandey, James Mkandawire, Mouhamadou Gueye, Aissa Diarra, and Sajeda Amin. 2021. "More Than Brides Alliance: Endline Evaluation Report." Population Council, New York.

Muralidharan, Karthik, and Nishith Prakash. 2017. "Cycling to School: Increasing Secondary School Enrollment for Girls in India." *American Economic Journal: Applied Economics* 9 (3): 321–50. https://doi.org/10.1257/app.20160004.

Neilson, Christopher, Francisco Gallego, and Oswaldo Molina. 2015. "The Impact of Information Provision on Human Capital Accumulation and Child Labor in Peru." Innovations for Poverty Action, New York. https://www.poverty-action.org /printpdf/21321.

Nguyen, Minh Cong, and Quentin Wodon. 2014. "Impact of Child Marriage on Literacy and Education Attainment in Africa." World Bank, Washington, DC.

Nguyen, Trang. 2008. "Information, Role Models and Perceived Returns to Education: Experimental Evidence from Madagascar." Unpublished manuscript. Massachusetts Institute of Technology, Cambridge, MA. https://www.povertyactionlab.org/sites /default/files/documents/Nguyen%202008.pdf.

Nour, Nawal M. 2006. "Health Consequences of Child Marriage in Africa." *Emerging Infectious Diseases* 12 (11): 1644–49. https://doi.org/10.3201/eid1211.060510.

Okurut, Jeje Moses. 2015. "Examining the Effect of Automatic Promotion on Students' Learning Achievements in Uganda's Primary Education." *World Journal of Education* 5 (5): 85–100.

Orozco-Olvera, Victor, Fuyuan Shen, and Lucie Cluver. 2019. "The Effectiveness of Using Entertainment Education Narratives to Promote Safer Sexual Behaviors of Youth: A Meta-analysis, 1985–2017." *PLOS ONE* 14 (2): e0209969. https://doi .org/10.1371/journal.pone.0209969.

Osili, Una Okonkwo, and Bridget Terry Long. 2008. "Does Female Schooling Reduce Fertility? Evidence from Nigeria." *Journal of Development Economics* 87 (1): 57–75. https://doi.org/10.1016/j.jdeveco.2007.10.003.

Oster, Emily, and Bryce Millett Steinberg. 2013. "Do IT Service Centers Promote School Enrollment? Evidence from India." *Journal of Development Economics* 104: 123–35.

Pellerano, Luca, Marta Moratti, Maja Jakobsen, Matej Bajgar, and Valentina Barca. 2014. "Child Grants Programme Impact Evaluation: Follow-Up Report." Oxford Policy Management, Oxford, UK.

Piper, Benjamin, Joseph Destefano, Esther M. Kinyanjui, and Salome Ong'ele. 2018. "Scaling Up Successfully: Lessons from Kenya's Tusome National Literacy Program." *Journal of Educational Change* 19 (3): 293–321. https://doi.org/10.1007/s10833 -018-9325-4.

Piper, Benjamin, and Abel Mugenda. 2014. "The Primary Math and Reading (PRIMR) Initiative: Endline Impact Evaluation." US Agency for International Development, Washington, DC. https://pdf.usaid.gov/pdf_docs/PA00K27S.pdf.

Psaki, Stephanie, Nicole Haberland, Barbara Mensch, Lauren Woyczynski, and Erica Chuang. 2022. "Policies and Interventions to Remove Gender-Related Barriers to Girls' School Participation and Learning in Low- and Middle-Income Countries: A Systematic Review of the Evidence." *Campbell Systematic Reviews* 18 (1): e1207. https://doi.org/10.1002/cl2.1207.

Randall, Jennifer, and Alejandra Garcia. 2020. "Let's Go Girls!: Evaluating the Effectiveness of Tutoring and Scholarships on Primary School Girls' Attendance and Academic Performance in the Democratic Republic of the Congo (DRC)." *FIRE: Forum for International Research in Education* 6 (3): 19–35.

Sabates, Ricardo, Pauline Rose, Benjamin Alcott, and Marcos Delprato. 2021. "Assessing Cost-Effectiveness with Equity of a Programme Targeting Marginalised Girls in Secondary Schools in Tanzania." *Journal of Development Effectiveness* 13 (1): 28–46. https://doi.org/10.1080/19439342.2020.1844782.

Sandefur, Justin. 2022. *Schooling for All Feasible Strategies to Achieve Universal Education*. Washington, DC: Center for Global Development.

Shah, Manisha, Jennifer Seager, João Montalvão, and Markus Goldstein. 2023. "Sex, Power, and Adolescence: Intimate Partner Violence and Sexual Behaviors." Working Paper 31624, National Bureau of Economic Research, Cambridge, MA. https://doi .org/10.3386/w31624.

Smarrelli, Gabriella Line Baago-Rasmussen, Susannah Hares, Dipak Naker, and DongYi Wu. 2024. "Violence in Schools: Prevalence, Impact and Interventions." Policy Brief, Center for Global Development, Washington, DC.

UNICEF (United Nations Children's Fund). 2024. "Delivery Care." UNICEF, New York. https://data.unicef.org/topic/maternal-health/delivery-care/.

Wang, Dongqing, Sachin Shinde, Tara Young, and Wafaie W. Fawzi. 2021. "Impacts of School Feeding on Educational and Health Outcomes of School-Age Children and Adolescents in Low- and Middle-Income Countries: A Systematic Review and Meta-analysis." *Journal of Global Health* 11: 04051. https://doi.org/10.7189/jogh .11.04051.

Williams, T., S. Mullen, A. Karim, and J. Posner. 2007. "Evaluation of the African Youth Alliance Program in Ghana, Tanzania, and Uganda: Impact on Sexual and Reproductive Health Behavior among Young People." Summary Report. JSI Research & Training Institute Inc., Rosslyn, VA.

Wilson, Nicholas. 2022. "Child Marriage Bans and Female Schooling and Labor Market Outcomes: Evidence from Natural Experiments in 17 Low- and Middle-Income Countries." *American Economic Journal: Economic Policy* 14 (3): 449–77.

World Bank. 2024. *Women, Business and the Law 2024*. Washington, DC: World Bank. doi:10.1596/978-1-4648-2063-2.

Yount, Kathryn M., Kathleen H. Krause, and Stephanie S. Miedema. 2017. "Preventing Gender-Based Violence Victimization in Adolescent Girls in Lower-Income Countries: Systematic Review of Reviews." *Social Science and Medicine* 192 (November): 1–13. https://doi.org/10.1016/j.socscimed.2017.08.038.

SPOTLIGHT 3

Quality Implementation of Safe Spaces Programs

Karen Austrian and Sara Troiano

Key Messages

- The past decade has witnessed a significant rise in the adoption of the "safe spaces" approach for adolescent girls' programs, supported by a growing evidence base and practical tool kits to guide implementers.
- Safe spaces are commonly discussed as a type of adolescent girls' program yet should be seen instead as a platform through which a range of girls' programs can be delivered.
- There is consensus among implementers on a key set of considerations for successful implementation of safe spaces, including guidance on community outreach, recruiting and supporting mentors, defining content, recruiting girls, group formation, monitoring and evaluation, and scaling up.

The Use of Safe Spaces Programs for Girls Has Grown over the Last 10 Years

Over the past decade, there has been an increasing use of "safe spaces" to refer to a programming approach targeting adolescent girls. In addition to a growing evidence base on the impact of programs using the safe spaces approach, there have also been many guides and tool kits published to guide program implementers (annex S3A). Safe spaces are commonly discussed as a type of adolescent girls' program yet should be seen instead as a platform through which a range of interventions can be delivered. The term "safe spaces" is often used interchangeably with "girls' empowerment clubs," "community-based girls' groups," "girls' groups," "girls' clubs," and similar terms. Safe spaces typically include a group of girls meeting regularly at a designated location and led by a mentor. Beyond that, the content and purpose of the meetings can vary widely, from sexual and reproductive health services to financial education to vocational skills training and more. Therefore, it is important to think of safe spaces as a platform for gathering adolescent girls in a setting where they can participate in a program—this platform allows for program delivery to focus

A reproducibility package is available for this book in the Reproducible Research Repository at https://reproducibility.worldbank.org.

on one or multiple thematic areas. Sometimes, safe spaces are implemented in combination with additional interventions that aim to engage girls' households, schools, and communities.

The evidence reviewed in chapters 3 and 4 underscores the mixed results of safe spaces programs, as a result of differences in programs' design and, most likely, differences in the quality of their implementation. Understanding the critical components of successful implementation is hence an essential companion to ultimately achieving impact with these programs. This spotlight provides a summary of key considerations when implementing safe spaces, based on curated references and consultations with safe spaces program implementers (governments, nongovernmental and civil society organizations, and development partners) representing 18 organizations from 12 countries. Key recommendations or implementation tips are organized along the programs' delivery chain (figure S3.1). The spotlight closes with a reflection on considerations for the scaling up of the safe spaces approach.

FIGURE S3.1 Safe Spaces Programs Should Follow a Specific Delivery Chain

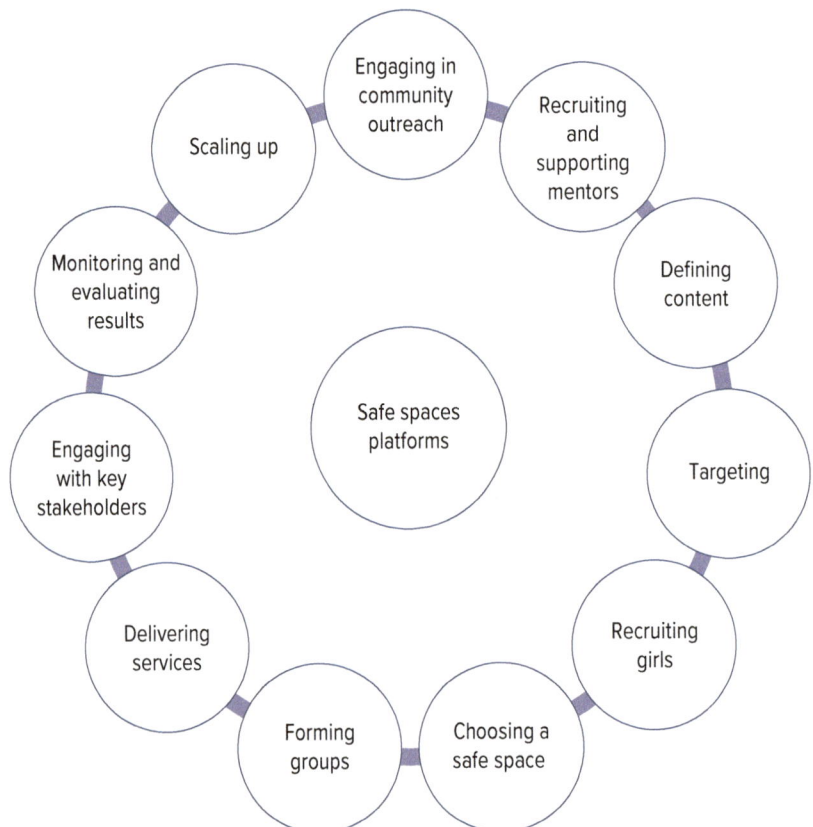

Source. Original figure for this report.

The Successful Delivery of Safe Spaces Programs Involves Critical Steps from Design to Evaluation

1. **Engaging in community outreach.** Involving the surrounding community during program preparation can be a way of building ownership and trust in a program, which helps with its sustainability. Community outreach should highlight the program's benefits to both girls and the community. Useful methods for engaging the community, both at the outreach stage and continuously during implementation, include organizing "family days" (to engage with the households of the program beneficiaries) and celebrations and home visits by program mentors. Implementers can leverage peer networks and influential community members to encourage participation, spread awareness, and engage families to ensure their support and address any concerns they might have regarding the program. For successful outreach, it is important to tailor messaging and outreach approaches to respect local customs, traditions, and sensitivities.

2. **Recruiting and supporting mentors.** Mentors—those facilitating the safe spaces—are critical to the quality of program implementation, as all the content delivered by a program flows through them. Preferred qualifications for mentors depend on context. Implementers share that positive performance has been associated with enrolling mentors who are female, come from the same communities as beneficiaries, speak the local language, and are older than beneficiaries but still close enough in age to be approachable. Preferably mentors have at least some basic literacy and good social and leadership skills, as girls may ultimately identify mentors as role models. Often, programs that remain in a community for a long period of time see girls who were once beneficiaries graduating into the mentor role. It should be kept in mind that mentors are program beneficiaries, too: they need not only up-front training but also ongoing supervision and support through local focal points and peer networks to succeed in their role.[1] Depending on the context, basic tools for mentors may include relevant resources, educational materials, and tools to facilitate discussions and activities within the safe space effectively; rain gear; tablets, mobile phones, and data and connectivity; and transport services (bikes, transport subsidies, or other) as relevant.[2] A stipend (in line with local standards) will motivate mentors, make them more respected by the community, and avert high turnover. Other nonfinancial incentives include prospects of career progression (for instance, through the promotion of best-performing mentors to supervisors) and recognition during public events.

3. **Defining content.** Although a program's curriculum depends on the program's specific objectives and targeted population, mentors', girls', and communities' perspectives should be taken into account as potential topics are assigned priorities. Overall, a balanced mix of topics that aligns with participants' aspirations while addressing key challenges they face should be ensured. Ideally, the curriculum should be tested through a pilot before implementing the program at scale. In general, life skills and basic literacy training is seen as a foundational basis for more "technical" training: information on sexual and reproductive health, human and legal rights, vocational training, financial literacy, savings practices, climate education, and other matters. The sequencing of topics is important: consideration should be given to starting with life skills training, or in general less controversial topics, to build trust among girls and their families and to give mentors time to gain confidence before covering more sensitive topics. Among initial topics, it might be useful to identify social norms and personal attitudes that, if changed as part of the program, could have positive impacts on participants' outcomes. As applicable and within the limits of the international regulations on child labor, activities to support the economic inclusion of older girls (microgrants, links to markets, among others) should be considered. To maximize the impact of safe spaces, it is important to link the content to complementary initiatives and services, referring participants to follow-up interventions to support them in their educational and economic pursuits, in order to leverage other resources in the community and help participants.

4. **Targeting.** Often a program will have to decide between reaching a larger number of girls in a particular community and operating in more communities. Collective experience has shown that change requires working with a critical mass of girls in an area, community, or school because part of the impact of safe spaces programs is that the host communities accept girls meeting regularly in public places, as well as having female leadership in the form of the program mentors. Therefore, this "threshold effect" needs to be considered when a program faces the trade-off between geographical scope and coverage. Reaching more girls in the same community should be prioritized before expanding to additional communities.

5. **Recruiting girls.** Outreach efforts need to be inclusive. Specific strategies should be planned to reach girls in vulnerable communities, younger girls, out-of-school girls, and girls at risk—those girls who may benefit more from a safe spaces program and are at the same time less likely to know about it or believe that such a program is suitable for them. Engaging

with community leaders is a necessary but not a sufficient step in the outreach process, as the spread of information may be limited to well-connected families. Door-to-door recruitment may be more effective in reaching girls in the most vulnerable families. When setting up a program, a survey or census to identify potential beneficiaries as well as their specific expectations and needs should be considered in order to maintain participation. The most vulnerable girls must feel their primary concerns are being addressed through the program.

6. **Choosing a safe space.** The location of the safe space platform needs to be identified together with the community (both adults and potential participants) to ensure appropriateness and ownership. The space should be easily accessible and within walking distance from the targeted population's residences. It should offer privacy (visual and auditory) with respect to nonparticipants in the community. Often safe spaces are in school classrooms when they are not being used, churches, community halls, or the compounds of mentors or community leaders. Ideally, the location meets water, sanitation, and hygiene needs, as well as accommodating breastfeeding and childcare needs, if relevant. The program should invest in making these spaces a pleasant environment in which the group feels ownership and should encourage the girls in the program to decorate the space. Equipping the space with resources the girls can use, as in a "library" model, should also be considered.

7. **Forming groups.** Within the constraints implied by budget and logistics considerations, safe spaces should be segmented according to characteristics such as age, marital status, whether or not participants have children, and educational enrollment status, as safe spaces for different segments may require different messaging, particularly in relation to sexual and reproductive health, social networks, and household dynamics. If only one characteristic can be given priority, it should be age, and separate groups should be formed for younger (10 to 14) versus older (15 to 19) adolescents. Special considerations might be needed when working with migrants or refugees and local populations in the same communities. Some targeted and intended heterogeneity can also trigger positive dynamics: for instance, when in-school girls become role models for out-of-school girls. Girls with disabilities should be included in all safe spaces.

8. **Delivering services.** There is no consensus on the optimal duration of a safe spaces program, but there is consensus on program intensity. Meetings should be regular and frequent (for example, once a week) to become routine, generate momentum, and reduce the risk of dropouts.

Sessions should be long enough to cover the training and to allow girls to provide feedback and ask questions. Participatory techniques should be considered: dramatization (dance and theater), play-based learning, sports (including self-defense techniques), and use of media. Training material (including messages and images) should be carefully designed so as not to reinforce existing gender stereotypes. Scripted discussions and content to guide safe spaces meetings will help mentors deliver accurate, quality, and consistent messaging. Beyond group dynamics, one-to-one interactions and the establishment of healthy peer relationships should be fostered. Throughout the program, it is critical to provide a safe, nonjudgmental environment for all participants regardless of background or identity. Consideration should be given to engaging with the most promising graduates as role models or mentors for future cohorts.

9. **Engaging with key stakeholders.** At the planning stage, it might be useful to conduct a stakeholder mapping to identify key stakeholders and potential champions of the program, as well as likely opponents. Local champions can be engaged as part of social and behavioral change campaigns. Parallel safe spaces can be set up to provide key information and training to strategic stakeholders around girls, particularly parents and boys. Occasionally, joint sessions between girls and these stakeholders can be envisaged to promote healthy dialogue, better mutual understanding, enhanced support systems, and community cohesion. However, this strategy also entails risks, including backlash from parents and boys shadowing girls and perpetuating existing power dynamics.

10. **Monitoring and evaluating results.** Having access to good monitoring data and understanding of where a program is succeeding and struggling, and for whom, will allow real-time adjustments to ensure the program is reaching the intended girls with the specified content. What monitoring, evaluation, and learning measures will be employed should be purposefully determined, with an emphasis on actionable information: data that will not be used should not be collected. What questions need to be answered should first be decided, and then monitoring, evaluation, and learning tools that will answer those specific questions can be developed. Mentors play a key role in collecting data at the local level, but care should be taken to ensure that trained monitoring and evaluation officials are deployed in relative proximity to communities to implement regular checks and progressively improve the quality of monitoring and evaluation. To leverage the potential of digital monitoring and evaluation or management information systems

in contexts of low connectivity, apps that allow offline work, with data then uploaded when internet service is available (rather than web-based apps), should be considered, and the cost of the internet connection for mentors should be included as part of the program budget. Setting up qualitative feedback mechanisms so that program quality can be improved based on girls' expressed experiences can also help with participation and success.

11. **Scaling up.** One of the potential limitations of the safe spaces approach is the ability to scale up to reach a large number of girls in a particular country. However, there are several examples of successful expansion of safe spaces programs. For example, through the Sahel Women's Empowerment and Demographic Dividend program, safe spaces are being implemented in nine countries and have reached more than 1 million girls.

Scaling Up a Safe Spaces Program Requires Careful Consideration of Related Issues

Those looking to expand a safe spaces program should think about how to address the following challenges related to scale:

- Although cost per beneficiary varies greatly depending on a program's scope, range of services offered via the safe spaces platform, and specific local markets, it is usually in a range between $50 and $300 (with the costs for most programs concentrated in the range of $100 to $200, including costs related to mentors, training, logistics, and other operational needs).

- Scale-up may be further limited by implementing capacity—a lack of adequately staffed and sufficiently organized implementers to operate at large scale.

- A lack of qualified mentors in any given location might also be a challenge. Cascading training or leveraging the most promising graduates from safe spaces as new mentors should be considered.

- When similar programs operate disjointedly, it leads to inefficiencies, duplicated efforts, and difficulties in aligning goals, hindering effective scale-up.

- Finally, when a program is trying to embed within a national system, those involved in the effort must keep in mind that adolescent girls are often not accorded a high priority in national development strategies, nor is it always clear which ministry or authority governs the national agenda on adolescent girls.

Successful scale-up should solve these challenges, typically by promoting partnerships among governments (for funding and policy support), nongovernmental organizations and community groups (for implementation and local engagement), and the private sector (including tech firms for digital access). Embedding a program within government infrastructure (for example, community health systems and schools) and having an intraministerial body, with one clear lead, that drives the agenda is pivotal to leverage government systems and public services' structures, promote coordination between implementers and programs, abate costs, and achieve widespread scale. For example, if a program is embedded within a country's ministry of health, community-level health volunteers may be able to facilitate safe spaces. In some cases, pursuing expansion at the subnational level may be promising, depending on the system of federalization in a particular country. In these cases, there are still critical roles for nongovernmental organizations to play in training and monitoring at the local level or in piloting and evaluating innovative features.

Annex S3A. Resources Relating to Girls' Groups

Useful resources on safe spaces implementation guidance include the following:

- **"Building Girls' Protective Assets: A Collection of Tools for Program Design" (Population Council)** is a collection of tools and exercises that enable those who design and implement programs for adolescent girls to integrate a "protective asset-building approach" into programming. Designed primarily for program staff and facilitators who are responsible for planning girl-centered programming, this tool kit follows a logical, stepwise approach to intentionally designing programs responsive to diverse realities. The collection includes multiple participatory activities to be conducted with girls, for example, the Ascertaining Sexual Relationship Types Tool. This tool is used within an established group to build girls' and program staff's understanding of whom girls in the community have sex with and the reasons for different relationships, through a guided exercise on how and why girls have sex with different types of people. The collection of tools is intended for implementers who are committed to extending their programs to reach the excluded subpopulations of girls and young women and helps programmers translate evidence into practice by focusing on strategies and programs that have been effective in reducing girls' risk and broadening their opportunities. The tool kit is available online in English, French, and Spanish at http://knowledgecommons.popcouncil.org/departments _sbsr-pgy/559.

- **"The Girl Roster: A Practical Tool for Strengthening Girl-Centered Programming" (Population Council)** is a digital information collection tool that can help program staff and practitioners understand who the girls and young women in their communities are and where they work, using a door-to-door mobile-phone-based questionnaire. Adult responses to a short series of nonsensitive questions shed light on the full universe of girls and young women, and this information is used to link girls and women to essential resources and services. Seeing the full reality of girls' lives within program areas can inform program design or modification to best serve them, especially those who are most likely to be excluded from programming without dedicated efforts to reach them. This tool kit has been used by 100 organizations in more than 35 countries and is available online in 15 languages, including Arabic, French, Hindi, Swahili, and Spanish at http://knowledgecommons .popcouncil.org/departments_sbsr-pgy/468.

- **"Making the Most of Mentors: Recruitment, Training, and Support of Mentors for Adolescent Girl Programming—Toolkit" (Population Council)** provides resources to support different aspects of group-based programming for adolescents that has a particular emphasis on mentoring. Filled with materials that can be adapted to fit the needs of different programs, this tool kit is designed to be practical and user-friendly for program planners, practitioners, mentor trainers, and mentors themselves. Information on topics ranging from job descriptions to monitoring is divided into four main categories—activities, case studies, guides, and tools—and identifies whether program planners, mentor supervisors, or mentors are the primary audience This tool kit is available online at http:// knowledgecommons.popcouncil.org/departments_sbsr-pgy/630.

- **"More Than a Backdrop: Understanding the Role of Communities in Programming—Action Guide" (Population Council)** highlights the important role communities play in girl-centered programming and the critical need to understand local communities to increase the chances of program success. With five key questions and tips on how to find the answers, this tool kit establishes the community as a key participant in programming and seeks to strengthen girls' programs by generating and using local information on community structures and resources in the program design. It is written for people who design, manage, and assess community-based programming and is relevant to programs that engage girls through other channels, including schools. It can also be useful for community-based programming with boys and parents This tool kit is available online at http://knowledgecommons.popcouncil.org/departments _sbsr-pgy/629.

- **"Building Assets Toolkit: Developing Positive Benchmarks for Adolescent Girls—Asset Cards" (Population Council)** provides program implementers, policy makers, advocates, and adolescents themselves with everything they need to conduct the Population Council's Building Assets Exercise, grappling with questions like, "By what age do girls need to know about sexual coercion?" This exercise includes a series of steps to define commonsense programmatic targets that are grounded in girls' realities, such as the information, skills, or physical assets (such as an ID card) girls need or demand in specific settings at specific ages. This information can help build and incorporate tailored content into girl-centered programming. First published in 2015, this tool kit is a living document, as it is perfected by users. The asset cards are available in English, French, Arabic, Spanish, Swahili, and Portuguese, and the Instruction Guide and Resource Manual for the tool kit is available online in English and French at http:// knowledgecommons.popcouncil.org/departments_sbsr-pgy/642.

- **"Adolescent Programming Toolkit Guidance and Tools for Adolescent Programming and Girls' Empowerment in Crisis Settings" (Plan International)** promotes adolescent-responsive programming, which is the intentional design and implementation of actions that meet the gender- and age-specific and diverse needs, priorities, and capacities identified by adolescents themselves, with special attention to girls and at-risk adolescents. The tool kit can be used in various crisis settings, ranging from rapid-onset emergencies to protracted crises and global pandemics. The guidance can be employed across a wide variety of settings and with diverse groups of adolescents globally and has been designed for practitioners working directly with and for adolescents in crisis settings. However, it can also be used by those working on emergency preparedness, business development, and humanitarian policy, advocacy, and research. The tool kit is available online at https://plan-international .org/publications/adolescent-programming-toolkit/.

- **"I'm Here: Steps and Tools to Reach Adolescent Girls in Crisis" (Women's Refugee Commission)** is an approach that emerged from a comprehensive 2013 study involving a literature review and interviews with more than 100 practitioners. The study revealed a need for practical guidance in translating commitments into actionable programs benefiting adolescent girls in crisis situations. In April 2014, the Women's Refugee Commission tested a new methodology in South Sudan, which led to the creation of the "I'm Here Approach." The framework established in this approach provides humanitarian actors with a series of steps and field tools designed to identify and reach the most vulnerable adolescent girls; ensure accountability for these girls' safety, health, and well-being; and guide actions from the initial stages of crisis response onward. This resource is available online in English and other languages at https://www .womensrefugeecommission.org/research-resources/im-here-steps -tools-to-reach-adolescent-girls-in-crisis/.

• **"The Girl Path" (EMpower)** has as its purpose to identify obstacles that prevent girls from fully participating in youth programs and then to brainstorm ways that programs can remove, reduce, or otherwise address those barriers. "The Girl Path" is currently available in English, Spanish, Hindi, and Russian, with imagery options of girls from East and Southeast Asia, India, Latin America, Europe, and Africa. The Girl Path brochure provides instructions on implementing the tools it provides, and the Girl Path icons can be clipped for use. The Girl Path resource is available online at https://empowerweb.org/assets/uploads/tools -resources/422/the_girl_path_2019_english.pdf.

Notes

1. A robust monitoring and evaluation system, possibly implemented through a digital platform, improves the quality of mentors' supervision.
2. Please refer to the resources profiled in annex S3A for more information on how best to empower mentors.

CHAPTER 4

What Do We Know about Enhancing Economic Success among Adolescent Girls in Africa?

Wei Chang, Estelle Koussoubé, and Clémence Pougue Biyong, with contributions from Kehinde Ajayi and Chiara Pasquini

Key Messages

- Significant evidence gaps persist, limiting understanding of effective strategies to enhance girls' agency, access to resources, and labor market outcomes across diverse contexts and girls' profiles.

- Despite their associated costs, which constrain their scalability, comprehensive economic empowerment initiatives that combine vocational or business training with additional interventions such as grants, on-the-job training, and mentoring have demonstrated effectiveness or promise in increasing various dimensions of girls' empowerment beyond education and health.

- Providing in-kind support for schooling, such as uniforms or bicycles, shows effectiveness in increasing girls' agency and promise for improving other aspects of girls' empowerment, but more research is needed on the effects of other education interventions on girls' empowerment.

- Emerging evidence from Africa and other regions suggests that interventions expanding employment opportunities for women, providing information on the return to education and training, and engaging boys, parents, and communities to transform restrictive gender norms could play an important role in empowering girls, but here also, more research is needed.

- Popular interventions like cash transfers, girls' groups, and financial inclusion programs yield mixed impacts on girls' empowerment, with their effects often dependent on program design, implementation quality, and context. Adapting these interventions to better serve girls' needs and evaluating them over longer time horizons could help enhance their impacts and cost-effectiveness at scale.

A reproducibility package is available for this book in the Reproducible Research Repository at https://reproducibility.worldbank.org.

Expanding Efforts Beyond Human Capital Fundamentals Is Key to Empowering Adolescent Girls

To empower adolescent girls to realize their potential and thrive in adulthood, it is imperative to expand the scope of efforts beyond those that merely establish human capital fundamentals. Although enhancing girls' human capital fundamentals is crucial, it alone does not guarantee a successful transition into productive employment or a significant reduction in gender gaps in economic achievement during adulthood. A number of other factors come into play, including marriage, childbearing, prevailing gender roles, and norms related to women's employment and household dynamics (Carvalho and Evans 2022; Elder and Kring 2016; Klasen 2019). Box 4.1 provides examples of traditional approaches in African societies that have historically supported adolescent girls' transition to economic success. These examples illustrate how some cultures have addressed the factors related to this transition.

BOX 4.1 Examples of Traditional Approaches for Building Pathways to Economic Success for Adolescent Girls in Africa

Many African societies have historically adopted practices to ensure the economic well-being of adolescent girls as they transitioned to adulthood. These practices were designed to build social cohesion, stimulate agency, equip adolescent girls with resources, and facilitate girls' economic achievements. Some examples of traditional practices from Yoruba culture can serve as an illustration.

- **Age-set systems.** The practice of organizing young people into age groups around the time of adolescence provided a platform for Yorubas to cultivate educational training and to nurture social capital (Williams and Ogunkoya 2021). Age groups served economic, social, religious, and recreational functions in communities, endowing adolescent girls with a core social unit as they entered adulthood.

- **Inheritance.** Adolescent Yoruba girls retained the right to inherit property from their family of birth (equal to their male siblings), providing them with lifelong access to their families' resources as a means of production, along with social identity and support (Oyěwùmí 1997, 50).

- **Accumulated wealth.** Yoruba mothers often accumulated a large wardrobe of expensive woven cloth to give their adolescent daughters an asset stock as they entered adulthood (Oyěwùmí 1997, 56).

- **Professional occupations.** Specialized professions and crafts were passed through family lineages, so adolescent Yoruba girls were positioned to acquire the necessary materials and skills to earn a living by pursuing their family's occupation (Oyěwùmí 1997, 68–71).

- **Esusu savings cooperatives.** Adolescent Yoruba girls could begin building savings through *Esusu* savings cooperatives: groups of people who pooled their resources in a rotating savings scheme. These cooperatives built social capital among members and encouraged financial inclusion and capital accumulation.

Opening the path toward success for adolescent girls involves providing them with enabling resources such as financial, digital, and social capital; fostering agency among them; and creating an environment conducive to supporting their economic achievements. Following the framework for adolescent girls' empowerment outlined in chapter 1, this chapter critically examines the existing evidence on adolescent girls' empowerment. It focuses on adolescent girls' outcomes related to resources (for example, knowledge and skills, financial capital, and social capital), agency (for example, aspirations, gender attitudes, and self-efficacy), and labor market outcomes (for example, employment, employment quality, and income). Table 4.1 provides a summary of the evidence and gaps, and annex 4A offers details on the criteria used to rate the strength of the evidence and a detailed mapping of the evidence for each category of intervention and domain of empowerment outcomes in the conceptual framework.

TABLE 4.1 Evidence Reveals Varying Degrees of Effectiveness of Interventions Aimed at Enhancing Adolescent Girls' Economic Success

Intervention category	Degree of effectiveness in enhancing adolescent girls' economic success
In-kind transfers for schooling	Effective
Comprehensive economic empowerment programs	Effective
School fee reduction or elimination	Promising
School feeding	Promising
Employment opportunities for women	Promising
Engaging boys, parents, and community	Promising
Information on return to education or training	Promising
Cash transfers	Mixed
Girls' group empowerment programs	Mixed
Other life skills training and mentoring and empowerment programs	Mixed
Financial inclusion programs	Mixed
Traditional vocational and business skills training	Mixed
Improving quality of instruction	Unknown
Child marriage ban	Unknown
Educational entertainment programs	Unknown
Health services	Unknown
Inheritance law reform	Unknown
School construction	Unknown
Sexual and reproductive health education	Unknown

Source: Original table for this report.

The chapter's goal is to illuminate current understanding, identify effective interventions—both policies and programs—and highlight areas in which knowledge gaps persist. It is organized into three sections. The first section reviews interventions with strong, well-documented evidence of effectiveness specifically within the African context. The second section explores interventions that have shown promising results in Africa or have demonstrated potential effectiveness in other regions, though the evidence from Africa remains limited. The final section discusses interventions with mixed results; although their effectiveness is not conclusively proven, they offer valuable insights and may benefit from further adaptation or refinement to suit the African context.

Evidence Reveals Effective Strategies for Empowering Adolescent Girls

Although none of the interventions reviewed show universal effectiveness across all dimensions and outcomes explored in this chapter, certain categories of interventions have demonstrated efficacy or promise in improving one or more dimensions of adolescent girls' empowerment. This section highlights interventions that have proven effective in enhancing at least one dimension of empowerment, without exhibiting negative or mixed impacts on other dimensions of empowerment studied.

Comprehensive Economic Empowerment Programs Effectively Increase Girls' Financial Capital and Improve Their Labor Market Outcomes

Comprehensive economic empowerment programs integrate business or vocational skills training with grants, on-the-job training, continuous mentorship, or some combination of the three. Evidence from Kenya, Liberia, and Zimbabwe suggests that these multicomponent programs are effective in improving financial capital and labor market outcomes, but their scalability may be hindered by their relatively high costs. For instance, the Empowerment of Adolescent Girls and Young Women program in Liberia provided six months of technical and life skills training in a classroom setting followed by six months of support aimed at helping participants secure wage employment or launch their own business. Six months after the classroom training, participants had increased savings, higher rates of employment, more earnings, and greater control over their incomes. However, it would take 3 to 12 years of sustained income for participants to fully recoup the costs of the program, posing challenges to the program's scalability (Adoho et al. 2014). A similar program in Kenya that provided three-month classroom-based technical training combined with a three-month internship resulted in greater savings, employment, and earnings for female participants, but researchers cautioned against drawing definitive conclusions owing to significant attrition observed at the end-of-program survey (Honorati 2015).

Comprehensive economic empowerment programs that target out-of-school girls often incorporate additional program elements to address the unique challenges faced by the most vulnerable adolescent girls. For instance, a "microfranchising" program in Kenya offered vocational and life skills training, together with start-up capital and ongoing business mentoring, to young women from Nairobi's poorest neighborhoods. The program led to large increases in earnings initially, with the increases driven by a shift from paid work to self-employment, but this impact dissipated in the second year following the program (Brudevold-Newman et al. 2023). Similarly, a program in Zimbabwe aimed at adolescent female orphans offered vocational training, life skills training, reproductive health services, grants, and guidance counseling. This comprehensive approach was effective in increasing income compared with solely offering life skills training and reproductive health services (Dunbar et al. 2014).

In-Kind Transfers for Schooling Increase Girls' Agency and Labor Market Success

In-kind transfers for schooling, including scholarships and the provision of school supplies such as textbooks, uniforms, or bicycles to ride to schools, have shown effectiveness in improving various dimensions of girls' empowerment, particularly girls' agency and labor market outcomes. For instance, a program in Zimbabwe that provided school fees, uniforms, and dedicated support from school staff to orphan girls in primary schools resulted in higher expectations regarding the completion of secondary and tertiary education. It also fostered more equitable gender attitudes (Hallfors et al. 2011).

Fiala et al. (2022) investigate the effects of a program in Zambia promoting girls' school attendance and commuting safety, which provided bicycles to in-school girls, conditional on their school attendance. The bicycles were provided either free of charge to the girls' parents or after a small up-front payment at the time of receiving the bicycle. The study reveals that the intervention improved the girls' locus of control, control over relevant domains of their lives, prosociality, and self-image, regardless of whether parents were required to pay a fee for the bicycle. However, the intervention led to increased aspirations among girls, increased desired age of marriage, and decreased desired fertility only when parents paid such a fee. The researchers suggest that up-front family payments signaled to girls their parents' desire to increase their investment in the girls' education and future.

Similar positive effects on girls' empowerment have been found in other contexts, such as Ghana. There, the provision of secondary school scholarships covering high school expenses for rural students boosted girls' aspirations for tertiary education. The scholarships also led to increases in digital capital, with female scholarship winners showing increased internet usage and media engagement. There were also gains in financial capital, with more female scholarship winners adopting bank accounts.

The scholarships also had positive impacts on girls' long-term labor market outcomes. Female scholarship winners were more likely to obtain higher-quality jobs, particularly in the public sector, and jobs with benefits. Although the scholarships did not lead to large overall increases in earnings, they did provide a protective effect for female winners during the COVID-19 lockdowns, with girls' earnings less negatively affected than those of the control group (Duflo, Dupas, and Kremer 2021).

Promising Approaches Are Emerging to Address Girls' Empowerment Challenges

Increasing Employment Opportunities for Women May Aid in Adolescent Girls' Empowerment

Given the growing size of the youth population in Africa as well as the structure of African labor markets (Bandiera et al. 2022), policies aimed at boosting employment opportunities on the continent are critical for its development prospects. Although general interventions, such as policies supporting highly skilled entrepreneurs, show promise for youth employment in Africa (Bandiera et al. 2022), understanding their potential impact on adolescent girls, especially those who are out of school or older, and tailoring these interventions to benefit girls is crucial. Although evidence on the effects on adolescent girls' empowerment outcomes in Africa of policies providing employment opportunities to women is scarce, findings from South Asia suggest promise for policy making. For instance, Heath and Mushfiq Mobarak (2015) find that exposure to garment factories in Bangladesh increased adolescent girls' and young women's labor force participation, along with generating improvements in their human capital fundamentals. Similarly, Jensen (2012) reports increased professional aspirations and labor force participation among adolescent and young women in rural India when they are provided with access to employment opportunities in the business process outsourcing industry, coupled with improvements in their human capital fundamentals.

Further research is needed to understand the potential impact of these interventions in the African context and to identify effective strategies for tailoring these interventions to benefit adolescent girls, particularly those who are out of school or older.

Providing Girls with Information on the Return to Education or Training May Change Their Labor Market Trajectories

The evidence on the effects of information on the return to education or vocational training in Africa is limited. Hicks et al. (2016) explore the impact of delivery of vocational education vouchers and information on labor market returns among out-of-school youth ages 17 to 28 in Kenya. They find that providing information on the return to vocational training seemed to address participants' misperceptions about the benefits of such training, and led to an increase in young women preferring and enrolling in traditionally male-dominated trades. These findings are consistent with those from a study evaluating the effects of providing information on trade-specific earnings on women's choice of trade in the Republic of Congo (Gassier, Rouanet, and Traore 2022). However, further research is needed to enable full understanding of the effects of providing information on the return to training on other aspects of girls' and young women's empowerment, including agency and long-term labor market outcomes. Additionally, research should explore the potential for integrating information on the return to education or training with other interventions, such as cash transfer programs or vocational training, to enhance their effectiveness.

Engaging Boys, Parents, and Community Can Increase Girls' Sense of Agency and Improve Their Health Outcomes

Engaging key stakeholders within adolescent girls' environments, such as parents, boys, and other community members, is a common complementary approach to girls' empowerment programs (Temin and Heck 2020). However, there is limited evidence regarding the effectiveness of this strategy, as it is often implemented as part of a bundled intervention. Nevertheless, emerging evidence from Africa and other regions suggests promise, particularly when it comes to engaging boys. For instance, Shah et al. (2023) find that in Tanzania, engaging boys through a soccer-based program dealing with sexual and reproductive health education led not only to improvement in girls' sexual and reproductive health outcomes, but also to increases in their sense of agency, as well as a reduction in their likelihood of experiencing intimate-partner violence. These improvements in girl's empowerment outcomes were found to be driven by changes in boys' attitudes regarding violence. Similarly, Boulhane et al. (2024) find that in Côte d'Ivoire, combining a girls' group intervention with an intervention targeting boys and men to equip them with life skills and knowledge regarding sexual and reproductive health, along with information on girls' and women's rights, resulted in enhanced socioemotional skills among girls, as well as positive gender attitudes, improved decision-making capacities, and increased engagement in income-generating activities. Further engagement with religious and community leaders led to similar improvements in girls' empowerment outcomes compared with the girls' group intervention alone, suggesting the effectiveness of an integrated approach.

Despite the promising evidence on the effectiveness of engaging boys, parents, and the community in girls' empowerment programs, there is a need for more research to enable understanding of the specific mechanisms through which these interventions affect girls' outcomes. Future studies should examine the relative effectiveness of engaging different stakeholders (for example, boys, parents, and community leaders) and identify best practices for integrating engagement strategies for these different stakeholders into girls' empowerment programs. Additionally, research should explore the potential for unintended consequences or backlash effects when engaging boys, parents, and the community and develop strategies for mitigating the risk of these effects.

Reducing or Eliminating School Fees May Improve Girls' Employment Outcomes

There is limited evidence regarding the broader impacts of interventions aimed at supporting girls' education in Africa, such as school feeding programs, school construction, and school fee elimination, beyond education outcomes like enrollment and achievement. However, existing evidence on the impacts of school fee reduction or elimination, in particular, on employment outcomes is promising.

A notable study by Brudevold-Newman (2021) finds that Kenya's 2008 secondary education expansion program, which reduced school fees and increased school capacity, shifted young women's employment away from agriculture and toward skilled work. Exposure to the program significantly increased the likelihood of skilled employment among girls and decreased their likelihood of agricultural employment.

Another study by Chicoine (2021) on the elimination of primary school fees in Ethiopia provides additional insights into the effects on girls' agency and labor market outcomes. The study finds that additional years of schooling resulting from the reform reduced women's acceptance of domestic violence, suggesting an improvement in attitudes related to gender-based violence. Furthermore, the elimination of school fees positively affected women's labor market outcomes, with each additional year of schooling increasing the likelihood of a woman working in a skilled or professional occupation. This increase in skilled employment appears to have been driven by a reduction in unskilled or agricultural work.

These findings suggest that school fee elimination can have lasting impacts on girls' labor market prospects. However, there is still a need for more research assessing the effects of school fee elimination on other aspects of girls' empowerment, such as agency and access to resources or skills. Further studies examining the long-term impacts of school fee elimination programs could provide valuable insights into the full potential of school fee elimination to enhance girls' empowerment in Africa.

Insights from Mixed Evidence Point to Potential Areas for Further Exploration

Cash Transfers May Yield Positive Effects, but Context Is Key

Cash transfers are a prominent intervention examined in this review, with both conditional and unconditional programs aimed at supporting adolescent girls in various ways, such as advancing their education or targeting the most vulnerable households through financial assistance. However, evidence regarding the impact of such transfers on dimensions of adolescent girls' empowerment beyond education shows mixed results.

For instance, the effects of cash transfers on savings, labor market skills, time allocation to income-generating activities, or participation in the labor market vary depending on the context, as well as implementation features, including the existence of conditionalities and the characteristics of the girls targeted (Asfaw et al. 2014; Baird, McIntosh, and Özler 2019; Brudevold-Newman et al. 2023; Kilburn et al. 2019; Palermo, Prencipe, and Kajula 2021). Nonetheless, promising findings suggest that cash transfers may contribute to enhancing adolescent girls' autonomy, as evidenced by girls' increased control over resources (Baird et al. 2016) and a higher likelihood of their being self-employed (Brudevold-Newman et al. 2023).

To increase the effectiveness of cash transfers in empowering adolescent girls, it is crucial to design cash transfer programs with girls' needs in mind. A recent review by Cirillo, Palermo, and Viola (2021) outlines several strategies throughout a program cycle for making social-protection programs—including cash transfers—sensitive to the needs of adolescent girls, enhancing their impacts on girls' well-being. According to the review, targeting strategies can play a key role in ensuring adolescent girls are included. For example, targeting strategies that focus on specific age groups and adjusting age thresholds when needed can be effective. Moreover, incorporating conditionalities relevant to girls, such as school attendance, health checkups, and participation in life skills or vocational training, can address their specific circumstances. However, these conditionalities should be balanced to avoid adding stress for adolescents or imposing responsibility on them. Additionally, considering adolescent girls the direct recipients of the transfers can empower them by giving them control over the resources, though this must be carefully managed to avoid household tensions. Complementary programming, including mentoring and life skills training, as well as links to health and social services can further address the multifaceted needs of adolescent girls, supporting a successful transition to adulthood.

The mixed evidence on the impact of cash transfers on adolescent girls' empowerment highlights the need for further research to enable understanding of the specific mechanisms through which these programs can enhance girls' outcomes, including agency and labor market outcomes. Future studies should examine the relative effectiveness of different targeting strategies, conditionalities, and complementary programming. Additionally, research should explore the potential for unintended consequences or backlash effects when cash transfers are provided directly to adolescent girls, their households, or both and should develop strategies for mitigating these risks (Cirillo, Palermo, and Viola 2021; see also box 4.2).

BOX 4.2 Potential Unintended Effects

Empowerment programs have yielded unintended effects on girls' outcomes, highlighting the importance of improved monitoring during program implementation. These unintended effects include increases in fertility rates and in the experience of gender-based violence.

(continued)

BOX 4.2 Potential Unintended Effects *(continued)*

Increased fertility

In Tanzania, an after-school program addressing reproductive health, healthy relationships, and gender-based violence inadvertently led to earlier initiation of relationships among participants. This premature onset of relationships subsequently resulted in elevated fertility rates among the girls. The researchers attributed this trend to societal pressures on girls to conceive once they enter a relationship (Berge et al. 2022).

Rise in gender-based violence

Research conducted in low-income areas of Kampala, Uganda, unveiled an unintended outcome of providing savings accounts to adolescent girls without the implementation of accompanying safe spaces programs focused on reproductive health and financial education. Although the savings accounts effectively boosted adolescent girls' savings, when provided alone, these savings accounts also led to a higher likelihood of girls experiencing unwanted sexual contact and harassment from men. This highlights the importance of reinforcing social assets, such as social networks, as well as providing reproductive health knowledge in conjunction with economic asset-building initiatives to protect vulnerable girls against the risk of sexual violence (Austrian and Muthengi 2014).

The Design of Girls' Group Empowerment Programs Determines Their Success

Girls' group empowerment programs are a well-studied approach for delivering life skills training, mentoring, and empowerment interventions. As noted in chapter 3, these programs are typically implemented in community settings outside schools, using designated safe spaces. Girls' group programs can take various forms, incorporating elements such as life skills training, financial education, health training, and more. Although the diversity in the design of these programs makes it challenging to draw clear conclusions regarding their effects, some key insights have emerged that can inform future programs.

First, girls' groups allow adolescent girls to build their knowledge and skills, as well as enlarge and diversify their social networks (Austrian et al. 2020; Bandiera et al. 2019; Buehren, Goldstein, et al. 2017; Cohen, Abubakar, and Perlman 2023; Stark et al. 2018). These groups facilitate discussions ranging from personal matters to career-oriented topics, fostering personal and professional bonds with both role models and peers.

Moreover, girls' group programs, especially those combining life skills training and reproductive health knowledge with additional components such as financial education, business training, or vocational skills training, have been shown to increase girls' financial skills and knowledge, as well as saving behaviors (Austrian et al. 2020; Austrian et al. 2021; Buehren, Chakravarty, et al. 2017; Buehren, Goldstein, et al. 2017; Cohen, Abubakar, and Perlman 2023; Özler et al. 2020).

However, although girls' groups have demonstrated positive impacts on girls' attitudes toward gender roles and self-efficacy in some contexts, results have been inconsistent across studies. For example, girls' groups have proven effective at changing adolescent girls' gender attitudes (Bandiera et al. 2020; Boulhane et al. 2024; Özler et al. 2020) and fostering adolescents' sense of agency, as captured by indicators of self-efficacy and self-perception (Austrian et al. 2020; Cohen, Abubakar, and Perlman 2023) and socioemotional skills (Boulhane et al. 2024). Yet other evaluations have shown no impacts on these same outcomes (for example, Austrian et al. 2020).

Additionally, girls' groups have shown mixed impacts on other outcomes for adolescent girls, including decision-making and employment outcomes (for example, Boulhane et al. 2024; Buehren, Chakravarty, et al. 2017; and Buehren, Goldstein, et al. 2017). However, they also show promise in regard to improving girls' time use, despite a limited number of studies reporting results on time use outcomes. For instance, Bandiera et al. (2019) report that in Sierra Leone, the Empowerment and Livelihood for Adolescents (ELA) girls' group program provided girls with an alternative use of their time as opposed to socializing with men, which also resulted in other positive empowerment outcomes.

Implementation lessons also emerge. First, including a specific focus on or content regarding the outcomes targeted by a particular intervention, be it life skills training or vocational training, matters for its impact. Second, implementation quality seems to matter, especially when these types of interventions are scaled up. For instance, evaluating the same program as Bandiera et al. (2020) but in Tanzania, Buehren, Goldstein, et al. (2017) find that the program had no impacts on girls' outcomes, which they attributed to low implementation quality in the Tanzanian context.

Finally, context plays a crucial role, with rural versus urban settings and conflict or disruptions influencing program impacts. For instance, results from the evaluation of the Adolescent Girls Initiative–Kenya show that the program had different impacts in rural and urban areas (Austrian et al. 2020). Similarly, studies conducted in Sierra Leone (Bandiera et al. 2019) and South Sudan (Buehren, Chakravarty, et al. 2017) show that the impact of ELA girls' clubs is influenced by the insecurity and vulnerability experienced by adolescents in conflict-affected regions and epidemics at the time of the studies.

Other Life Skills, Mentoring, and Empowerment Programs Provide Girls with Practical Skills but Demonstrate Mixed Results in Other Areas

Other life skills, mentoring, and empowerment programs, including sexual and reproductive health education, are designed to equip girls with practical skills, tailored to the objectives of each initiative. Delivered outside of girls' group platforms, these programs provide access to practical resources for informed decision-making. Like girls' groups, they have shown effectiveness in enhancing girls' knowledge and skills. However, their impact on outcomes such as social capital, goal setting, sense of agency, and labor market outcomes varies.

For instance, the Marriage: No Child's Play project implemented by the More than Brides Alliance demonstrated increases (in India, Malawi, Mali, and Niger) in girls' knowledge about the legal age of marriage (Melnikas et al. 2021). Similarly, the IMpower program, focused on self-defense training, increased girls' self-defense knowledge in Kenya and Malawi (Decker et al. 2018).

Regarding the effects of these interventions on social capital, the existing evidence, though limited, suggests no impact in the context of the Marriage: No Child's Play project in Malawi, Mali, or Niger, as measured by girls' involvement in clubs or groups (Melnikas et al. 2021). Further research is needed to enable full understanding of the impacts of these interventions.

The impacts of life skills training on goal setting and sense of agency appear mixed, varying across contexts, whereas emerging evidence of the effects of such training on autonomy is promising. For instance, in Somalia, the Choices program, aimed at promoting equitable gender attitudes and behaviors among adolescents, led to positive shifts in attitudes and increased educational aspirations (Brar et al. 2023). Similarly, in the context of the ELA program in Tanzania, Shah et al. (2023) evaluate the effect of a goal-setting intervention aimed at improving girls' sexual and reproductive health outcomes through the adoption of safe behaviors. They find that the intervention helped girls set concrete strategies to improve their health, achieve their desired results, and increase their control over their sexual health. However, not all programs show such positive results. The Marriage: No Child's Play project showed divergent results in this regard across Malawi, Mali, and Niger, with gender-equitable attitudes worsening in

Malawi and Mali, whereas no discernible impact was observed in Niger (Melnikas et al. 2021).

When it comes to the effects of life skills programs on girls' labor market outcomes, they have generally shown minimal impact (Berge et al. 2022; Honorati 2015; Melnikas et al. 2021).

Financial Inclusion Programs Have Had a Mixed Degree of Success

Financial inclusion programs, which provide savings accounts, financial literacy training, or both, have demonstrated mixed effects on knowledge and behaviors, with research mainly focusing on highly marginalized adolescent girls (Austrian and Muthengi 2014; Austrian et al. 2021; Burke et al. 2020; Ssewamala et al. 2010). For example, in South Africa, a financial education program that covered budgeting and savings options for orphans and children affected by HIV or AIDS increased girls' participation in savings groups and their intention to save for education, although it did not increase financial knowledge or raise savings amounts (Burke et al. 2020). Financial inclusion programs seem to benefit boys and girls equally, as shown in a program that offered matched savings accounts for AIDS orphans in Uganda (Ssewamala et al. 2010).

However, there is little evidence on the impact of financial inclusion programs in nonfinancial domains, such as agency, or their effects on longer-term economic achievement. Notably, two studies of girls' empowerment groups examine the impact of bundling financial inclusion programs with girls' groups programs, providing suggestive evidence that multicomponent programs may have additional benefits or protective effects (Austrian and Muthengi 2014; Austrian et al. 2021). As part of the Adolescent Girls' Initiative–Kenya, researchers studied the impact of adding a wealth creation component to a safe spaces program that encompassed violence prevention, conditional cash transfers, and health education. Two years after the intervention, the wealth creation component, which consisted of financial education, piggy banks or savings accounts, and a small cash incentive, had sustained positive effects on saving behaviors among both rural and urban participants, but effects on financial literacy and household wealth were observed only among urban participants (Austrian et al. 2021). Similarly, in Uganda, providing savings accounts to adolescent girls increased their savings amounts and financial assets (Austrian and Muthengi 2014). However, girls who received only savings accounts, compared with those who also participated in safe spaces groups that targeted health knowledge and social assets, were at greater risk of sexual violence, which indicates that solely boosting financial assets may increase certain vulnerabilities for girls in this context (Austrian and Muthengi 2014; see also box 4.2). Complementary programming could provide protective measures against potential backlashes, which aligns with recent findings from a review on financial inclusion programs' impact on young women's well-being (Deshpande and Koning 2023). Although evidence on financial inclusion programs for adolescent girls is still emerging, insights from research on adult women's financial inclusion may offer valuable lessons for designing effective interventions for adolescent girls (box 4.3).

BOX 4.3 Lessons from Promoting Women's Financial Inclusion

Although the existing evidence on the impact of promoting financial inclusion among adolescent girls is limited, there is a more substantial body of research focusing on young and older women.

Evidence from research involving adult women suggests that increased privacy of savings accounts or cash transfers may increase the effectiveness of these interventions for adolescent girls. For instance, in a laboratory experiment in rural Kenya, it was shown that women are willing to forgo investment returns to keep their income hidden (Jakiela and Ozier 2016). This preference for income privacy suggests that women expect that their income will be "taxed" by their family members or relatives, a phenomenon often referred to as "kin taxation" in the economic literature. Such expectations can significantly influence financial decision-making and saving behavior. Similarly, a study among factory workers in Côte d'Ivoire demonstrated the potential benefits of private savings accounts. Workers who were provided with private savings accounts were more inclined to use them, compared with those with access to standard, nonprivate savings accounts. Providing private accounts not only increased account use but also led to improved worker attendance and higher earnings, compared with both workers without any account and workers with standard, nonprivate accounts (Carranza et al. 2022).

Taken together, these studies suggest that savings technologies that provide privacy (such as digital financial services) may increase adolescent girls' control over their financial resources. However, it is important to tailor such services to the specific needs of adolescent girls, considering the potential necessity of parental supervision for safety reasons.

Training in Traditional Vocational and Business Skills May Have Positive Impacts

Programs providing training in traditional vocational and business skills aim to equip participants with the essential "hard skills" or business practices needed for a successful transition to the labor market. Unlike comprehensive economic empowerment programs, these initiatives typically involve classroom-based sessions without on-the-job training or ongoing business mentoring. Such skills training interventions can be implemented within formal educational settings or tailored for those not following a traditional academic path.

Whereas there is a growing body of rigorous evidence on the effects of vocational and business training in low- and middle-income countries, including African countries (McKenzie 2021; McKenzie et al. 2023), there is a lack of evidence specifically on the impact of these trainings in the African context when they target older adolescent girls. Among the few existing studies, an evaluation of entrepreneurship training targeted at unmarried girls in secondary schools in Tanzania revealed positive impacts across multiple domains of empowerment, including enhanced business knowledge and more gender-equitable attitudes, leading to significant gains in long-term self-employment and income observed three to four years after the intervention (Berge et al. 2022), regardless of whether the training was coupled with reproductive health education. Conversely, in Kenya, providing vouchers for vocational training to out-of-school youths had limited effects on employment or earnings, although offering information on the return to vocational education prompted more women to enroll in training programs focused on traditionally male-dominated trades (Hicks et al. 2016).

Because of a lack of robust evidence, the efficacy of such skills training programs in improving adolescent girls' empowerment outcomes remains uncertain. However, it's worth noting that broader evidence on the effectiveness of these training programs in low- and middle-income countries suggests limited impacts on employment and earnings: the primary empowerment dimensions these initiatives were expected to affect (McKenzie 2021; McKenzie et al. 2023). Although emerging evidence suggests some innovative approaches—such as psychology-based training in business, as well as more tailored job training policies that consider the characteristics and needs of both employers and beneficiaries (Carranza and McKenzie 2024; McKenzie et al. 2023)—are promising, it remains an open question how these approaches can be adapted, including which additional interventions are necessary, to benefit older out-of-school adolescent girls in particular.

Promising Avenues, as Well as Substantial Knowledge Gaps, Shape Considerations for Future Directions

This narrative review has highlighted significant knowledge gaps in interventions aimed at enhancing girls' economic success while also underscoring promising avenues for policy actions. The review finds that a number of interventions have shown effectiveness or promise in improving girls' empowerment outcomes beyond health and education, including comprehensive economic empowerment programs; in-kind transfers for schooling; providing employment opportunities to women; offering information on the return to education or training; engaging boys, parents, and the community; and school fee reduction or elimination. However, the review emphasizes that there is no one-size-fits-all solution, as no single intervention category has consistently demonstrated success across all dimensions of girls' empowerment. This underscores the multiple challenges girls encounter and emphasizes that programs must be deliberate about their specific goals within the realm of empowerment. It is important to recognize that improvements in one dimension of empowerment may not always translate into improvements in other dimensions, as also highlighted in spotlight 2.

Despite the extensive body of evidence assessing programs designed to empower adolescent girls in Africa, certain crucial dimensions have been consistently overlooked. Although many indicators related to resources and agency are widely studied, other outcomes of the framework for adolescent girls' empowerment used in this report are rarely measured or reported in studies. These include outcomes such as control over time allocation, decision-making, and access to digital assets. Moreover, whereas changing the context at the institutional or macro level might be beyond the scope of any single program, several programs, including girls' groups and other empowerment programs, have the potential to shift household dynamics and social norms, provided there is an intentional component aimed at creating an enabling environment, such as engaging the girls' entourages in their communities. However, few studies have reported outcomes beyond those observed in respect to the girls themselves. There is also a need for long-term follow-up data to measure programs' impact on labor market outcomes in adulthood and deepen understanding of the sustained implications of these programs for the economic trajectory of adolescent girls.

Additionally, evidence from large-scale programs is also critically needed. This is particularly important for multicomponent interventions that require significant coordination among stakeholders to ensure quality and effective implementation. Such programs can be challenging to scale up on account of the complexity involved in maintaining consistent standards across different contexts. Therefore, robust evidence from large-scale implementations will be essential to enable understanding of how these multicomponent interventions can be feasibly scaled up while maintaining their effectiveness.

Moreover, studies often lack detailed insights into how interventions can be tailored to girls' diverse backgrounds and profiles (annex 4A). Whereas some programs aim to address the needs of girls within or outside the school environment, very few programs are designed specifically for married girls or those with children (Edmeades, Lantos, and Mekuria 2016). Similarly, there is often a lack of analysis on heterogeneous intervention effects based on girls' characteristics even in regard to indicators that have been widely studied. Future research that considers, in intervention design and impact evaluation, the unique needs of adolescent girls at various stages of life would offer valuable insights for the scale-up of effective policies and programs.

Finally, although some studies do report the costs associated with the interventions they examine, this remains the exception rather than the norm among the studies reviewed in this chapter. In addition to evaluation of the effectiveness of specific programs, cost-effectiveness analysis is essential for informed policy making, particularly when considering scaling up programs in contexts in which resources are limited. However, it is important to recognize that cost-effectiveness should not be overemphasized at the expense of other important considerations. Some interventions may have delayed benefits that are difficult to quantify or translate into monetary terms. These benefits, such as increasing girls' agency, may not be fully captured in cost-effectiveness analysis but are just as important for girls' empowerment as those that can be completely quantified. Therefore, although this report strongly urges implementers and researchers to collect and report cost-related information, it is essential to consider cost-effectiveness alongside other factors, such as the potential for long-term social impact and the broader benefits that may be harder to quantity or translate into monetary terms.

Annex 4A. Evidence Overview Methodology

Study Selection and Analysis

Chapter 3 and this chapter provide a comprehensive narrative review of the recent evidence on programs and policies designed to empower adolescent girls. Both chapters build on existing literature reviews, while also examining additional studies. Chapter 3 primarily draws upon studies from recent literature reviews of interventions to improve education and health outcomes (Bergstrom and Özler 2023; Evans and Yuan 2022;

Malhotra and Elnakib 2021; Meherali et al. 2021; Psaki et al. 2022). This chapter primarily draws upon studies from recent literature reviews focused on economic and financial empowerment (Deshpande and Koning 2023; Emezue et al. 2021; Haberland et al. 2021; Temin and Heck 2020). Additionally, in both chapters, other relevant studies meeting the following inclusion criteria are included:

- They evaluate interventions targeting adolescent girls (ages 10 to 19) or interventions with broader target groups that present age- and sex-disaggregated results.
- They evaluate interventions implemented in Sub-Saharan Africa.
- They report results on at least one of the outcomes in the adolescent girls' empowerment framework introduced in chapter 1.
- They employ experimental or rigorous quasi-experimental methods that enable causal identification.
- They were published before March 2024.

Studies that report only education or health outcomes, as part of the evidence on human capital fundamentals, are covered in chapter 3.

Assessing what works to support adolescent girls is challenging for several reasons (box 4A.1). Nonetheless, mapping of the evidence identifies a total of 19 distinct categories of interventions encompassing both policies and programs designed to address specific challenges faced by, and opportunities available to, adolescent girls in the African context (table 4A.1).[1] Rather than a formal meta-analysis, the goal is to provide concise yet nuanced takeaways, delineating effective strategies and areas requiring attention for policy audiences. Additionally, gaps in the literature are highlighted for future research.

BOX 4A.1 Challenges in Assessing What Works to Support Adolescent Girls

Adolescent girls' empowerment is multidimensional

Most reviews of evidence relating to adolescent girls' empowerment focus on what works to improve a single outcome (for example, learning-adjusted years of schooling for educational interventions or income for economic empowerment) or assess the effects of a single type of intervention (for example, cash transfers). Understanding what works, in contrast, entails examining how multiple types of policies and interventions affect multiple outcomes (that is, human capital fundamentals, enabling resources, agency, context, and economic achievements). Interventions that have an impact on one component of adolescent girls' empowerment may not

(continued)

BOX 4A.1 Challenges In Assessing What Works to Support Adolescent Girls *(continued)*

be effective at addressing other components. To address this complexity, this report discusses interventions that affect human capital fundamentals in chapter 3 and then interventions that affect the remaining components of adolescent girls' empowerment in this chapter.

The time horizon of impacts is long

While some intervention outcomes are observed immediately, others take longer to emerge. For example, increases in school enrollment may be evident relatively quickly, whereas changes in agency may take years to become apparent. Understanding the long-term impacts of interventions in early adolescence is crucial, yet it is challenging without longitudinal data, which are currently lacking (Baird and Özler 2016).

Jurisdiction over adolescent girls' outcomes differs by context

The age of majority differs across contexts, in both customs and formal law, and by sector. For instance, the age at which adolescent girls can make independent decisions about their sexual and reproductive health without parental or spousal consent varies. Similarly, the legal age at which they can open a bank account differs. These variations pose challenges in standardizing interventions and policies across different contexts and complicate the assessment of their impacts.

Multisectoral approaches complicate assessment of impacts

Some issues concerning adolescent girls' empowerment cut across multiple sectors, including education, health, social services, finance, labor, gender, and family affairs. A significant challenge in assessing interventions aimed at empowering adolescent girls is that many are bundled, incorporating components from several sectors. This report follows existing reviews and builds on existing classifications when available (for example, Bergstrom and Özler 2023; Evans, Mendez Acosta, and Yuan 2024). When these classifications are not available, the report categorizes interventions based on an assessment of their primary components.

Cost-effectiveness is important but should not be overemphasized

Evaluating the cost-effectiveness of interventions is crucial for understanding their feasibility and scalability. Whereas some interventions may show immediate impacts, others may have delayed benefits. Additionally, whereas some benefits are easily quantifiable, others, especially those related to empowering girls, are difficult to quantify and may not be fully captured in cost-effectiveness analysis. Focusing solely on cost-effectiveness can result in researchers and policy makers overlooking significant social impacts and broader benefits that are harder to measure but equally important for girls' empowerment.

With these challenges in mind, this report examines what is known about how to address adolescent girls' empowerment, highlighting outstanding questions and emerging solutions from reviewing the state of evidence.

TABLE 4A.1 Interventions to Empower Adolescent Girls in Africa Show Evidence of Varying Degrees of Effectiveness, and There Are Numerous Gaps

Intervention category	Education	Health	Knowledge and skills	Financial capital	Physical and digital capital	Social capital	Time	Goal setting	Sense of agency	Autonomy	Labor market outcomes
In-kind transfers for schooling	Effective	Promising	—	—	Promising	—	—	Effective	—	—	—
Comprehensive economic empowerment programs	—	Mixed	—	Promising	Promising	—	—	—	—	Promising	Effective
School fee reduction or elimination	Effective	Promising	—	—	—	—	—	—	—	—	Promising
School feeding	Effective	—	—	—	—	—	Promising	—	—	—	—
Sexual and reproductive health education	—	Effective	—	—	—	—	—	—	—	—	—
Improving quality of instruction	Effective	—	—	—	—	—	—	—	—	—	—
Cash transfers	Effective	Mixed	Mixed	Effective	Promising	—	Mixed	—	Mixed	Promising	No effect
Health services	Mixed	Effective	—	—	—	—	—	—	—	—	—
Employment opportunities for women	—	—	—	—	—	—	—	—	—	—	—
Engaging boys, parents, and community	—	Promising	Promising	—	—	—	—	—	Promising	Promising	—
Information on return to education or training	—	—	—	—	—	—	—	Mixed	—	—	—

(continued)

TABLE 4A.1 Interventions to Empower Adolescent Girls in Africa Show Evidence of Varying Degrees of Effectiveness, and There Are Numerous Gaps (continued)

Intervention category	Education	Health	Knowledge and skills	Financial capital	Physical and digital capital	Social capital	Time	Goal setting	Sense of agency	Autonomy	Labor market outcomes
Child marriage ban	—	—	—	—	—	—	—	—	—	—	—
Edutainment programs	—	Promising	—	—	—	—	—	—	—	—	—
Inheritance law	—	—	—	—	—	—	—	—	—	—	—
School construction	Promising	—	—	—	—	—	—	—	—	—	—
Girls' group empowerment programs	Mixed	Mixed	Effective	Effective	—	Effective	Promising	Mixed	Mixed	Mixed	Mixed
Other life skills training and mentoring and empowerment programs	Mixed	Mixed	Effective	Mixed	—	—	—	Mixed	Mixed	Promising	Mixed
Financial inclusion programs	—	—	Promising	Mixed	—	—	—	—	—	Mixed	—
Traditional vocational and business skills training	—	—	—	—	—	—	—	—	—	Mixed	—

Source: Original table for this report.

Note: — = intervention has unknown effect or there is insufficient evidence to evaluate the effect.

The strength of evidence regarding the effect of different intervention categories on specific indicators of empowerment is rated using the following criteria:

- Effective: at least three rigorous studies showing positive, statistically significant impacts of the intervention, supported by most of the studies.

- Promising: fewer than three rigorous studies showing positive, statistically significant effects of the intervention.

- Mixed: fewer than three-quarters of available rigorous studies showing statistically significant effects of the intervention in the same direction.

- No effect: at least two rigorous studies showing no statistically significant effect of the intervention.

- Unknown or little evidence: fewer than two rigorous studies investigating the intervention's effect.

In addition to synthesizing the vast body of research for policy audiences and highlighting the evidence gaps, chapters 3 and 4 contribute to the literature by highlighting what has been proven to be effective specifically in Africa. This focus on Africa is particularly valuable, as it addresses a notable gap in existing reviews. For instance, evidence on how to expand and enhance girls' education in low- and middle-income countries has grown considerably in recent years (Evans and Yuan 2022; Evans et al. 2023; JPAL 2017; Psaki et al. 2022; Sperling and Winthrop 2016; Wodon et al. 2018),[2] but few previous reviews have focused expressly on Africa. Similarly, Bergstrom and Özler (2023) review interventions aimed at improving girls' well-being across low- and middle-income countries.

Overview of Studies' Characteristics

Distribution of Interventions

The interventions studied for this report are diverse, with cash transfers (18 interventions) and girls' group empowerment programs (15 interventions) being the most-evaluated interventions (figure 4A.1). This reflects in part policy makers' significant focus on financial support and group-based programs as strategies to empower girls. Sexual and reproductive health education is also a major focus (9 interventions), reflecting the importance placed on knowledge in this area as a component of empowerment. Other interventions, such as health services, fee reductions or eliminations, and life skills training delivered outside of girls' groups, are evaluated slightly less frequently (7 interventions each). The least commonly studied interventions include inheritance law reforms and edutainment, indicating a need for more evidence on their impact.

FIGURE 4A.1 Cash Transfers and Girls' Group Empowerment Programs Are the Most Commonly Evaluated Interventions

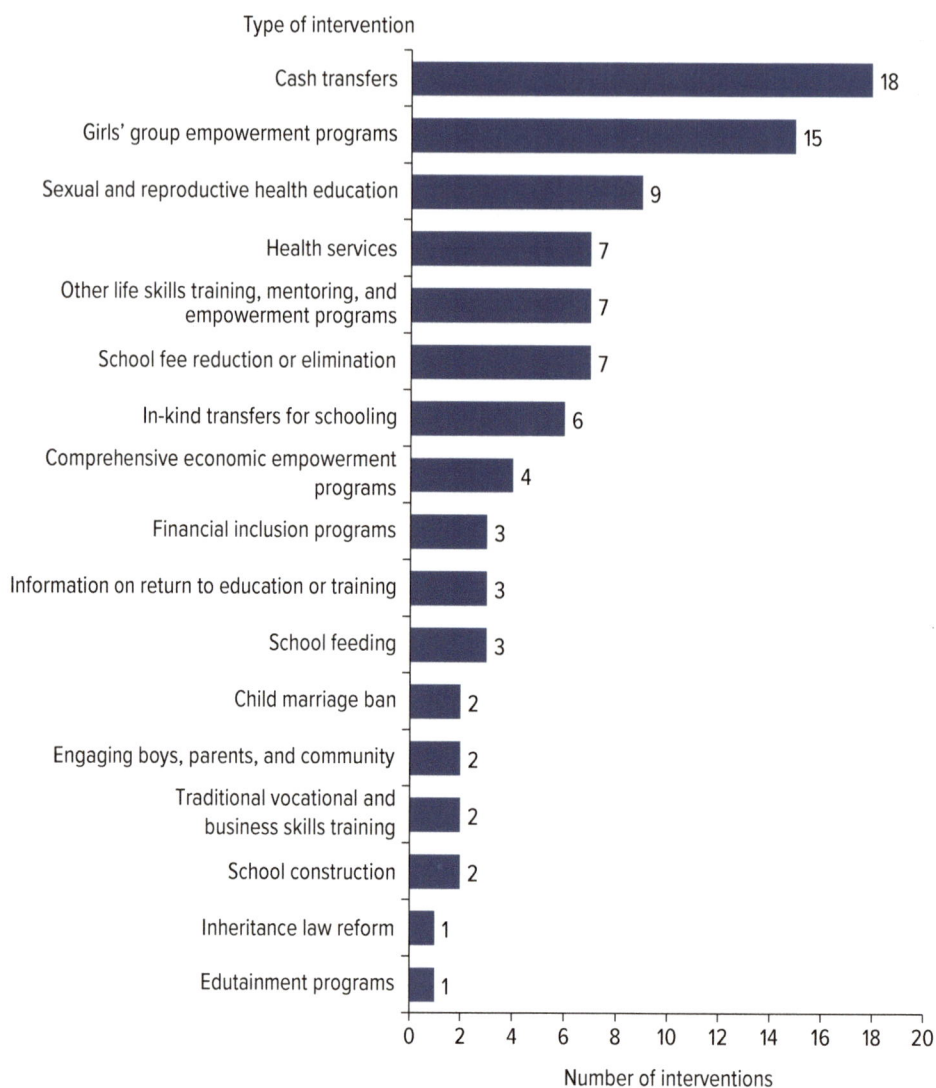

Source: Original figure for this report.

Distribution of Studies by Region

The geographic distribution of the studies reveals a predominant focus on East Africa, where 53 percent of the research was conducted. Southern Africa and West Africa were also represented, though to a lesser extent, with about 21 percent and 23 percent of the studies conducted there, respectively (figure 4A.2). Central Africa was the focus of the fewest studies, only about

FIGURE 4A.2 Research Studies on Africa Show a Predominant Geographic Focus on East Africa

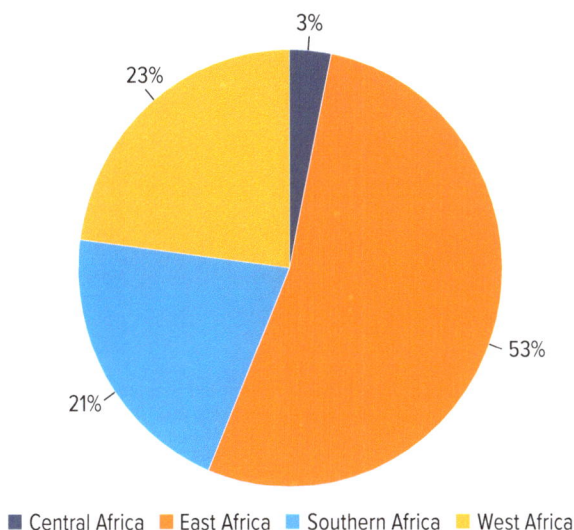

Source: Original figure for this report.
Note: Numbers in the figure show the percentage of research studies on Africa that focus on each specific subregion of the continent.

3 percent of the total, suggesting a critical gap in research regarding this region. The distribution of the studies underscores the varying levels of research attention across different regions, which may reflect differing regional priorities or challenges in accessing certain areas.

Distribution by Age

The studies reviewed show a significant focus on both younger and older adolescents between 10 and 19 years of age, with 44 studies (51 percent) covering this age span (figure 4A.3). Studies focused exclusively on younger adolescents (10 to 14 years) account for 28 percent (24 studies), and those focused on older adolescents (15 to 19 years) make up 22 percent (19 studies). Although most of the studies include a broad range, the comprehensive approach suggests that empowerment strategies are being designed to address the needs of girls across different stages of adolescence.

FIGURE 4A.3 Studies Tend to Include Both Younger and Older Adolescent Girls

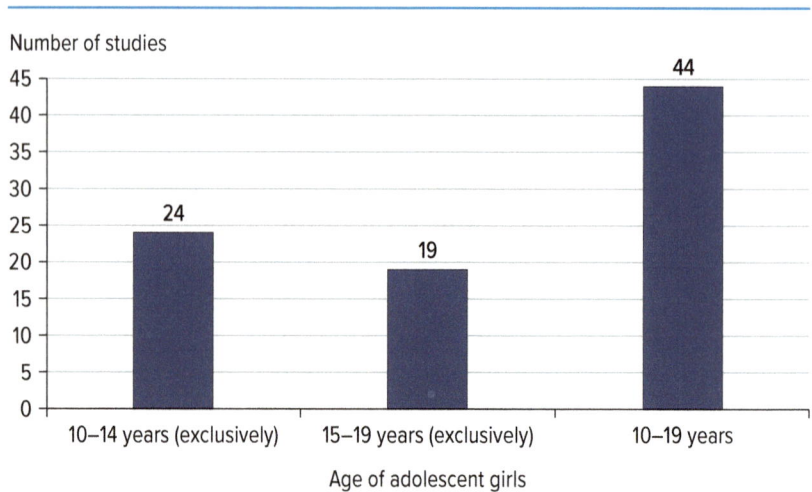

Number of studies

Age of adolescent girls

Source: Original figure for this report.

Distribution by School Enrollment Status

Most of the studies (60 percent, 52 studies) focus on adolescent girls who were actively enrolled in school at the time of the start of the intervention (figure 4A.4). However, a significant proportion (32 percent, 28 studies) include both in-school and out-of-school girls. Only a small number of studies (8 percent, 7 studies) look specifically at interventions targeting out-of-school adolescent girls. This distribution indicates that most evidence to date has centered on schoolgirls, whereas the needs of and constraints faced by out-of-school girls remain underexplored.

Distribution by Marital Status

A significant number of studies examined in the report—more than a third (38 percent, 33 studies)—do not report the marital status of participants (figure 4A.5). Most of the studies that do report marital status (62 percent, 54 studies) include both married and unmarried girls at baseline (43 percent, 37 studies). However, a far greater proportion of studies (18 percent, 16 studies) focus exclusively on unmarried girls, compared with the very few (1 percent, 1 study) that look at married girls only. The evidence base appears skewed toward unmarried girls, whereas as highlighted in this report, married adolescents represent an important population facing distinct vulnerabilities.

FIGURE 4A.4 Most Studies Have Focused on Adolescent Girls Who Are
Enrolled in School

Number of studies

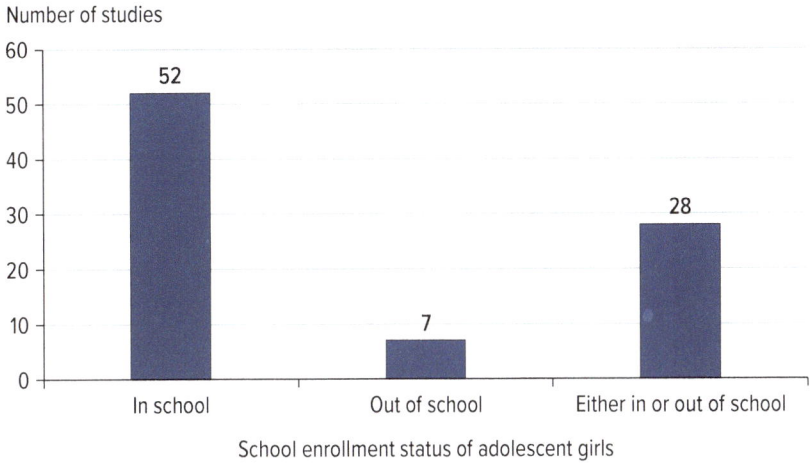

School enrollment status of adolescent girls

Source: Original figure for this report.

FIGURE 4A.5 More Than One-Third of Studies Do Not Report Adolescent
Girls Marital Status

Number of studies

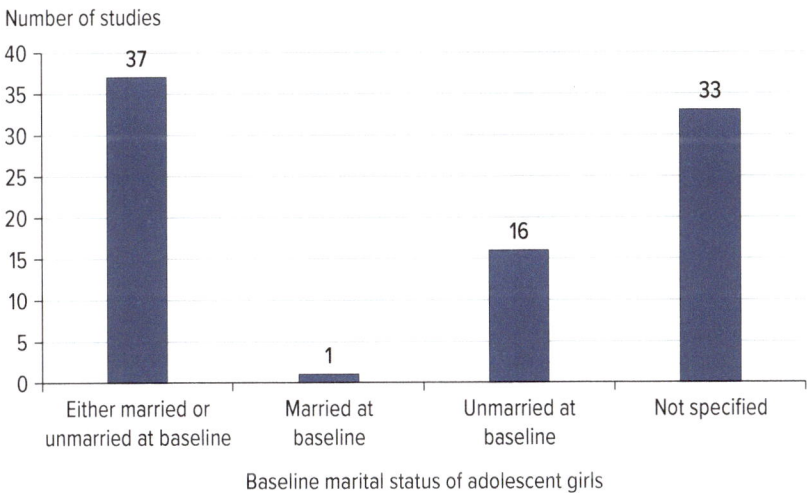

Baseline marital status of adolescent girls

Source: Original figure for this report.

Heterogeneous Effects by Key Adolescent Girl Characteristics

Many studies examined in the report do not analyze heterogeneous effects
across key adolescent girl characteristics such as age, grade, school enrollment
status, and marital status (figure 4A.6). In regard to age, only 39 percent

(34 studies) report heterogeneous results. Heterogeneous effects by marital status, schooling status (that is, whether a girl is in or out of school), and grade level or years of schooling are even less frequently reported. Only 14 percent of studies (12 studies) report differences between married and unmarried adolescent girls, and an even smaller proportion report differences by participants' schooling status (9 percent, 8 studies) or by grade level or years of schooling (10 percent, 9 studies). This highlights an important knowledge gap, as the evidence provides limited insights into how interventions may need to be tailored based on characteristics such as girls' age, marital status, schooling status, or educational attainment.

FIGURE 4A.6 Most Studies Do Not Report Heterogeneous Effects across Key Adolescent Girl Characteristics

Number of studies

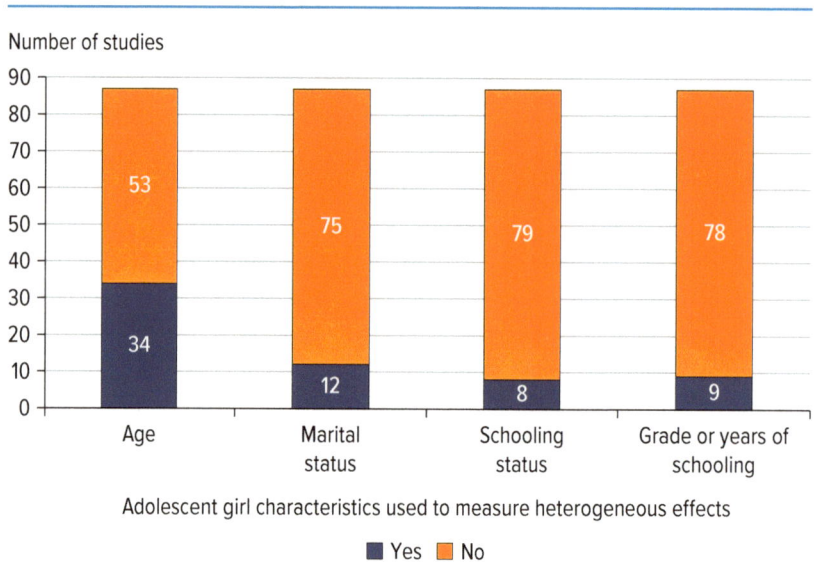

Adolescent girl characteristics used to measure heterogeneous effects

■ Yes ■ No

Source: Original figure for this report.

Notes

1. Most of the programs reviewed include a variety of interventions, either directly targeting adolescent girls or indirectly engaging with their communities. These interventions are categorized according to their core components, which include cash transfers, school fee reduction or elimination, girls' group empowerment programs, vocational training, financial literacy, or a combination of these components.

2. The cumulative number of experimental and quasi-experimental evaluations of impact on education increased 15-fold between 2000 and 2016 (Wodon et al. 2018). Many of these evaluations either focus on girls' education or present

evidence on girls' education within the context of a program that benefits both boys and girls (Evans and Yuan 2022). They measure both intermediate education outcomes, such as enrollment and attendance, and final education outcomes, such as completion and student learning.

References

Adoho, Franck, Shubha Chakravarty, Dala T. Korkoyah, Mattias Lundberg, and Afia Tasneem. 2014. "The Impact of an Adolescent Girls Employment Program: The EPAG Project in Liberia." Policy Research Working Paper 6832, World Bank, Washington, DC. https://doi.org/10.1596/1813-9450-6832.

Asfaw, Solomon, Benjamin Davis, Josh Dewbre, Sudhanshu Handa, and Paul Winters. 2014. "Cash Transfer Programme, Productive Activities and Labour Supply: Evidence from a Randomised Experiment in Kenya." *Journal of Development Studies* 50 (8): 1172–96. https://doi.org/10.1080/00220388.2014.919383.

Austrian, Karen, Erica Soler-Hampejsek, Jere R. Behrman, Jean Digitale, Natalie Jackson Hachonda, Maximillian Bweupe, and Paul C. Hewett. 2020. "The Impact of the Adolescent Girls Empowerment Program (AGEP) on Short and Long Term Social, Economic, Education and Fertility Outcomes: A Cluster Randomized Controlled Trial in Zambia." *BMC Public Health* 20 (1): 349. https://doi.org/10.1186/s12889-020-08468-0.

Austrian, Karen, Erica Soler-Hampejsek, Beth Kangwana, Yohannes Dibaba Wado, Benta Abuya, and John A. Maluccio. 2021. "Impacts of Two-Year Multisectoral Cash Plus Programs on Young Adolescent Girls' Education, Health and Economic Outcomes: Adolescent Girls Initiative–Kenya (AGI-K) Randomized Trial." *BMC Public Health* 21 (1): 2159. https://doi.org/10.1186/s12889-021-12224-3.

Austrian, Karen, and Eunice Muthengi. 2014. "Can Economic Assets Increase Girls' Risk of Sexual Harassment? Evaluation Results from a Social, Health and Economic Asset-Building Intervention for Vulnerable Adolescent Girls in Uganda." *Children and Youth Services Review* 47 (December): 168–75. https://doi.org/10.1016/j.childyouth.2014.08.012.

Baird, Sarah, Ephraim Chirwa, Jacobus de Hoop, and Berk Özler. 2016. "Girl Power: Cash Transfers and Adolescent Welfare: Evidence from a Cluster-Randomized Experiment in Malawi." In *Human Capital*, edited by Sebastian Edwards, Simon Johnson, and David N. Weil, 139–64. Vol. 2 of *African Successes*. Chicago: University of Chicago Press. https://www.nber.org/books-and-chapters/african-successes-volume-ii-human-capital/girl-power-cash-transfers-and-adolescent-welfare-evidence-cluster-randomized-experiment-malawi.

Baird, Sarah, Craig McIntosh, and Berk Özler. 2019. "When the Money Runs Out: Do Cash Transfers Have Sustained Effects on Human Capital Accumulation?" *Journal of Development Economics* 140 (September): 169–85. https://doi.org/10.1016/j.jdeveco.2019.04.004.

Baird, Sarah, and Berk Özler. 2016. "Sustained Effects on Economic Empowerment of Interventions for Adolescent Girls: Existing Evidence and Knowledge Gaps." Background Paper, Center for Global Development, Washington, DC.

Bandiera, Oriana, Niklas Buehren, Robin Burgess, Markus Goldstein, Selim Gulesci, Imran Rasul, and Munshi Sulaiman. 2020. "Women's Empowerment in Action: Evidence from a Randomized Control Trial in Africa." *American Economic Journal: Applied Economics* 12 (1): 210–59. https://doi.org/10.1257/app.20170416.

Bandiera, Oriana, Niklas Buehren, Markus Goldstein, Imran Rasul, and Andrea Smurra. 2019. "The Economic Lives of Young Women in the Time of Ebola: Lessons from an Empowerment Program." Policy Research Working Paper 8760, World Bank, Washington, DC. https://doi.org/10.1596/1813-9450-8760.

Bandiera, Oriana, Ahmed Elsayed, Andrea Smurra, and Céline Zipfel. 2022. "Young Adults and Labor Markets in Africa." *Journal of Economic Perspectives* 36 (1): 81–100. https://doi.org/10.1257/jep.36.1.81.

Berge, Lars Ivar Oppedal, Kjetil Bjorvatn, Fortunata Makene, Helgesson Sekei, Vincent Somville, and Bertil Tungodden. 2022. "On the Doorstep of Adulthood: Empowering Economic and Fertility Choices of Young Women." Norwegian School of Economics, Norway.

Bergstrom, Katy, and Berk Özler. 2023. "Improving the Well-Being of Adolescent Girls in Developing Countries." *World Bank Research Observer* 38 (2): 179–212. https://doi.org/10.1093/wbro/lkac007.

Boulhane, Othmane, Claire Boxho, Désiré Kanga, Estelle Koussoubé, and Léa Rouanet. 2024. "Empowering Adolescent Girls through Safe Spaces and Accompanying Measures in Côte d'Ivoire." Policy Research Working Paper 10721, World Bank, Washington, DC.

Brar, Rajdev, Niklas Buehren, Sreelakshmi Papineni, and Munshi Sulaiman. 2023. "Rebel with a Cause: Effects of a Gender Norms Intervention for Adolescents in Somalia." Policy Research Working Paper 10567, World Bank, Washington, DC. https://doi.org/10.1596/1813-9450-10567.

Brudevold-Newman, Andrew. 2021. "Expanding Access to Secondary Education: Evidence from a Fee Reduction and Capacity Expansion Policy in Kenya." *Economics of Education Review* 83 (August): 102127. https://doi.org/10.1016/j.econedurev.2021.102127.

Brudevold-Newman, Andrew, Maddalena Honorati, Gerald Ipapa, Pamela Jakiela, and Owen Ozier. 2023. "A Firm of One's Own: Experimental Evidence on Credit Constraints and Occupational Choice." Working Paper 646, Center for Global Development, Washington, DC. https://www.cgdev.org/sites/default/files/firm-ones-own-experimental-evidence-credit-constraints-and-occupational-choice.pdf.

Buehren, Niklas, Shubha Chakravarty, Markus Goldstein, Vanya Slavchevska, and Munshi Sulaiman. 2017. "Adolescent Girls' Empowerment in Conflict-Affected Settings: Experimental Evidence from South Sudan." Unpublished, World Bank, Washington, DC.

Buehren, Niklas, Markus Goldstein, Selim Gulesci, Munshi Sulaiman, and Venus Yam. 2017. "Evaluation of an Adolescent Development Program for Girls in Tanzania." Working Paper 7961, World Bank, Washington, DC. https://doi.org/10.1596/1813-9450-7961.

Burke, Holly M., Mario Chen, Kate Murray, Charl Bezuidenhout, Phuti Ngwepe, Alissa Bernholc, and Andrew Medina-Marino. 2020. "The Effects of the Integration of an Economic Strengthening and HIV Prevention Education Programme on the Prevalence of Sexually Transmitted Infections and Savings Behaviours among Adolescents: A Full-Factorial Randomised Controlled Trial in South Africa." *BMJ Global Health* 5 (4): e002029. https://doi.org/10.1136/bmjgh-2019-002029.

Carranza, Eliana, Aletheia Amalia Donald, Florian Grosset, and Supreet Kaur. 2022. "The Social Tax: Redistributive Pressure and Labor Supply." Policy Research Working Paper 10155, World Bank, Washington, DC.

Carranza, Eliana, and David McKenzie. 2024. "Job Training and Job Search Assistance Policies in Developing Countries." *Journal of Economic Perspectives* 38 (1): 221–44. https://doi.org/10.1257/jep.38.1.221.

Carvalho, Shelby, and David Evans. 2022. "Girls' Education and Women's Equality: How to Get More out of the World's Most Promising Investment." Center for Global Development, Washington, DC. https://www.cgdev.org/publication/girls -education-and-womens-equality-how-get-more-out-worlds-most-promising -investment.

Chicoine, Luke. 2021. "Free Primary Education, Fertility, and Women's Access to the Labor Market: Evidence from Ethiopia." *World Bank Economic Review* 35 (2): 480–98. https://doi.org/10.1093/wber/lhz042.

Cirillo, Cristina, Tia Palermo, and Francesca Viola. 2021. "Non-contributory Social Protection and Adolescents in Lower- and Middle-Income Countries: A Review of Government Programming and Impacts." United Nations Children's Fund, New York.

Cohen, Isabelle, Maryam Abubakar, and Daniel Perlman. 2023. "Pathways to Choice: A Bundled Intervention against Child Marriage." Center for Effective Global Action Working Paper 230, University of California, Berkeley. https://doi.org/10.26085 /C31C71.

Decker, Michele R., Shannon N. Wood, Esther Ndinda, Gayane Yenokyan, Jacob Sinclair, Nankali Maksud, Brendan Ross, Benjamin Omondi, and Martin Ndirangu. 2018. "Sexual Violence among Adolescent Girls and Young Women in Malawi: A Cluster-Randomized Controlled Implementation Trial of Empowerment Self-Defense Training." *BMC Public Health* 18 (1): 1341. https://doi.org/10.1186 /s12889-018-6220-0.

Deshpande, Rani, and Antonique Koning. 2023. "The Impact of Financial Inclusion on Young Women's Well-Being: A Survey of Evidence and Recommendations for Practitioners." CGAP, Washington, DC. https://www.cgap.org/research/publication /impact-of-financial-inclusion-on-young-womens-well-being-survey-of-evidence.

Duflo, Esther, Pascaline Dupas, and Michael Kremer. 2021. "The Impact of Free Secondary Education: Experimental Evidence from Ghana." NBER Working Paper 28937, National Bureau of Economic Research, Cambridge, MA. https://doi.org /10.3386/w28937.

Dunbar, Megan S., Mi-Suk Kang Dufour, Barrot Lambdin, Imelda Mudekunye-Mahaka, Definate Nhamo, and Nancy S. Padian. 2014. "The SHAZ! Project: Results from a Pilot Randomized Trial of a Structural Intervention to Prevent HIV among Adolescent Women in Zimbabwe." *PLOS ONE* 9 (11): e113621. https://doi.org /10.1371/journal.pone.0113621.

Edmeades, Jeffrey, Hannah Lantos, and Feven Mekuria. 2016. "Worth the Effort? Combining Sexual and Reproductive Health and Economic Empowerment Programming for Married Adolescent Girls in Amhara, Ethiopia." *Vulnerable Children and Youth Studies* 11 (4): 339–51. https://doi.org/10.1080/17450128.2016.1226529.

Elder, Sara, and Sriani Kring. 2016. "Young and Female: A Double 'Strike' for Women Entering the Workforce." Work4Youth Publication Series 32, International Labour Organization, Geneva. https://www.semanticscholar.org/paper/Young-and-female -a-double-strike-Gender-analysis-of-Elder-Kring/ad4aca13ee8592c02b9379b 6cb022ec9d93c9abe.

Emezue, Chuka, Cristina Pozneanscaia, Greg Sheaf, Valeria Groppo, Shivit Bakrania, and Josiah Kaplan. 2021. "The Impact of Educational Policies and Programmes on Child Work and Child Labour in Low-and-Middle-Income Countries: A Rapid Evidence Assessment Study Protocol." United Nations Children's Fund—Innocenti, Florence, Italy. https://www.unicef.org/innocenti/reports/impact-educational -policies-and-programmes-child-work-and-child-labour.

Evans, David K., Susannah Hares, Peter A. Holland, and Amina Mendez Acosta. 2023. "Adolescent Girls' Safety in and out of School: Evidence on Physical and Sexual Violence from across Sub-Saharan Africa." *Journal of Development Studies* 59 (5): 739–57. https://doi.org/10.1080/00220388.2023.2172333.

Evans, David K., Amina Mendez Acosta, and Fei Yuan. 2024. "Girls' Education at Scale." *World Bank Research Observer* 39 (1): 47–74. https://doi.org/10.1093/wbro /lkad002.

Evans, David K., and Fei Yuan. 2022. "What We Learn about Girls' Education from Interventions That Do Not Focus on Girls." *World Bank Economic Review* 36 (1): 244–67.

Fiala, Nathan, Ana Garcia-Hernandez, Kritika Narula, and Nishith Prakash. 2022. "Wheels of Change: Transforming Girls' Lives with Bicycles." IZA Discussion Paper Series 15076, Institute of Labor Economics (IZA), Bonn, Germany.

Gassier, Marine, Lea Rouanet, and Lacina Traore. 2022. "Addressing Gender-Based Segregation through Information: Evidence from a Randomized Experiment in the Republic of Congo." Policy Research Working Paper 9934, World Bank, Washington, DC.

Haberland, Nicole, Thomas de Hoop, Sapna Desai, Sarah Engebretsen, and Thoai Ngo. 2021. "Adolescent Girls' and Young Women's Economic Empowerment Programs: Emerging Insights from a Review of Reviews." ECWG Working Paper 03, Evidence Consortium on Women's Groups, Washington, DC. https://doi.org /10.31899/pgy17.1031.

Hallfors, Denise, Hyunsan Cho, Simbarashe Rusakaniko, Bonita Iritani, John Mapfumo, and Carolyn Halpern. 2011. "Supporting Adolescent Orphan Girls to Stay in School as HIV Risk Prevention: Evidence from a Randomized Controlled Trial in Zimbabwe." *American Journal of Public Health* 101 (6): 1082–88. https://doi .org/10.2105/AJPH.2010.300042.

Heath, Rachel, and A. Mushfiq Mobarak. 2015. "Manufacturing Growth and the Lives of Bangladeshi Women." *Journal of Development Economics* 115 (July): 1–15. https://doi.org/10.1016/j.jdeveco.2015.01.006.

Hicks, Joan Hamory, Michael Kremer, Isaac Mbiti, and Edward Miguel. 2016. *Evaluating the Impact of Vocational Education Vouchers on Out-of-School Youth in Kenya.* 3ie Impact Evaluation Report 37. New Delhi, India: International Institute for Impact Evaluation. https://doi.org/10.23846/ow1064.

Honorati, Maddalena. 2015. "The Impact of Private Sector Internship and Training on Urban Youth in Kenya." Policy Research Working Paper 7404, World Bank, Washington, DC. https://doi.org/10.1596/1813-9450-7404.

Jakiela, Pamela, and Owen Ozier. 2016. "Does Africa Need a Rotten Kin Theorem? Experimental Evidence from Village Economies." *Review of Economic Studies* 83 (1): 231–68.

Jensen, Robert. 2012. "Do Labor Market Opportunities Affect Young Women's Work and Family Decisions? Experimental Evidence from India." *Quarterly Journal of Economics* 127 (2): 753–92. https://doi.org/10.1093/qje/qjs002.

JPAL (Abdul Latif Jameel Poverty Action Lab). 2017. "Roll Call: Getting Children into School." Policy Bulletin, JPAL, Cambridge, MA.

Kilburn, Kelly, James P. Hughes, Catherine MacPhail, Ryan G. Wagner, F. Xavier Gómez-Olivé, Kathleen Kahn, and Audrey Pettifor. 2019. "Cash Transfers, Young Women's Economic Well-Being, and HIV Risk: Evidence from HPTN 068." *AIDS and Behavior* 23 (5): 1178–94. https://doi.org/10.1007/s10461-018-2329-5.

Klasen, Stephan. 2019. "What Explains Uneven Female Labor Force Participation Levels and Trends in Developing Countries?" *World Bank Research Observer* 34 (2): 161–97. https://doi.org/10.1093/wbro/lkz005.

Malhotra, Anju, and Shatha Elnakib. 2021. "20 Years of the Evidence Base on What Works to Prevent Child Marriage: A Systematic Review." *Journal of Adolescent Health* 68 (5): 847–62. https://doi.org/10.1016/j.jadohealth.2020.11.017.

McKenzie, David. 2021. "Small Business Training to Improve Management Practices in Developing Countries: Re-assessing the Evidence for 'Training Doesn't Work.'" *Oxford Review of Economic Policy* 37 (2): 276–301. https://doi.org/10.1093/oxrep/grab002.

McKenzie, David, Christopher Woodruff, Kjetil Bjorvatn, Miriam Bruhn, Jing Cai, Juanita Gonzalez-Uribe, Simon Quinn, Tetsushi Sonobe, and Martin Valdivia. 2023. "Training Entrepreneurs." *VoxDevLit* 1 (3). https://voxdev.org/voxdevlit/training-entrepreneurs.

Meherali, Salima, Komal Abdul Rahim, Sandra Campbell, and Zohra S. Lassi. 2021. "Does Digital Literacy Empower Adolescent Girls in Low- and Middle-Income Countries: A Systematic Review." *Frontiers in Public Health* 9. https://doi.org/10.3389/fpubh.2021.761394.

Melnikas, Andrea J., Grace Saul, Michelle Chau, Neelanjana Pandey, James Mkandawire, Mouhamadou Gueye, Aissa Diarra, and Sajeda Amin. 2021. "More Than Brides Alliance: Endline Evaluation Report." Population Council, New York.

Oyĕwùmí, Oyèrónké. 1997. *The Invention of Women: Making an African Sense of Western Gender Discourses.* Minneapolis: University of Minnesota Press.

Özler, Berk, Kelly Hallman, Marie-France Guimond, Elizabeth A. Kelvin, Marian Rogers, and Esther Karnley. 2020. "Girl Empower—A Gender Transformative Mentoring and Cash Transfer Intervention to Promote Adolescent Wellbeing: Impact Findings from a Cluster-Randomized Controlled Trial in Liberia." *SSM Population Health* 10 (April): 100527. https://doi.org/10.1016/j.ssmph.2019.100527.

Palermo, Tia, Leah Prencipe, and Lusajo Kajula. 2021. "Effects of Government-Implemented Cash Plus Model on Violence Experiences and Perpetration among Adolescents in Tanzania, 2018–2019." *American Journal of Public Health* 111 (12): 2227–38. https://doi.org/10.2105/AJPH.2021.306509.

Psaki, Stephanie, Nicole Haberland, Barbara Mensch, Lauren Woyczynski, and Erica Chuang. 2022. "Policies and Interventions to Remove Gender-Related Barriers to Girls' School Participation and Learning in Low- and Middle-Income Countries: A Systematic Review of the Evidence." *Campbell Systematic Reviews* 18 (1): e1207. https://doi.org/10.1002/cl2.1207.

Shah, Manisha, Jennifer Seager, João Montalvão, and Markus Goldstein. 2023. "Sex, Power, and Adolescence: Intimate Partner Violence and Sexual Behaviors." Working Paper 31624, National Bureau of Economic Research, Cambridge, MA. https://doi .org/10.3386/w31624.

Sperling, Gene B., and Rebecca Winthrop. 2016. *What Works in Girls' Education: Evidence for the World's Best Investment.* Washington, DC: Brookings Institution Press.

Ssewamala, Fred M., Leyla Ismayilova, Mary McKay, Elizabeth Sperber, William Bannon, and Stacey Alicea. 2010. "Gender and the Effects of an Economic Empowerment Program on Attitudes toward Sexual Risk-Taking among AIDS-Orphaned Adolescent Youth in Uganda." *Journal of Adolescent Health* 46 (4): 372–78. https://doi.org/10.1016/j.jadohealth.2009.08.010.

Stark, Lindsay, Khudejha Asghar, Ilana Seff, Gary Yu, Teame Tesfay Gessesse, Leora Ward, Asham Assazenew Baysa, Amy Neiman, and Kathryn L. Falb. 2018. "Preventing Violence against Refugee Adolescent Girls: Findings from a Cluster Randomised Controlled Trial in Ethiopia." *BMJ Global Health* 3 (5): e000825. https://doi.org/10.1136/bmjgh-2018-000825.

Temin, Miriam, and Craig J. Heck. 2020. "Close to Home: Evidence on the Impact of Community-Based Girl Groups." *Global Health: Science and Practice* 8 (2): 300–324. https://doi.org/10.9745/GHSP-D-20-00015.

Williams, Catherine, and Niyi Ogunkoya. 2021. "Women and the Age-Group System among the Ijebu of Southwestern Nigeria." *Yoruba Studies Review* 1 (December): 123–36. https://doi.org/10.32473/ysr.v1i1.130018.

Wodon, Quentin, Claudio E. Montenegro, Hoa Nguyen, and Adenike Onagoruwa. 2018. "Missed Opportunities: The High Cost of Not Educating Girls." World Bank, Washington, DC.

SPOTLIGHT 4

Focusing on Change: Analyzing the Political Economy of Adolescent Girls' Empowerment Initiatives in Africa

Michael Kevane and Estelle Koussoubé

Key Messages

> *Too many children still die, too many mothers are lost to complications of childbirth, and too few girls are in secondary school. So we need to do much more.* —Mahamadou Issoufou, former president of Niger

- There is a significant gap in research related to the political economy of adolescent girls' empowerment and its implications. Current research primarily focuses on the impacts of adolescent girls' empowerment policies and programs, underscoring the need for greater exploration of the political economy factors that influence the success of programs and legal reforms.

- In recent decades, there has been a substantial increase in interest in and funding for adolescent girls' empowerment initiatives in Africa. This trend reflects a growing global interest in the empowerment of adolescent girls, but much more effort is needed to achieve this objective.

- To achieve success in adolescent girls' empowerment programs, four key areas require attention: government support, framing and persuasion that emphasizes economic benefits, engagement with leaders and key stakeholders in communities, and regional coordination and collaboration.

- Successful legal reforms, such as laws against child marriage, depend on five key elements: having a champion, establishing a solid analytical foundation that demonstrates the benefits of gender equality and legal reforms, creating an enabling environment for law enforcement through community engagement, building a large coalition of partners, and engaging the legal community.

A reproducibility package is available for this book in the Reproducible Research Repository at https://reproducibility.worldbank.org.

Navigating Power Dynamics in Adolescent Girls' Empowerment

There is scarce research in the field of the political economy of adolescent girls' empowerment in Africa, indicating a gap in understanding of this important topic.[1] The very nature of empowerment implies a transformative change in power dynamics, wherein previously disempowered individuals or communities gradually acquire power, that is, influence and control, in various spheres. Such a change involves various actors and institutions that have differing interests and strategies, with significant implications for the outcomes of the change process.

In the case of adolescent girls' empowerment, in this report's conceptual framework (chapter 1), empowerment manifests itself at various levels: at the individual level, through the acquisition of skills and agency; at the household and community levels, with shifts in attitudes and norms, such as marriage norms and norms related to work; and at the societal or state level, through changes in laws and the expansion of economic labor opportunities. Key actors involved in driving the transformative changes implied by these various routes for manifestation include individuals; households; religious, ethnic, and other affinity communities; political parties; organizations; corporations; and various additional groups at the national and international levels. Actors exhibit considerable variation in their immediate interests, underlying values, and beliefs concerning adolescent girls' empowerment issues. The interactions among actors determine the success of initiatives (Jones et al. 2018; Shearer et al. 2016).

This spotlight examines the role of key actors, institutions, and ideas in influencing the adoption and implementation of programs and policies, as well as legal reforms, aimed at empowering adolescent girls in Africa. It is important to note that the analysis presented here does not aim to provide a comprehensive overview of all the political economy factors influencing changes in policy regarding adolescent girls' empowerment. Instead, its focus is on highlighting key areas of attention or essential lessons drawn from successful adoption and implementation of adolescent girls' empowerment programs and legal reforms. A review of existing literature, as well as consultations with key stakeholders—including World Bank staff, government officials, and activists—informs the analysis.

The spotlight explores key areas of attention for preparing and implementing adolescent girls' empowerment programs and for legal reforms aimed at adolescent girls' empowerment. Although some key areas of attention overlap, some substantive differences should be highlighted, especially given the broader implications that policies and reforms hold for a particular country. In addition, it's important to understand the broader context of international support for adolescent girls' empowerment initiatives in Africa. Box S4.1 provides an overview of the changing landscape, including international commitments, increased funding, and the factors driving the growing focus on adolescent girls' empowerment. This context is crucial for understanding the environment in which programs and legal reforms are being implemented.

BOX S4.1 The Changing Landscape of International Support for Adolescent Girls' Empowerment Programs and Policies

Over the past few decades, driven by international and regional efforts involving various stakeholders such as women's and girls' organizations, activists, and international organizations, African governments have made significant commitments to promoting gender equality and empowering women and girls. These commitments include signing and ratifying numerous international, regional, and subregional agreements and instruments. Notable among them are crucial legal frameworks like the "Convention on the Elimination of All Forms of Discrimination against Women," the "Beijing Declaration and Platform for Action," and the "Protocol to the African Charter on Human and Peoples' Rights on the Rights of Women in Africa" (commonly referred to as the "Maputo Protocol"), as well as the Sustainable Development Goals. The fifth of these goals has the specific aim to achieve gender equality and empower all women and girls (see OECD 2021 for an overview of the legal framework in Africa regarding women's rights). However, it is essential to note that although some countries have incorporated these standards into their legal frameworks and policies, others have not done so yet (chapter 2).

Low- and middle-income countries have made steady progress in the pursuit of gender equality over the past few decades. This progress is particularly evident in areas such as education, health, and labor market outcomes. While these improvements can be partly attributed to the efforts described in the previous paragraph, there is a consensus that much more needs to be accomplished to fully achieve gender equality (UN Women 2023; UNICEF, UN Women, and Plan International 2020; World Bank 2012).

Progress made in domains such as girls' education and health also reflects the higher priority given to these domains in the agendas and public discourse of international donors, as well as in their financial investment priorities (Carvalho and Evans 2022; Devonald, Guglielmi, and Jones 2023). For example, a 2022 analysis of financial investments by the World Bank and the United Kingdom's Foreign, Commonwealth and Development Office reveals a significant increase in education spending in the preceding two decades (Carvalho and Evans 2022). At the World Bank, the analysis found, spending rose from an average of $29 million in 2000–05 to $1.65 billion in 2015–20; at the Foreign

(continued)

BOX S4.1 The Changing Landscape of International Support for Adolescent Girls'
Empowerment Programs and Policies *(continued)*

Commonwealth and Development Office, it increased from an average of $69 million to $481 million. Despite the increased level of priority being assigned, donors continue to underinvest in efforts to dismantle many of the gender-specific constraints faced by girls, such as child marriage, adolescent pregnancy, and inadequate menstrual hygiene, as well as the underlying causes of gender inequality in education outcomes (Carvalho and Evans 2022). Moreover, investments in adolescent girls and gender equality represent only a small fraction of total development assistance: less than 6 percent from the 10 top gender equality donors in 2020 (Devonald, Guglielmi, and Jones 2023).

Several factors could explain the increased attention and priority given to adolescent girls' empowerment. This spotlight focuses on three key political economy factors. First, the shift can be partly attributed to the demand from high-level political figures, including heads of state like the former president of Niger, Mahamadou Issoufou, who have advocated for more significant efforts to empower girls. President Issoufou's call for action triggered subsequent calls and endorsements by other heads of state in the Sahel region, prompting responses from international organizations, including the United Nations and World Bank. These responses have taken the form of investments in initiatives aimed at enhancing the human capital of adolescent girls and reducing gender inequality in countries in the region.

Another contributing factor is the growing body of evidence that supports initiatives focused on girls' empowerment. Specifically, there is increasing evidence showing the importance of investing in girls' empowerment for reducing poverty and fostering economic development, as well as the cost of inaction (for example, Chaaban and Cunningham 2011; Levine et al. 2008; Sheehan et al. 2017; Wodon et al. 2017; Wodon et al. 2018; World Bank 2019). The prevalence of the economic argument for promoting empowerment in the public discourse (Carvalho and Evans 2022) highlights the importance of this evidence for the adoption of programs and policies that benefit girls. For example, evidence concerning the cost of gender inequality in Niger, produced in 2019, likely played a pivotal role in the government's subsequent decision to implement policy and legal reforms aimed at eradicating early marriage and ensuring girls' access to education (World Bank 2019).

Additionally, besides the growing evidence of the economic and social benefits of investing in adolescent girls' empowerment, there has been a steady increase in the availability of evidence on effective strategies for empowering girls across a range of domains (as discussed in chapters 3 and 4). This evidence appears to have been leveraged in an iterative process to design second- and third-generation programs for implementation by governments and nongovernmental organizations that will have a greater impact across the continent (for example, BRAC and UNFPA 2023; World Bank 2023).

Increasing Adolescent Girls' Empowerment through Evidence-Based Interventions

Four key areas of attention have been identified that influence the preparation and implementation of evidence-based interventions aimed at empowering adolescent girls: government champions, economically linked framing, engaging influential community members, and regional coordination and collaboration.

Government Policy Makers' Support

Informants for this spotlight emphasized the importance of having government officials champion projects, promote interministerial coordination, and engage key ministries beyond those focused solely on gender or women's issues, including those responsible for youth and education. This is important at the preparation phase of a project as well as during its implementation. However, political support by governments should not be assumed to be automatic, and it is not certain that governments will fund programs without external financing. For instance, the success of the adolescent girls' empowerment programs analyzed as part of this spotlight can be attributed to the advocacy of high-level figures in governments, including ministers of finance and planning or equivalent, along with other influential (male and female) politicians. Presentations of evidence on the benefits of gender equality and empowering girls, along with the costs of not doing so, to other governments and political leaders has helped ensure support for these projects. Although high-level champions are needed, securing buy-in at all levels of government plays a role in the sustainability of programs in case of changes in leadership.

Framing and Persuasion

Economic analysis demonstrating the returns on investments for empowering adolescent girls is crucial. Having solid analytical work is essential for supporting the actions of potential champions as well as for securing the needed buy-in from various governmental and societal bodies. Additionally, it can be strategically beneficial to frame adolescent girls' empowerment projects as youth initiatives, as economic investments, or as both, instead of solely using a rights-based framing. Adolescent girls' empowerment projects have sometimes been perceived as social-protection efforts rather than economic investment programs, which may have led some governments to be hesitant about borrowing to pay for them. Some government officials may need convincing that social-protection programs as well as adolescent girls' initiatives yield high returns in terms of increased economic activity in both the short and longer terms among women and girls. The integration of interventions targeting a broader audience, including boys, even if only through gender-sensitive trainings, can also be beneficial to persuade policy makers and a larger constituency.

Engaging Leaders and Key Stakeholders

Collaboration with (community and religious) leaders, as well as other key stakeholders such as parents, is essential to secure the necessary support for the smooth implementation of program activities. Highlighting both the social and economic benefits of initiatives, leveraging trusted sources to disseminate messages, and emphasizing the role of the community in realizing the benefits are all crucial aspects. For example, in Mauritania and Niger, as part of government-implemented adolescent girls' empowerment projects, the involvement of experts in Islam and development facilitated discussions with religious leaders on critical issues such as child marriage, girls' education, and family planning. Parental discussions and gender-sensitive training programs targeting boys have also played a crucial role in instilling a sense of ownership of adolescent girls' empowerment initiatives within communities, thereby gaining community support for the initiatives.

Regional Coordination and Collaboration

Engaging with regional political and economic bodies and institutions, such as the African Union and other subregional entities, is a crucial aspect of regional programs aimed at empowering adolescent girls in Africa. The primary goals of these regional partnerships include codifying political and legal reforms to ensure that they are well structured and recognized; facilitating peer-to-peer exchanges between countries to encourage the sharing of experiences, best practices, and lessons learned in the context of adolescent girls' empowerment; and communicating progress to raise awareness of successful initiatives and foster a sense of accountability among governments and stakeholders. Support in strengthening these institutions may be a necessary initial step in enabling them to fulfill their intended roles effectively and in preventing delays in the implementation of critical activities.

From Programming to Policy Making to Legal Reforms

This section explores key lessons from successful efforts at reforming or establishing crucial laws that affect the well-being of adolescent girls, particularly laws related to child marriage. As emphasized in chapter 3, there is evidence that laws banning child marriage, when enforced, can effectively reduce child marriage and childbearing. Although laws banning child marriage, especially strong ones that criminalize it, may not be sufficient on their own to drive change in situations in which they significantly deviate from prevailing social norms or in which there is little adherence to legal regulations, such laws still play a role in creating an enabling environment for girls' empowerment (Svanemyr et al. 2013). Implementing positive changes requires strategic approaches. Box S4.2 offers valuable insights from a leader in adolescent girls' empowerment programs, providing a practical perspective on bringing about change in this critical area.

Effective legal reform has five key components:

- **Having a champion.**
- **Having a solid analytical foundation** that demonstrates the benefits of gender equality and legal reforms for empowering adolescent girls.
- **Creating an enabling environment** for the enforcement of a particular law through engagement with various parts of society, starting with key stakeholders in communities, and through widespread dissemination and explanation of the law's objectives.
- **Building a large coalition of partners** that includes government bodies, as well as local and international nongovernmental organizations, donors, and other stakeholders.
- **Engaging the legal community.**

Although the first three of these components are the same as those emphasized for adolescent girls' empowerment programs, they become even more critical in the context of legal reforms. Convincing stakeholders to invest in girls' education is one challenge, but persuading them to establish a law that defies established norms presents a distinct set of obstacles.

BOX S4.2 Recipe for Success: Advice from a Leader of an Adolescent Girls' Empowerment Program to Those Who Want to Bring About Change and Work on Empowering Adolescent Girls

- Begin by assessing the terrain and the presence of analytical work and a champion. Without these elements, it may be challenging to proceed.
- Boldness and a proactive approach are crucial attributes.
- Develop a deep understanding of the local context. Building rapport with authorities; establishing trust; and demonstrating passion, honesty, and a willingness to engage in dialogue are all vital components of success.

Moreover, building a large coalition of partners that includes government bodies—as well as local and international nongovernmental organizations, donors, and other stakeholders—is crucial. Such a coalition not only demonstrates internal and external support for a reform but also serves to raise awareness about the issues addressed by the reform and to gain support from opponents.

When it comes to fostering the enforcement of laws, which may be the most challenging aspect of the change process, a key informant for this spotlight mentioned that "a law is necessary but not sufficient. After the law is passed, we must provide households with opportunities for their girls to thrive." This highlights the significance of leveraging existing adolescent girls' empowerment programs that are active within communities as catalysts for enforcing laws. In other words, gaining acceptance for laws that postpone child marriage within communities becomes more achievable when girls have access to education and economic opportunities. Child marriage, though fundamentally rooted in gender-inequitable norms, is also influenced by factors such as poverty and the limited economic prospects available to girls (Petroni et al. 2017).

> *In school, we receive advice about our future, and we are well educated. On the other hand, when we drop out of school, we easily get married.*
>
> —In-school girl, age 10 to 14, Perma, Benin

Additionally, engaging the legal community plays a key role in both enforcement and monitoring of laws. Building the capacity of the legal community facilitates the enforcement of existing laws that support girls' empowerment in countries where such laws exist and advocates for the enactment of laws promoting girls' empowerment in countries where there are legal gaps. For example, one World Bank–funded adolescent girls' empowerment project analyzed as part of this spotlight has established a regional legal platform comprising senior lawyers, judges, parliamentarians, and in some cases, supreme court justices. This platform aims to support the implementation of legislative reforms in target communities by enhancing the application of existing laws on gender; providing capacity building for actors within the judicial system, with a focus on texts and good practices related to the rights of girls and women; conducting a community-based dissemination of information about women's and girls' rights through community dialogues to dispel misconceptions and myths surrounding potential conflicts between laws and customary or religious practices; and supporting legal reforms, including the adoption of new legislation and revisions to discriminatory legal texts.

Although legal reforms play a crucial role in advancing adolescent girls' empowerment, it's also important to consider the impact of broader social movements and evolving forms of activism. Box S4.3 explores the landscape of youth-led social movements and the emerging role of digital media in advocating for adolescent girls' rights across Africa.

BOX S4.3 Evolving Social Practices

Adolescent girls' empowerment is a complex process influenced by various actors operating at different levels. Whereas there has been a great deal of emphasis on the role of the private sector in youth employment and young women's empowerment in Africa (Ayele, Glover, and Oosterom 2018; Beegle and Christiaensen 2019; Filmer and Fox 2014; Fox et al. 2020), the role of social movements remains underexplored.

Youth-Led Social Movements

Traditional social movements—involving, for instance, marches or protests—that advocate for adolescent girls' rights may pursue various strategies, including promoting consciousness raising at the individual level, coordinating changes in social norms, lobbying government officials, providing training for judges to bring about legal changes, and advocating for constitutional amendments. However, there are few well-documented examples of significant youth-led social movements or political parties in African countries in the past two decades with substantial engagement among adolescent girls or young women. In fact, women's movements more broadly are relatively marginalized in almost all African countries (Dieng 2023; Tripp et al. 2008). This dearth of youth-led movements constitutes a significant gap in the empowerment landscape.

In contrast, several Latin American countries, including Argentina with its Ni Una Menos movement, as well as countries in the Middle East and North Africa, have witnessed significant social movements and political agendas centered on adolescent girls or addressing issues relevant to them. These movements have played a crucial role in advocating for the rights and empowerment of adolescent girls (Belotti, Comunello, and Corradi 2021; Cohen 2022; Ennaji 2021; Friedman and Rodríguez Gustá 2023; Taft 2010).

However, some African countries have experienced youth-oriented social movements engaging adolescent boys, such as the Mungiki movement in Kenya. While the Mungiki movement started with a focus on reviving traditional cultural practices among youth, it rapidly expanded to urban centers, especially among young men. Despite its secretive and violent nature, during its peak it garnered substantial support among young men (Henningsen and Jones 2013; Kagwanja 2006; Rasmussen 2010; Wamue 2001). It's worth noting that some national-level youth movements in Africa

(continued)

BOX S4.3 Evolving Social Practices *(continued)*

are dominated by young men adhering to a heteronormative gender regime that constrains young women to dependent, domestic roles (for example, Crossouard and Dunne 2015). Their effectiveness remains unclear.

Digital Media and the Changing Landscape

The rise of digital media and social networks has marked a new era for adolescent empowerment. Digital media challenge traditional cultural gatekeepers and create opportunities for youth activists to disseminate empowering messages. Although both girls and boys are increasingly using social media platforms, gender disparities in digital access, along with differences in access to digital technologies between urban and rural areas, continue to impede broader participation (Begazo, Blimpo, and Dutz 2023; Wang et al. 2023). These disparities, coupled with challenges related to misuse and the spread of misinformation, limit the potential of digital activism to empower the most vulnerable.

Nevertheless, social media platforms facilitate various types of activism across Africa, including activism centered on addressing political issues, access to education, feminist issues, and more (see, for example, Nwaolikpe 2021; Reneses and Bosch 2023; and Sebeelo 2021). Notably, many African countries are witnessing the expansion of the cultural-production sector through online youth activists who actively generate and spread content and discourses resonating with adolescents, particularly girls (de Bruijn 2022; de Bruijn and Oudenhuijsen 2021). For instance, francophone Africa has seen the emergence of digitally active "slameuses" who use a fusion of hip-hop and poetry in slam performances—a form of spoken-word poetry that often addresses social and political issues— to convey messages of empowerment for adolescent girls. However, although social media and subsequent digital activism have transformed the nature of social movements, their influence on political party agendas, legislative outcomes, and government interventions related to adolescent girls' issues in Africa requires further examination.

Despite the growing global attention to and investments in adolescent girls' empowerment, there is a notable gap in research on its political economy, emphasizing the need for further investigation into the factors shaping this domain. The recipe for success in implementing evidence-based programs and legal reforms for adolescent girls' empowerment involves government support, preparation of evidence for a sound analytical underpinning, engagement with key stakeholders, and collaboration with a diverse range of stakeholders. Understanding and addressing the political economy of adolescent girls' empowerment is essential for fostering positive change in the lives of adolescent girls across Africa. As work continues toward gender equality and girls' empowerment, the insights that result from such work will serve as valuable guidance for policy makers, practitioners, and advocates dedicated to this crucial cause.

Note

1. It is worth acknowledging the large literature on the political economy of gender inequality and women's empowerment more broadly as well as in specific areas such as politics. For an example of a study on the politics of policy and program implementation for advancing adolescent girls' well-being in Ethiopia, see Jones et al. (2018).

References

Ayele, Seife, Dominic Glover, and Marjoke Oosterom. 2018. "Youth Employment and the Private Sector in Africa." *IDS Bulletin*, February 1. https://api.semanticscholar.org/CorpusID:158332689.

Beegle, Kathleen, and Luc Christiaensen. 2019. *Accelerating Poverty Reduction in Africa*. Washington, DC: World Bank. https://doi.org/10.1596/978-1-4648-1232-3.

Begazo, Tania, Moussa Blimpo, and Mark Dutz. 2023. *Digital Africa: Technological Transformation for Jobs*. Washington, DC: World Bank.

Belotti, Francesca, Francesca Comunello, and Consuelo Corradi. 2021. "*Feminicidio* and #NiUna Menos: An Analysis of Twitter Conversations during the First 3 Years of the Argentinean Movement." *Violence against Women* 27 (8): 1035–63. https://doi.org/10.1177/1077801220921947.

BRAC (Bangladesh Rural Advancement Committee) and UNFPA (United Nations Population Fund. 2023. "Adolescent Empowerment at Scale: Successes and Challenges of an Evidence-Based Approach to Young Women's Programming in Africa." BRAC, Dhaka, Bangladesh, and UNFPA, New York. https://www.unfpa.org/publications/adolescent-empowerment-scale-successes-and-challenges-evidence-based-approach-young.

Carvalho, Shelby, and David Evans. 2022. *Girls' Education and Women's Equality: How to Get More out of the World's Most Promising Investment*. Center for Global Development, Washington, DC. https://www.cgdev.org/publication/girls-education-and-womens-equality-how-get-more-out-worlds-most-promising-investment.

Chaaban, J., and W. Cunningham. 2011. "Measuring the Economic Gain of Investing in Girls: The Girl Effect Dividend." Policy Research Working Paper 5753, World Bank, Washington, DC.

Cohen, Paulina. 2022. "Not One Woman Less: An Analysis of the Advocacy and Activism of Argentina's Ni Una Menos Movement." *UCLA Journal of Gender and Law* 29 (1): 107–46.

Crossouard, Barbara, and Máiréad Dunne. 2015. "Politics, Gender and Youth Citizenship in Senegal: Youth Policing of Dissent and Diversity." *International Review of Education* 61 (1): 43–60. https://doi.org/10.1007/s11159-015-9466-0.

de Bruijn, Mirjam. 2022. "Slam Poetry in Chad: A Space of Belonging in an Environment of Violence and Repression." *Conflict and Society* 8 (1): 242–57.

de Bruijn, Mirjam, and Loes Oudenhuijsen. 2021. "Female Slam Poets of Francophone Africa: Spirited Words for Social Change." *Africa* 91 (5): 742–67.

Devonald, Megan, Silvia Guglielmi, and Nicola Jones. 2023. *Investing in Adolescent Girls: Mapping Global and National Funding Patterns from 2016–2020 Report*. London: Gender and Adolescence: Global Evidence (GAGE). https://doi.org/10.13140/RG .2.2.35019.05922.

Dieng, Rama Salla. 2023. "From Yewwu Yewwi to #FreeSenegal: Class, Gender and Generational Dynamics of Radical Feminist Activism in Senegal." *Politics and Gender, First View*: 1–7. https://doi.org/10.1017/S1743923X2200071X.

Ennaji, Moha. 2021. "Women, Social Movements and Political Activism in North Africa." In *The Palgrave Handbook of African Women's Studies*, edited by Olajumoke Yacob-Haliso and Toyin Falola, 1347–63. Cham: Springer International Publishing. https://doi.org/10.1007/978-3-030-28099-4_4.

Filmer, Deon, and Louise Fox. 2014. "Youth Employment in Sub-Saharan Africa." World Bank, Washington, DC.

Fox, Louise, Philip Mader, James Sumberg, Justin Flynn, and Marjoke Oosterom. 2020. "Africa's 'Youth Employment' Crisis Is Actually a 'Missing Jobs' Crisis." *Development Policy Review* 39: 621–43.

Friedman, Elisabeth Jay, and Ana Laura Rodríguez Gustá. 2023. "'Welcome to the Revolution': Promoting Generational Renewal in Argentina's Ni Una Menos." *Qualitative Sociology* 46 (2): 245–77. https://doi.org/10.1007/s11133-023 -09530-0.

Henningsen, Erik, and Peris Jones. 2013. "'What Kind of Hell Is This!' Understanding the Mungiki Movement's Power of Mobilisation." *Journal of Eastern African Studies* 7 (3): 371–388.

Jones, Nicola, Elizabeth Presler-Marshall, Bekele Tefera, and Bethelihem Gebre Alwab. 2018. "The Politics of Policy and Programme Implementation to Advance Adolescent Girls' Well-Being in Ethiopia." In *Empowering Adolescent Girls in Developing Countries*, edited by Caroline Harper, Nicola Jones, Anita Ghimire, Rachel Marcus, and Grace Kyomuhendo Bantebya, 62–80. London and New York: Routledge.

Kagwanja, Peter Mwangi. 2006. "'Power to Uhuru': Youth Identity and Generational Politics in Kenya's 2002 Elections." *African Affairs* 105 (418): 51–75.

Levine, Ruth, Cynthia Lloyd, Maurice Green, and Caren Grown. 2008. *Girls Count: A Global Investment & Action Agenda*. Center for Global Development, Washington, DC.

Nwaolikpe, Onyinyechi Nancy. 2021. "Women, Social Media, and Culture in Africa." In *The Palgrave Handbook of African Women's Studies*, edited by Olajumoke Yacob-Haliso and Toyin Faiola, 2045–61. London: Springer Nature.

OECD (Organisation for Economic Co-operation and Development). 2021. *SIGI 2021 Regional Report for Africa*. Social Institutions and Gender Index. Paris: OECD Publishing. https://doi.org/10.1787/a6d95d90-en.

Petroni, Suzanne, Mara Steinhaus, Natacha Stevanovic Fenn, Kirsten Stoebenau, and Amy Gregowski. 2017. "New Findings on Child Marriage in Sub-Saharan Africa." *Annals of Global Health* 83 (5–6): 781–90. https://doi.org/10.1016/j.aogh.2017 .09.001.

Rasmussen, Jacob. 2010. "Mungiki as Youth Movement: Revolution, Gender and Generational Politics in Nairobi, Kenya." *Young* 18 (3): 301–19.

Reneses, Pablo A., and Tanja Bosch. 2023. "The Limitations of Hashtag Feminist Activism on South African Twitter: A Case Study of #Menaretrash and #Womenaretrash." *Men and Masculinities* 26 (4): 585–603.

Sebeelo, Tebogo B. 2021. "Hashtag Activism, Politics and Resistance in Africa: Examining #ThisFlag and #RhodesMustFall Online Movements." *Insight on Africa* 13 (1): 95–109.

Shearer, Jessica C., Julia Abelson, Bocar Kouyaté, John N. Lavis, and Gill Walt. 2016. "Why Do Policies Change? Institutions, Interests, Ideas and Networks in Three Cases of Policy Reform." *Health Policy and Planning* 31 (9): 1200–11. https://doi.org/10.1093/heapol/czw052.

Sheehan, Peter, Kim Sweeny, Bruce Rasmussen, Annababette Wils, Howard S. Friedman, Jacqueline Mahon, George C. Patton, Susan M. Sawyer, Eric Howard, John Symons, Karin Stenberg, Satvika Chalasani, Neelam Maharaj, Nicola Reavley, Hui Shi, Masha Fridman, Alison Welsh, Emeka Nsofor, and Laura Laski. 2017. "Building the Foundations for Sustainable Development: A Case for Global Investment in the Capabilities of Adolescents." *Lancet* 390 (10104): 1792–806. https://doi.org/10.1016/S0140-6736(17)30872-3.

Svanemyr, Joar, Elisa Scolaro, V. Chandra-Mouli, K. Blondeel, and Marleen Temmerman. 2013. "The Contribution of Laws to Change the Practice of Child Marriage in Africa." Inter-Parliamentary Union, Geneva.

Taft, Jessica K. 2010. *Rebel Girls: Youth Activism and Social Change across the Americas.* New York: NYU Press.

Tripp, Aili Mari, Isabel Casimiro, Joy Kwesiga, and Alice Mungwa. 2008. *African Women's Movements: Transforming Political Landscapes.* Cambridge: Cambridge University Press.

UN (United Nations) Women. 2023. *Progress on the Sustainable Development Goals.* Progress on the Sustainable Development Goals Series. Bloomfield: United Nations Research Institute for Social Development.

UNICEF (United Nations Children's Fund), UN (United Nations) Women, and Plan International. 2020. *A New Era for Girls: Taking Stock of 25 Years of Progress.* New York: UNICEF, UN Women, and Plan International. https://www.unwomen.org/en/digital-library/publications/2020/03/a-new-era-for-girls-taking-stock-on-25-years-of-progress-for-girls.

Wamue, Grace Nyatugah. 2001. "Revisiting Our Indigenous Shrines through Mungiki." *African Affairs* 100 (400): 453–67.

Wang, Dongqing, Sachin Shinde, Roisin Drysdale, Alain Vandormael, Amare W. Tadesse, Huda Sherfi, Amani Tinkasimile, Mary Mwanyika-Sando, Mosa Moshabela, Till Bärnighausen, Deepika Sharma, and Wafaie W. Fawzi. 2023. "Access to Digital Media and Devices among Adolescents in Sub-Saharan Africa: A Multicountry, School-Based Survey." *Maternal and Child Nutrition* (April): e13462. Published ahead of print, April 4, 2023. https://doi.org/10.1111/mcn.13462.

Wodon, Quentin, Chata Male, Ada Nayihouba, Adenike Onagoruwa, Aboudrahyme Savadogo, Ali Yedan, Jeff Edmeades, Aslihan Kes, Neetu John, Lydia Murithi, Mara Steinhaus, and Suzanne Petroni. 2017. "Economic Impacts of Child Marriage: Global Synthesis Report." World Bank and International Center for Research on Women, Washington, DC.

Wodon, Quentin, Claudio E. Montenegro, Hoa Nguyen, and Adenike Onagoruwa. 2018. "Missed Opportunities: The High Cost of Not Educating Girls." World Bank, Washington, DC.

World Bank. 2012. *World Development Report 2012: Gender Equality and Development.* Washington, DC: World Bank.

World Bank. 2019. "Economic Impacts of Gender Inequality in Niger." World Bank, Washington, DC.

World Bank. 2023. "Gender Equality in Development: A Ten-Year Retrospective." World Bank, Washington, DC.

CHAPTER 5
Conclusions

Kehinde Ajayi, Estelle Koussoubé and Fatima Zahra

Key Messages

- Every adolescent girl has the potential to make a unique contribution to the world.
- Sustained progress improving the lives of adolescent girls requires concerted action.
- Six practicable steps can set adolescent girls in Africa on a pathway to prosperity:
  - Build human capital.
  - Enhance economic success.
  - Focus on the most vulnerable girls.
  - Adopt a holistic approach.
  - Address data and evidence gaps.
  - Mobilize diverse stakeholders.
- The cost of inaction is high. The time for change is now.

Where Do We Go from Here?

Every adolescent girl has the potential to thrive and make a distinctive contribution to the world. How can those around them ensure that each girl realizes her fullest potential as she transitions into adulthood? Society has a collective responsibility, driven not only by a moral imperative, but also by an economic incentive, to support each girl on her unique journey. Appropriately tailored interventions can transform trajectories for all African girls (figure 5.1), from the most vulnerable among them, like 12-year-old Mariam, who enter

---

A reproducibility package is available for this book in the Reproducible Research Repository at https://reproducibility.worldbank.org.

adolescence in challenging contexts facing the highest risks of school dropout, early marriage, and childbearing, to those like 10-year-old Grace, who are still on track to stay in school and have bold ambitions yet encounter mounting obstacles to fulfilling their aspirations. With tools and evidence-based guidance, vital support can be provided to adolescent girls navigating complex life transitions, from new labor market entrants like 19-year-old Chantal, transitioning from education to employment and seeking fulfilling, dignified work, to those like 15-year-old Imani, driven by determination amid the dual challenges of work and education, and to married adolescents and mothers like 18-year-old Aya, who must balance multiple responsibilities.

FIGURE 5.1   Appropriately Designed Interventions Can Empower Adolescent Girls at Any Age and in Any Circumstance

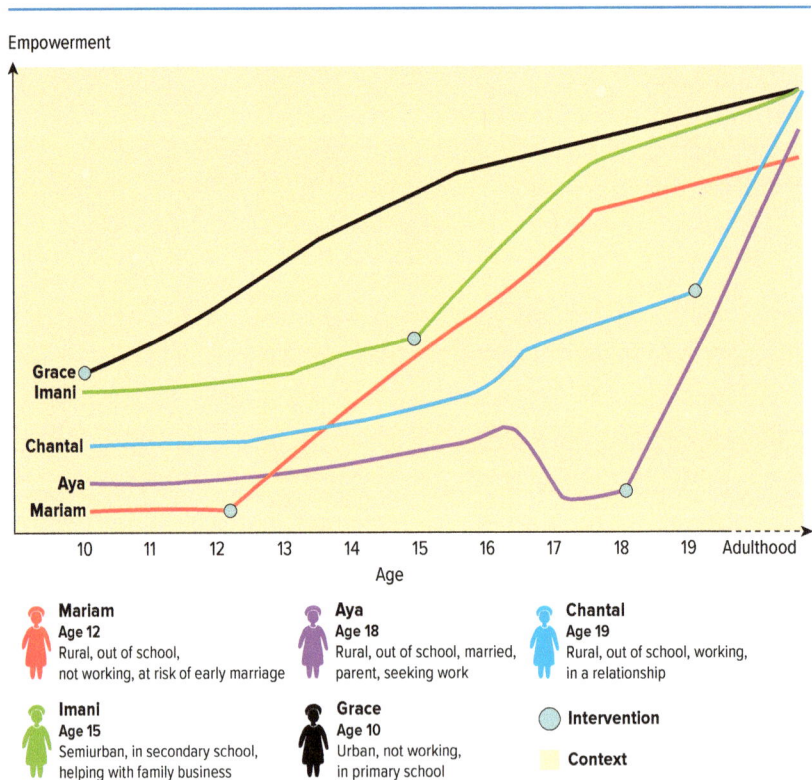

Source: Original figure for this report.

The past two decades have provided inspiring examples of countries that have made great strides toward improving the lives of adolescent girls. They have also revealed discouraging examples of setbacks and stagnation. The path to sustained progress requires concerted action. The conceptual framework, data analysis, and evidence reviews in this report outline six actionable steps forward.

- **Keep girls on the path to success by building human capital fundamentals through investments in education and health early on.** Concerted intervention from early adolescence (age 10) onward can provide a buffer for adolescent girls and equip them with a solid foundation that will enable them to navigate any challenges they may face on their path to adulthood. Policies and programs that reduce direct and indirect costs of education to students and their families have been found to be consistently effective in improving education outcomes, particularly for girls. In contexts in which child marriage is prevalent, education incentives also reduce child marriage and early childbearing. In communities in which access to education remains restricted or the quality of education is poor, interventions that work to alleviate these barriers can bolster the development of girls' human capital fundamentals. Although evidence on what works to improve health outcomes for adolescent girls in Africa is relatively thin, emerging studies and global evidence point to providing sexual and reproductive health education and youth-friendly services as the most effective approaches.

- **Complement human capital investments with interventions that provide girls with the essential resources and agency and a supportive environment conducive to their success.** Empowering adolescent girls for success goes beyond establishing human capital fundamentals. Market-aligned vocational training, business support, and life skills training need to be integrated to boost employment and income for girls, especially those who are out of school. Additionally, investment should be made in promising approaches to expand and improve the services and opportunities to which girls have access, including employment opportunities for women. Interventions should be customized to address contextual factors such as relevant legal frameworks, labor market structures, fragility and conflict, and community and household contexts to ensure sustainable improvements in girls' empowerment outcomes.

- **Tailor interventions to address the diverse circumstances and needs of girls, putting a priority on the most vulnerable.** Various groups of girls, particularly the most vulnerable girls—including those from the poorest households, rural areas with limited resources, and areas affected by violence—should be identified, and their needs should be made a priority. Definitions of vulnerability may extend to many circumstances and characteristics in addition to those just specified, such as ethnicity, religion, or disabilities. Girls balancing dual roles of working while attending school or taking care of children require tailored programs to support their needs for continuing education, accessing childcare, and earning income. Young mothers and married girls face unique obstacles to continuing their education and need support to enhance their human capital fundamentals and accumulate other resources.

- **Adopt a holistic approach in the design of interventions.** Potential challenges at different stages of program development and implementation can be anticipated and addressed. Factors such as program costs, implementation capacity, and alignment with existing initiatives must be carefully considered. Additionally, leveraging digital tools and platforms can be beneficial for reaching girls who are out of school, marry early, or reside in rural areas, given evidence of expanding digital access across different countries, demographics, and socioeconomic groups. Technological innovations can also lower costs given the challenges of tight fiscal space.

- **Address data and evidence gaps.** Measures in areas in which measurement is lacking, such as aspects of context, digital capital, and job quality, need to be developed and tested. Evidence must be generated and then programs designed that allow assessment of not only what works, but what works for whom, including for married adolescents and girls with children, who have often been overlooked. Priority should be given to measuring program quality from the program outset, using detailed indicators for assessing implementation effectiveness. Additional insights about cost-effectiveness are needed to advance understanding of the trade-offs among promising interventions. Effective avenues for scale-up are necessary so that the scope of proven approaches can be expanded.

- **Mobilize key stakeholders and foster collaboration.** Support should be rallied from a diverse range of stakeholders, including community, national, and regional leaders; governmental bodies; the private sector; civil society; nongovernmental organizations; and other development partners. Both the social and economic benefits of empowering adolescent girls must be emphasized, with support from a robust analytical framework. Collaboration can be facilitated among stakeholders to effectively implement evidence-based interventions, encompassing both programs and policy and legal reforms.

This report adds a crucial perspective to the discourse on adolescent girls in Africa, emphasizing not whether, but how policy makers, practitioners, and researchers should act to enhance adolescent girls' empowerment. An opportunity exists to catalyze a net benefit of trillions of dollars by investing in adolescent girls in Africa. The cost of inaction is high. The time for change is now.

www.ingramcontent.com/pod-product-compliance
Lightning Source LLC
Chambersburg PA
CBHW050906210326
41597CB00002B/39